A Message of Love

MESSAGES TO
INSPIRE,
EMPOWER
&HEAL

BOOK 1

S G RUDDY

4th Edition

A Message Of Love

An Introduction

The intention of this book is to offer you advice, support and guidance in a simple, well explained and empowering way. It aims to cover a wide range of subjects and topics such as love, hurt, success, failure, pain, confidence, anger, positivity and much much more. The messages contained within this book will help to clarify spiritual concepts in a straightforward and concise way.

The aim of this book is to support you in the process of becoming your best self. Each of the messages and lessons contained within this book will help to encourage you to take back creative control of your life. They will help to inspire you to dream big and take action, with each message gently supporting you in the process of letting go of the past, embracing the present and welcoming in the future. The quotes contained within this book aim to help you to connect with yourself, and all those around you, at a much deeper level and allow you to consistently live your life from a place of love, peace and power.

This book will support you in the process of becoming your best self and help you to consistently see things how your higher self (or inner self) sees things. This book will supply you with simple yet powerful reminders and tools which will help to bring you back into harmony and alignment with who you really are and how things are at the highest 'vibrational' level. The messages of love contained within this book will help you to open up a space that will begin to allow in your highest blessings and desires.

Regardless of how far along you currently are on your spiritual journey this book will be able to help you in some manner. It is especially useful for those of you who are looking for a book that can summarise and simplify all of the spiritual knowledge that you have already begun to learn, or more accurately, remember.

For convenience sake, many of the messages shared within this book are short and to the point, with each of the messages aiming to help offer you a spiritual and practical solution in a clear and concise way, no matter what circumstance or situation that you are currently facing.

At times you may feel like the messages overlap or repeat themselves, however rest assured that each message is written with a different intention and from a different perspective to help allow you to see the same core message from another frequency or point of view. Each message that you will subsequently read in this book will help to expand, explain and clarify the previous concepts even further for you, and help add a little more depth and detail to that particular subject.

The ideas, advice and messages of love contained within this book manifested from no particular process. Some have manifested from asking my 'higher self' a question, and some have come from overhearing other people's problems and meditating upon them. Many of the lessons naturally manifested from encountering other people on different frequencies and from viewing the world around me with an open heart and a curious mind. Many of the spiritual concepts also came from my own personal experiences and challenges, however the vast majority of them came from my own meditations.

Many of the messages contained within this book came to me in those moments of silence. To explain it in simpler terms, every time that I would ask the universe or my higher self a question about a particular subject or scenario, or I would happen to talk about a certain subject, a sort of 'magic' would occur.

The universe would begin to provide me with an answer, almost every time, as long as I would have access to something to write down the thoughts and answers that I received. The universe would seem to 'download' a spiritual solution into my consciousness either immediately, or later that day when I least expected it. As long as I kept an open heart, and had the intention of helping others (and as long as it all came from a place of love) the solutions, guidance and lessons would continue to appear and continue to reveal themselves to me.

I now come to recognise this process as 'opening up' and allowing my higher or inner self to communicate directly with me, which I hope that this book can allow you to do for yourself too.

I don't like claiming ownership of the messages (although it is all my own work) as I feel as though they don't really belong to me. I don't have to consciously think of an answer, the answers seem to come through me, for you and for anyone else who they can help and offer healing to. The messages continue to evolve and expand everyday, which is why I called this 'Book 1'.

Please understand that the single aim of this book and every single message written within it, is not to get you to listen to or rely upon me, but to listen to yourself and your own inner and higher self. Please note that the words 'higher self' can be switched to similar words such as 'inner self', your 'inner being' or 'soul', which I will explain in more detail later. My aim is for these messages to help you to see things from another perspective, to encourage you to look within and allow insight and clarity to bring you new and exciting breakthroughs in every single area of your life. I hope that the messages will help ignite a spark within you which will allow you to change your own life for the better. I hope to hold that space for you to have your very own 'light bulb' moments.

Before we go on any further, I need to make this clear. I'm not perfect, I don't live the 'perfect life'. I don't have all of the answers and I forget my own lessons from time to time too, so this book is for me just as much as it is for you. However since these messages seem to help me to consistently be my best self, I thought that they might be able to help you too.

I made the decision a few years ago that I was going to continue to share any of the messages that I received, just as long as they were at their core, messages of love. (The story of how 'A Message Of Love' came about can be found at the end of this book).

Please understand that this book is just one way of seeing things. There is always more than just one way of perceiving something, just like 1+8 = 9, 10-1 = 9 too. There are many different ways to get the same answer or result, and many different approaches to unveil the same inherent truth. No one method is better than the rest. As long as the method used and the messages that they provide come from a place of love and compassion and they promote peace and happiness for all, I personally feel that they should all be listened to and learned from. Ultimately we're all teachers for each other, we're all answering each other's questions in subtle little ways. I have found that at any given moment we are either being called to learn from others or we're being called to help teach others.

As with all things in life, no one single sentence can solve every problem. Some people will read these messages and think, "What about this experience?" or "That doesn't apply to this situation". You'll always be wrong to someone. In those cases take what you can and leave the rest. As we are all on different frequencies, with different needs (and on different journeys) I advise that you take what works for you and that which resonates as the truth in this book and apply it in your own life, and just leave the rest. What is the 'truth' for one person may not be the truth for another, and that is perfectly OK.

Any message that you read within this book that you feel somehow is meant for you, really is meant for you. There is no such thing as coincidence. Any message that speaks directly to you and resonates deeply within you, is meant for you. It in fact came from you. Trust that your higher self helped to guide and direct you towards that particular message at that particular time. Your higher self was actually involved in the process of its creation. Your current vibration allowed in that particular message for a greater reason, and on this occasion I had the privilege of being the person that the universe chose to channel and deliver that message through. I was the path of least resistance this time. Your higher self is always directing you towards answers, places and people often without you even being consciously aware of it.

Finally, this book isn't necessarily like other spiritual and self help books, it has no particular order. You can use this book in lots of different ways. Some of the possible ways that you could use it are:

- Traditionally reading it from the beginning to the end, just going chronologically page by page through the book.
- You could open up the book in a 'random' place and read the first message that you see. Maybe you could ask your higher self to help provide guidance, support and clarity with a certain issue

and then open up the book at a random place or choose a random page number and read that particular message.
- Or maybe you could even read a 'random' message from the book every morning or every night before you go to bed, or maybe even read a message in your free time.

No matter how you choose to use this book or where you decide to pick up and read, there will always be a message of love ready to help assist and support you no matter what you are going through.

Get to know the lingo

Before we get started, I have included a brief explanation below of what some of the most common words and 'lingo' used in this book mean, which will allow you to have a better understanding of what each message is expressing.

God / The Universe

Any time that I use those words, I'm talking about that supreme, loving and all knowing energy that is within you and I. I'm talking about that formless and nameless energy that we are all a part of, not apart or separated from. God isn't 'out there' it is beside you and within you, it's a part of all things. In essence it is who you are. You are the universe and the power of God in disguise. You are a part of all things, and all things are a part of you. God isn't a person, it is genderless, it's not that condemning and judging presence that we have all been told that it is. Remember that God came before any religion, so God is not about religion, it's about love. That is often why I don't use the word 'God' in these messages of love, as it is likely going to be misunderstood by many. Most people view the word 'God' through a fear based belief, definition or experience. 'The universe' is a much lighter word that leaves room for it to reveal its true power to you. Please understand that the universe (or God) is the energy that creates all things. It does the creating, and we do the 'allowing' in of that creation. It will reflect back to you that which you 'put out'. It will place on your path and bring into your conciousness, awareness and reality all of those things which are vibrating in harmony with you and your current frequency. In addition, please note that any time that I talk about angels, guardian angels or your ancestors I'm talking about that power too, that loving and limitless energy that they (and we) return to when we leave this form / body. Finally, if the word 'God' works for you when I use the words 'the universe' then please use that, and vice versa.

Vibration / Vibrating In Harmony With / Wavelength / Frequency

At the core level everything is 'vibrating'. Ask any scientist and they'll tell you that every single thing in our reality, at the deepest level (under a microscope) is moving and vibrating. That nothing is ever really 'still' or even 'solid'. At the core level you too are vibrating. The 'Law of Attraction' in essence states that the frequency in which you're vibrating at determines what you are currently able to 'attract' and allow into your reality. Whatever frequency you vibrate at helps to determine what you can see / perceive and what you can allow into your consciousness and reality. Therefore your reality is a reflection and a manifestation of your resonance or frequency.

From this point on think of your emotions as being translators of your frequency. Your current emotions are letting you know which frequency you are currently vibrating at, and which frequency you are seeing things from. Your emotions can be used to make you aware of what you're currently allowing in, or even what you're currently holding back. In essence, when you feel 'good' (which is when you're focussing upon feelings such as love, joy, hope, faith and appreciation) you're vibrating at a higher frequency and you are vibrating in harmony with that which you desire, and that which you are at the highest level. When you feel good you're on the same frequency and spectrum as everything that feels good to you, which is calling onto your path and 'allowing' into your consciousness and reality everything and everyone that feels like that joy. When you feel good you're letting in everything that feels good to you, which includes thoughts, events and people that feel that way or will leave you feeling that way. When you're feeling 'down' (and when you're consistently focussing upon feelings such as anger, fear or hate) that is a manifestation of, or more accurately an indication of, your current lower frequency, and that which you are currently vibrating in harmony with and allowing into your reality.

When you feel 'down' please understand that you aren't actually creating more situations that feel like that. Instead see it as an indication that you're currently holding back that which you already have and already are at the highest frequency, which is why it feels so bad to you to focus upon those lower frequency feelings such as anger or fear.

Please note, this will all be discussed and explained in more depth and detail later, so don't worry about trying to understand it all fully now.

So to clarify it for you, you're not 'attracting' things into your reality, you're just allowing them in. So ask yourself, "What am I currently allowing in?". You can only allow into your conciousness and reality that which you're on the same frequency as and that which you're vibrating in harmony with. Knowing this, What are you resonating with? What resonates with you? As that is an indication of your frequency and that which you're currently allowing into your reality.

In regards to the term 'wavelength', have you ever heard the phrase, "We are on the same wavelength". Do you ever have those moments where you and someone close to you happen to say the same thing at the exact same time? The reason why this happens isn't due to a coincidence, it is because you were 'vibrating' in harmony with each other (on the same wavelength or on a similar wavelength) at that particular moment, or you were vibrating in harmony with each other in regards to that particular subject or thing. You both had access to the same ideas that were on a particular frequency. If you feel as though you're on the same wavelength as someone else, it is because you are.

Essentially the frequency that you're currently vibrating at - and the wavelength that you're on, determines not only your perspective and the thoughts that you will receive or have access to, however it will also help to determine whether or not you're currently allowing in 'positive' or 'negative' thoughts. It also determines the path which will unfold in front of you. Your frequency is always pulling you towards a future (or more accurately towards a newer version of the present) that will bring you even more things that are on the same wavelength as you, including all of those thoughts, feelings, people and circumstances that are on the same spectrum as how you currently feel now, that is until you change. Changing and determining your own vibration and frequency is the key to being your best self and living your best life. By guiding your attention and awareness purposefully, and intentionally focussing upon that which lifts up your frequency (or that which makes you feel better) you will begin to change your life for the better.

Higher Self / Highest Self

Think of your higher self as being the best version of yourself. It's who you are at the highest level. It is that part of you that resides on the highest frequencies. Your highest self has consistent and unlimited access to the power of the entire universe, its 'essence' is centred there. Your higher self always has the highest perspective in regards to everything. It can see the whole map of your life, when you can only see the next step. Your higher self is the most 'complete' version of yourself. It is who you were before you came into this physical body.

When you're feeling good and when you're at peace or when you're feeling any of those high frequency feelings such as appreciation and joy (or any of those feelings which bring you 'up') you will automatically and naturally begin to increase your frequency which will cause you to vibrate in harmony with your higher self. When you do that consistently you will begin to allow in everything that you're seeking, including everyone that resides at those higher frequencies. When you're in alignment with your highest self (which is when you're currently seeing things how the best and most unlimited version of yourself would see things, and when your thoughts and feelings are consistently in harmony with who you really are and that which you desire to be and see, and when your actions are supporting that) you will begin to open up a space that will allow you to consciously receive and 'download' not only the guidance, insight and clarity that resides at those higher frequencies, but those blessings and miracles too. You will also allow 'the way' or the 'path' to reveal itself to you. That which you're seeking and that which is in your highest good will also begin to effortlessly reveal itself to you. You will begin to 'go with the flow' of life.

Inner Being / Inner Self

This is who you really are. It is that silent yet powerful awareness and presence that is deep within you. It is that power that gives life to whatever it observes, whatever it becomes aware of and whatever it focuses upon. Please understand that you are not your thoughts. You are the awareness that gives life to those thoughts. Thoughts are powerless without your attention, focus and awareness (or in essence, your energy and power). Your inner self is who you are beyond your thoughts. When you meditate you will begin to access your inner and higher self.

The words 'higher self' and 'inner self' can be used interchangeably, they point to the same inherent truth, which is the best version of yourself, and your true power. Think of your inner self as being the receiver that picks up on the information which your higher self and the universe is continuously beaming down. Your inner being is the channel in which your higher self flows its energy through.

Your inner self is where all insight can be found, it is where your happiness, peace and power is. See your inner self as being a 'computer' which is connected to the 'internet' of the universe. Your inner being is constantly downloading and accessing the insight and wisdom that your higher self and the universe provides it with, which your mind is able to 'translate'.

Your inner being is the space within you that contains all wisdom, clarity and insight (hence that is why it is called 'insight', because it is found by looking within). You will naturally be able to access this peace, power and joy within you when you're not focussing upon or holding onto anything that would take you 'down' (which is anything of a lower frequency). You don't have to do anything to get in touch with your inner self, it's not called the 'inner doing', it's called the 'inner being' for a reason. When you take your attention and awareness of anything that is distracting you from feeling and connecting with the peace and power that is within you, your inner being comes alive. It will begin to make its presence known.

Before we begin

Before we begin, I want to personally thank you for choosing to read this book. I hope that it can leave you with a renewed sense of clarity and peace, and help to reveal to you the power that you have as a conscious creator.

I hope that the messages contained within this book can help offer you some sort of support and encouragement as you 'level up' and become your best and most empowered self.

May they help you to know and recognise (and never underestimate or undermine) your own inner worth, power and purpose from here on out. I hope that these messages of love will allow you to accept, appreciate, love, value and care for yourself even more than ever before.

I started my spiritual journey and 'spiritual awakening' by reading self-help books, magazines and spiritual texts, such as this one, from incredible teachers and spiritual mentors such as Abraham Hicks, Eckhart Tolle and Oprah Winfrey, and I hope that this book can now be a part of that process for you.

This is my attempt at paying it forward.

Much love as always,

S G Ruddy

THE FEELING IS KEY

The purpose of visualising success and visualising yourself being your best self in the environment that you desire to be in, is to get you into the feeling place or emotional state of already having it now. How you feel now is what really matters (which in time becomes matter) and visualisations allow you to activate the state of being that you prefer which will begin to allow in everything which vibrates in harmony with that feeling. From that high frequency you will then begin to 'attract' (or more accurately allow in) 'real' feelings and experiences that match that vibration. When you feel good now, you will begin to allow in everything that feels joyful and good to you, and that which you have defined as joyful. When you start to activate those higher feeling frequencies it will naturally and automatically begin to draw to you (and also draw you to) everything and everyone that will make you feel like that.

THE MASTER KEY TO YOUR DESIRES

Imagine that genuine feelings of love, appreciation and faith are the keys to the universe. If you imagine that everything that you have ever wanted (and that which has yet to manifest) is locked behind a door of resistance (beyond feelings such as lack and unworthiness). Imagine that combined feelings of joy, appreciation and love, act exactly like a master key that will allow you to open up and unlock that door. Your desires are waiting patiently for you to remove your attention and awareness long enough from any of those lower frequency and resistant feelings which will begin to allow them in (which is the only thing that is separating you from your desires and your best self). Remember that the door opens with focus, not force. If the door doesn't open with love, then it is not worth opening.

THINGS KEEP GOING WRONG FOR YOU?

Do you ever find that when one thing goes wrong in your life, that multiple things tend to go wrong at the same time too? The main reason why is often because when something upsets you (and you allow that to become your main point of focus or attention) you will tend to stick around on the same frequency as how that problem or circumstance feels, which will begin to allow into your life even more things that feel like that. The 'door' is open to allow in those 'negative' things. However this principle also applies whenever you're feeling good too. Once good things start to happen and once you begin to focus upon them, even better things start to occur, and things often just keep getting better and better. So in future when things go wrong, learn to allow them, however don't allow them to steal your attention or determine your state of being. Change your point of focus and awareness, view things from a higher perspective.

IT IS SETTING YOU UP FOR SUCCESS

One day, sooner than you even realise, you're going to look back and wonder why you ever doubted yourself or doubted the universe. You'll be able to look back and see the perfection and the perfect timing of it all, and how every single interaction and apparent moment of 'coincidence' was guiding you towards something greater. You'll be able to understand and see that all of those struggles that you faced weren't actually holding you back, they were in fact propelling you forward, giving you the opportunity to become your best self. It was all setting you up for success. Knowing this, understand that any struggle that you're currently facing is ultimately setting you up for more.

COPING WITH PAIN AND SHAME

Please understand that you don't have to cope with feelings such as guilt or shame, you just need to let them go. Although that sentence is simple in theory, it's often much more difficult in practise. However please understand that any negative emotion that is in your awareness is trying to move on, it's ready to leave you, that's the only reason why it's there. Painful memories from your past only ever awaken and come to the surface when they're ready to be understood, healed and released. So when negative feelings rise up within you, be still, tune in within, and let them move through you. Set them and yourself free. The moment that you begin to take your attention and awareness of that which isn't you (e.g feelings such as pain or fear), you will immediately start to elevate back up to your original high frequency. You will find yourself again, and maybe even find peace for the first time.

YOU'RE ABOUT TO LEVEL UP

You have gone through some of the toughest trials, challenges, failures and setbacks that one person can face, however you didn't allow that to define or defeat you. Take a moment now to recognise and appreciate just how far you've come. You're still here, be proud of yourself. You continued to courageously move towards your peace, purpose and joy in spite of it all. You chose to not only go through it, but to grow through it too. This message is here to reassure you that very soon things are about to turn around for you. You're about to 'level up' in every single area of your life. Just like in a video game, you're about to reach the next level. That situation that you're currently dealing with is giving you the opportunity to step back and get a running jump towards what is next. You're about to springboard into your blessings.

NOT EVERYONE IS AGAINST YOU

Just because one particular person doesn't like you or doesn't understand you, doesn't mean that everyone is against you and that no one 'gets' you. When you are facing someone who makes you feel that way, it is often hard to remember that. Your primary point of focus tends to become their disapproval, which not only lowers your frequency but also begins to allow in even more thoughts, feelings, situations and people that will make you feel like that. Although not everyone is against you, please understand that not everyone is 'for' you either, and that is perfectly OK. That is just a natural part of life. However learn to focus upon how you feel about yourself, rather than fighting against or imagining what other people are thinking about you. Stop giving energy and 'weight' to their negative comments. Empower your own perspective.

THINKING OF GIVING UP?

If you're about to give up on that which you desire, especially from a place of fear, anger, frustration or irritation, please understand that you're not seeing things clearly. The only reason why you're currently getting thoughts and feelings that are convincing you to give up, is because you're on the same frequency as those perspectives. Centre yourself and allow your higher self to provide you with thoughts, perspectives and feelings regarding that which you're observing or experiencing, and not your pain, past or ego. Only then can you allow what is best for you to unfold in your reality. Sometimes giving up is the right and best course of action, however if it is, the idea will come through clearly when you're at peace. Only ever give up on something from a place of peace and clarity.

DEFINE YOUR OWN DESTINY

Only you have the privilege and honour of defining who you are and what you're capable of doing and becoming. However when you allow the past or someone else to define, limit or create who you are or what is possible for you, you will start to go 'off course'. You will begin to believe in their vision of you, instead of believing in your vision of yourself, which will immediately limit your potential and purpose. You will unknowingly hand creative power over to someone else and start to lose connection with who you really are. You've got to define your own destiny. Place your faith in the vision that your higher self holds of you, instead of believing in someone else's limited perspective of you.

TAKE THINGS UP AN OCTAVE

Right now your higher self is encouraging you to take things to the next level. It's time to take things up an 'octave' and time for you to rise up to the next level, or more accurately to a higher frequency. You're ready. Give up sitting around waiting for the world to find you, and for other people to understand you or appreciate your work. Turn that potential and passion within you into purpose. Work on those inspired ideas, develop them fully, meet the universe half way. Trust that your passion and faith will create or unveil the path that you're seeking. Make that product or start that business, it's time to do the work. It's time to promote your work and your message. Show the world who you are, and start today.

STILL DENYING HOW YOU FEEL?

Continuing to deny how you really feel will continue to persist your pain, and continue to cause problems and blocks to appear in your life and on your 'path'. Denial of how you feel denies you the opportunity to heal and move on. It's important to understand that the pain that you feel now likely isn't because of the past, but because you are still not accepting, appreciating or loving yourself fully now. Your resistance against how you feel, against 'what is' and against all those opportunities for healing that the universe has sent you, is what is causing the majority of the problems in your present. Once you bring full acceptance to everything, you will stop persisting that which is blocking your healing.

BULLIED IN THE PAST?

Growing up did you feel as though you had to defend yourself against the world? That you had to constantly explain yourself to someone? Or that you had to constantly justify yourself to others? If you did, that tends to have a 'knock on' affect on your entire life, that is until you find healing. Those who have been ignored, abandoned and above all else bullied in the past, be it physically, mentally or spiritually, must find healing. Those who were 'neglected' must find peace too, especially those who were made to feel as though they didn't matter, that they weren't wanted or that they wouldn't result to anything. Those feelings of worthlessness can affect your entire life if you let them. If you still haven't healed you will more than likely still be unconsciously responding to life, others, yourself and your dreams from that place of pain and fear now. However once you begin to allow 'what was' and you start to acknowledge, accept and move through and beyond those feelings, you will begin to heal and move on.

RISE TO THE CHALLENGE

Too many times we talk ourselves out of moving towards those opportunities which the universe has presented us with, opportunities which would have very likely helped to bring us closer to our desires and our best life. We unknowingly let our fears and doubts determine our destiny and potential, but no more. That 'big' opportunity that you turned down is coming back around again in another disguise for you very soon, but this time you're going to move towards it with courage and faith. You're not going to shrink back or hide away from life in fear any longer. You're going to rise to the challenge and grow to the level that is required for you to succeed.

SAVE YOURSELF

Too often people try in vain to save a toxic relationship before trying to save themselves. The reason being is because they feel at some level that they have invested too much of themselves in the stability of that relationship, and that it would be a failure at some level to admit 'defeat' and have to walk way. Only the ego hates to admit 'defeat', however please understand that the ego has no real love to give, it can't love. If you're seeing 'love' and a relationship from that level, then it's not love, it's dependence and attachment in disguise. Be willing to fight for yourself and your own happiness and peace as much as you're fighting to save that toxic relationship. Be as loyal to yourself and your boundaries as you are being to that relationship.

DOING THIS WILL CHANGE EVERYTHING

Appreciation is one of the most powerful feelings in the entire universe. It has the power to completely transform your life. Simply repeating the phrase, 'Thank you, Thank you, Thank you', from a feeling of heartfelt appreciation and gratitude, will have a profound affect on your entire life. Please note, this isn't about saying 'thank you' to make anything happen or from the feeling of 'I'm not worthy of having it', it is expressing gratitude knowing and affirming your power and worthiness. It's called gratefulness and not great-emptiness for a reason. A loving and joyful expression of appreciation is key.

YOU'RE GOING TO STUMBLE AND FALL

Just like a child that is learning to walk for the first time, you will often stumble through life until you get your footing and until you find your balance. You can expect to fall down a few times when you're learning to 'stand on your own two feet'. However as adults what tends to happen is we focus upon and remember how many times we have fallen down, rather than counting how many steps forward we have taken. When you continue to count and recall your failures and falls, you'll end up calling into your life even more things that will trip you up. You've got to stop counting your failures, and start counting your blessings. Take it easy on yourself, you're going to fall down and fail spectacularly a few times, but that's just a part of the bigger plan. You were supposed to fall down so that you could learn how to lift yourself back up again, and so that you could recognise your true power.

WHERE ARE THE 'BIG' CHANGES?

Have you been thinking lately, "Where are those big changes that I have been visualising?". Please understand that the 'big' changes that you are seeking, either within yourself or in your outside reality, rarely happen overnight. They're often the result of subtle little changes that go unnoticed by us, with each small change adding up and leading to the next, all unfolding in perfect timing and divine order. There is purpose to each sequence of change. Your visualisations have set those changes into motion, however please let the universe decide how and when those changes will manifest. There is no rush. There is a time and a season for everything, and the universe knows when that is, so trust it.

DOES THEIR TALENT INTIMIDATE YOU?

When you know what you have of value within yourself, other people's beauty, talent or success won't have the power or ability to make you feel bad about yourself. Their greatness or success won't intimidate you, it will instead inspire and empower you. If you feel and believe that someone else's success or greatness is somehow taking away from yours, that is an indication and a reminder to centre yourself and to vibrate higher. Only an ego feels insecure and intimidated by others and believes that someone else has the power or ability to affect them. No person or thing has the ability to take away your power, purpose or talent. Who you really are can't be affected by anyone or anything.

WENT THROUGH IT, OR GOT STUCK IN IT?

You went through that painful past, but did you unconsciously get stuck in it? Did you move beyond it or did you stay with it? Have you continued to live in that place of pain ever since? When you go through something painful, it is so important that you move the whole way through it in order for you to come out the other end of it, which is your reconnection with who you really are. You've got to move past your past. You can't move through something or begin to let it go if you're still holding onto, fighting against or refusing to acknowledge it. You have got to move through your emotions in order for you to heal and reach your highest potential.

GOING AGAINST YOUR GUT INSTINCT?

When you feel pressured or forced to do something that is against your gut instinct just to please others, or to not cause a fuss, things will immediately start to go wrong. You will start to betray yourself, your morals, your values and your purpose. Your uphill battle to please others (or to be liked by them) will always take you off your path and further away from that which was meant for you. Life is not supposed to be a constant upward battle, think of it instead as a downward flow. When a course of action doesn't feel right to you or right for you, that's because it's not in alignment with your highest purpose. It can't bring you or anyone else any peace, joy or success. Your inner self knows at all times whether or not you're doing that which is in your highest good, so listen to it, it won't steer you wrong.

LEAVE RUDENESS 'AT THE SCENE'
Those people who don't know how to communicate effectively will often come across as rude or abrupt whenever they try to express how they're really feeling. The way that they speak to you is often the way that they were spoken to in the past or the way that they speak to themselves in the present. Those people who express themselves in a forceful or rude way often only speak that way now because they didn't have an opportunity to speak loudly or openly about how they felt and what they thought growing up. Their rudeness has nothing to do with you or with what is going on, you just got in the way of their pain. So don't take it personally and don't take their rudeness with you, leave the insult and upset at 'the scene'.

CAN'T SEE A WAY FORWARD?
When you can't see a way forward, that isn't a sign that you should give up, it's a sign that you need to step back, rise up and start seeing things from a higher perspective. Imagine those type of hopeless feelings or situations as being a low laying fog that covers up your path and restricts your view. In order to see things clearly, you've got to rise above the fog (or more accurately change your current way of seeing things). Don't allow how things look right now to trick you into believing that this is how things will always be. The fog always clears eventually, until then allow yourself to be supported through it.

MONEY IS JUST PAPER
Are you still seeing money as this big, all powerful and unattainable thing which is constantly illusive to you? At its basis, remember that money is just numbers on a screen and paper

(sometimes it can be plastic too). You see numbers on a screen all day, and you see and touch paper (and plastic) all of the time, so why are you seeing money as being any different in your mind? Paper isn't removed from you, it isn't out of your control, it isn't bigger than you or rarely in your environment, it's all around you, there is an abundance of it everywhere every single day. Start to see money that way too. When you change the way that you're seeing money, you'll begin to change the way that you will experience it too.

NO MORE HOLDING BACK YOUR BLESSINGS

That which you have desired from the depth of your being (not from your ego) is created the moment that you desire it. What your heart desires, the universe has already created, all you have to do is the allowing in of that thing by being a consistent and genuine match to how it feels, or by matching the frequency that it resides at. When you feel good (or more accurately when you vibrate higher) you will begin to allow in everything that feels good to you, which often includes your highest desires. You only have to allow in your blessings, you don't have to create them or force them in. Remember, you can't miss what is meant for you, however you can continue to hold it back unconsciously. Let it in.

FEEL LIKE YOU CAN'T GO ON?

When you feel like you can't go on, that just means that you can't go on living the way that you're currently living (or carry on seeing things the way that you're currently seeing them). Your higher self is making you aware through those feelings that something needs to change, that is why it feels so bad to you. That feeling is the difference between feeling who you really are and feeling what you're currently limiting yourself to. Right now your current perspective is preventing you from seeing yourself and your future clearly. Clarity, peace and the strength to carry on will come in time once you have begun to acknowledge and accept 'what is'. It's time to process your feelings and prioritise your own healing.

LOVE IS BLIND

Relationships can't be founded upon hope alone, nor the promise of what things can be. Please understand that it's not your job to see the potential in a relationship or a partner, especially when they're not doing the same for you. You have got to take the 'rose tinted glasses' off and have the courage to open up your eyes and see things for what they are and as they really are. Love is blind when you're seeing love from that limited or distorted perspective. If there isn't consistency, commitment, compassion and open and honest communication, then there isn't love or a stable relationship there.

YOUR IDEAS ARE A 'SPINNING TOP'

Think of your ideas as being a 'spinning top'. When you begin to develop your ideas and take action upon your inspiration, your spinning top begins to spin. However it often takes a while for things to gain momentum, to reach their highest potential and to start going in the direction that you prefer. However, once you get started, those ideas that are meant to go the distance tend to pick up speed fast and continue to gain momentum. The difficulty is often in getting those ideas off the ground, however once they get started, and they are given enough time and energy, they can spin into something incredible.

RUN AN ANALYSIS

It is important that you take some time to see whether or not your current way of seeing and doing things is helpful and is supporting the life that you desire to live. Run an analysis within. This isn't about over analysing anything, it's about running an analysis from time to time to see if there are any 'viruses' in your way of thinking, and in your way of seeing and doing things. Run an analysis from the intention of bettering yourself, rather than doing it to point out your mistakes. The results of that 'scan' and that period of self reflection will reveal themselves to you when you centre yourself and you tune in within. It will bring into your awareness that which needs healing, that which needs to change and that which is ready to move on.

TIME FLIES WHEN YOU'RE HAVING FUN

The same way that time 'flies' when you're having fun (and that time seems to go by faster when you're not looking at it) your desires will often manifest much faster when you're having fun and when you're not focussing upon the lack of them in your current reality or consciousness. Your attention to the 'lack' is slowing them down. In addition when you feel like your desires are taking a long time, they tend to go even slower, your faith in the 'slowness' of their arrival, slows them down even more. When you just let go and have fun, not only will time 'fly by' but you'll allow your desires to arrive into your reality much quicker than expected.

SELF LOVE BEFORE THEIR LOVE

A relationship should never come above or before your own inner happiness, peace and stability. It is so important that you find and strengthen the connection and relationship between yourself and your higher / inner self before trying to find a connection or a relationship with someone else. Until you do, you'll end up seeking their love, acceptance and validation, rather than loving, validating and accepting yourself. What you're really looking for is self love, self worth and self acceptance, and you won't find that in another person until you find it within yourself. Know that your worth and value isn't defined by what happened in the past, or even by how others treat you in the present, it is defined solely by you.

CLEAR VISION

When you're going from 'here' to 'there' it is important that you don't lose sight of where you're going and who you're becoming. When you have a clear and consistent vision you'll be able to see through and beyond 'what is' to the bigger picture. You'll also be able to acknowledge 'what is' without allowing it to determine what will be and what you believe, or allow it to blur or distort how you see yourself, your desires or your future. Without a clear vision you'll tend to get lost. If you lose your way, gain perspective and refocus your faith and feelings upon the bigger picture. Remind yourself of where you're going and what is already promised for you. Don't give up.

IRRITATED BY THEM?

If someone expresses who they really are, and at some level it irritates you or angers you, that is often a sign that you're not vibrating in alignment with your best self. The perspective that brings you negative thoughts and commentary when others are being themselves, is often a reflection of your failure to honour and be who you really are, essentially that you're not living on purpose. Their uniqueness shouldn't have the power or ability to upset or irritate you, it should instead inspire, empower and encourage you to do the same.

DOWNLOAD GREATNESS

Something that we fail to recognise is that we have access to the same ideas that all of the great minds of the past had. They weren't any different than us. However what made them 'special' was that they found a way to access and receive those ideas and that inspiration from the universe. They were able to increase their frequency and allow those life changing ideas (which resided at the highest frequencies) to download into their consciousness. The universe is constantly beaming those ideas down to you too, all that you have to do is vibrate higher, raise up your 'antenna' and allow them in.

THE 'CUP' OF PAIN

Those who are 'lost' in feelings of fear, hurt, despair and pain will often continue to project those feelings onto everyone else unintentionally, that is until they heal and release the hurt of the past. They're in essence hurting others to the same degree that they have been hurt, and hurting everyone else to the degree that they're still hurting themselves. They're showing us on the outside how much pain they're in on the inside. In addition some people may even hurt you because that is how they get the attention, validation, power, control or worth that they're seeking, all of which they feel that they are currently missing within themselves. People do strange things when they're in pain. To them you're often just a distraction or a 'cup' for them to pour their pain into. They're pouring it out and onto you (and others) in an attempt to get rid of it within themselves, but don't hold onto their pain or store it away. It wasn't yours to begin with. Just focus upon filling up your own inner cup with feelings of love, joy and appreciation.

YOUR 'CURRENT' REALITY

What frequency are you currently residing at? Think of your current frequency as being a supplier of energy. Your current reality has a constant current of energy and power flowing through it at all times. Your frequency flows through you and everything that you do and everywhere that you go. It energises all things and gives life to that which you're observing. In addition the frequency that you're currently residing at is allowing in everything that is on the same frequency as it. Your current reality is where your power lays. When you change your current perspective, and you begin to change your point of focus or awareness, everything changes.

FACING A CRISIS?

Crises help us to find out who we really are, they help to reveal our true power and purpose (just as long as we don't let ourselves get lost in them). When the world feels like it is coming crashing down around you and you feel like you're losing your mind, take that as an indication that you're just finding yourself or letting go of who you thought you were. Crises help us to get clear on who we are and what we really desire, they have purpose. The word 'crisis' finds its origins in the word 'decide', and the term 'decisive point'. Decide that this crisis will be the turning point that you have been looking for.

THE SELF CLEANING PROCESS OF LIFE

Your life, mind and reality are constantly going through a self cleaning process. Feelings, people and things which are no longer in your highest good are constantly removing themselves from your life. That which has served its highest purpose in your life will remove itself from your environment (be it thoughts, feelings or people). When you centre yourself and vibrate higher, your mind will automatically and naturally do this. It will bring any 'negative' or unhelpful thoughts, feelings, beliefs and memories into your awareness (that are no longer serving you) for you to acknowledge, heal and then release them. What appears in your awareness today is ready to go.

EXPECTING IT FROM LACK?

Are you expecting greatness and blessings knowing and believing in them from the feeling and mentality of abundance? Or are you expecting greatness and your desires from the feeling of lack and limitation? You have got to stop expecting abundance from those lower frequency feelings, and start accepting the state of being that would allow in those type of results, which is genuine feelings of joy, love, appreciation and abundance. All you need to do is have a positive expectation and a relaxed faith regarding all things, that is all that is needed to work wonders on your life.

WHAT DISCOURAGED REALLY MEANS

Often when you can't see definitive proof that things are changing for the better, you can be left feeling discouraged. However please understand what those feelings of discouragement really mean. Feeling discouraged is just the opposite of feeling courageous. Feeling discouraged doesn't mean that you should give up on something, it just means that how you're currently seeing things is stopping you from accessing the courage within you to keep going. Feelings of discouragement are always reminding you to choose courage and to see things from a higher perspective.

DECISIONS FROM PAIN OR PEACE?
From what space are you making the major decisions in your life from? Are they reaction based, from a place of fear? Or are you responding to life from a place of peace and love? Before every major decision and choice that you make, or before you react to a particular situation, ask yourself, "Is this decision that I'm about to make, coming from a place of power and peace, or pain and fear?". Contemplate your highest good and highest purpose first before taking action or reacting. Ask yourself, "Will doing this or saying that (or failing to do it or say it) bring me closer into alignment with who I desire to be, and who I really am? Or will it take me further away from it?". When you make yourself aware of the energy that you are bringing to your decisions you can start to see the intention and reason for them, and how that will always directly affect the result. The intention determines the energy that flows into everything that you do and calls onto your path everything and everyone that resonates at that same level. It is up to us to step back, centre ourselves and consciously respond to life from peace, rather than automatically reacting from pain.

WHEN LOVE COMES AND GOES
Often when a love interest comes and goes we can often be left thinking, 'What went wrong?' Especially when it didn't work out to begin with. However that 'failed' relationship had purpose. Its purpose may have been to awaken within you not only how love looks and feels to you, but what you are truly worthy of. The universe may have placed that person in front of you in order for you to get clear on how love looks and feels to you, which the universe will then use to filter people through, bringing people onto your path that fit that description. That love interest helped to ignite a spark and a desire within you for love. That brief encounter with love also allowed you to get onto a higher frequency which will help to allow the 'right' relationship into

your reality (just as long as you're not only focussing upon the one that got away). It's important to understand that when you say it has to be that one particular person (the one that got away) you will unintentionally limit what you're worthy of. You will end up stopping the 'right' relationship and true love from getting to you. If you're waiting for that person to come back in order for you to feel happy or feel good enough, you'll often end up unhappy while you watch them move on and find their 'right' relationship, simply because they let go and allowed in 'true' love. Above all else connect to the love within yourself without worrying if they'll come back, you can't miss what is meant for you. The love that you're seeking on the outside will only come (and stick around) once you love, validate and appreciate yourself fully. Once you do that, you will begin to allow in the love that you're worthy of, until then you'll settle for less than you desire and deserve.

IT'S TIME TO FOCUS ON YOU NOW
You have sacrificed so much for everyone else, you have continued to put them first and continued to neglect yourself and your own inner peace, purpose and happiness. It's time to focus upon you now. No more hiding away, being apologetic and making yourself small. Build yourself up. Know and claim your greatness. You've put yourself last for the last time. It's never too late to claim your gift and purpose, and become the person that you were meant to become. It's time to step into your best self and show the world who you really are. This is your time now.

NO FRIENDS?
Do you find yourself with very few close friends? There is often a reason for that. The universe often gives those people with the biggest purpose, a brief period in their life where they feel disconnected and removed from others. That alone time is teaching them to rely upon and think for themselves. You will have friends very soon, who are on the same wavelength as you, just as long as you let people in, and you let them see who you really are. If you're pretending to be someone else, you'll end up

attracting those people into your life who weren't meant for you. In order to allow in real and lasting friendships you're going to have to be your true authentic self.

DISAGREEMENTS

Not everyone that you encounter will have the same intentions, mindset, opinions or beliefs that you have and that's OK. Disagreements and differences at their core are healthy, there is no need to be afraid of them. It's important to understand that someone else having a different opinion than you isn't necessarily an attack on who you are, what you believe or what you do. There is no need to take it personally. Only someone who bases who they are on the reaction or opinions of others will fear disagreements. As long as someone else's different opinion isn't based on ignorance, prejudice or fear, let them be.

YOUR 'FLAWS' HAVE PURPOSE

Your insecurities and 'flaws' only look and feel that way when you are looking at things from a lower frequency or perspective. The things that you least like about yourself are often the things which the universe will use to align you with your purpose and those who are meant for you. Your insecurities are assets and strengths in the eyes of the universe. They have a higher purpose, they add to your overall growth and experience. The universe will use them to rearrange your path and life. It will use your 'weaknesses' to give you opportunities and instil true strength and worth within you. They will be the vehicle that will take you to success.

YOU DON'T HAVE TO SETTLE FOR IT

Just because you're spiritual doesn't mean that you shouldn't stand up for yourself, have an opinion or speak out when you come across ignorance. It doesn't mean that you're a 'push over' either. Being spiritual allows you to see through and rise above that which tries to push or tear you down. It allows you to have clear boundaries and to let people know in a respectful manner when they've crossed the line. Just because you're 'positive' and 'spiritual' doesn't mean that you have to keep quiet. You don't have to settle for it. Stand up and speak out.

THOSE WHO FIND FAULT WITH YOU
At times in life you'll encounter those people who constantly seem to ridicule what you do and who you are. No matter what you do, it will never be good enough for them, they'll always seem to find something wrong with what you did. Don't take it personally though. It's not you, it's them. You just got in the way of their pain. Their opinion of you is just a reflection of their own perspective and their own inner pain. They're viewing everything from a lower frequency, including you and themselves. They can't see themselves clearly, so how can they see you clearly? Until they heal, they'll continue to find fault with everything and everyone, and continue to have a reason to be upset.

SEEING 11:11? IT'S REFLECTION TIME...
Do you find yourself constantly seeing reoccurring numbers or words? That is often the universe's way of getting your attention. That aligned time, is often an indication to take some time to step back and reflect. Since they are often numbers that read the same backwards as they do forwards (reflected time) they're often a sign that a time of reflection is need. This doesn't mean that anything bad is going to happen, quite the contrary, it's just a reminder that before your blessings can manifest you have got to centre yourself. It's also a sign that you're being supported, cared for and being divinely protected and guided.

IT WON'T DEFEAT YOU
Struggles often instil within us courage, tenacity and strength, however before they do, they often leave us feeling defeated and drained. Please understand that this struggle and situation that you're currently dealing with hasn't got the power to defeat you, it's here to liberate you. What first knocks you down, often lifts you higher when you come out the other end of it. You will get through this struggle. However if you define it as being impossible

to overcome (or you see yourself as not being strong enough to handle it) then you'll continue to hold yourself back from the blessings that are just beyond this current lesson.

ARE YOUR ACTIONS IN ALIGNMENT?

Are your current outer actions in alignment with the person that you are becoming on the inside? Are you letting fear stop you from taking action upon that which you desire to be or do? What you act upon is what you're most sure of, which is what the universe will respond to. The universe will take that as an indication of and a preference for what you want. If you continue to act upon or give into fear, then you will often get back even more fearful thoughts and events. So what are you acting upon? Boredom or your purpose? When you change what you are acting upon, things start changing. Remember that the universe can only ever meet you half way, once you have already started to take aligned and inspired action towards your goals and your desires. Do the inner work and take those leaps of faith when opportunities arise. The universe will rise to meet you every single time, however the staircase will only appear once you have jumped.

ALLOW WHAT IS, JUST DON'T SETTLE FOR IT

Allow 'what is', learn to make peace with it without settling for it. Being content with where you are doesn't mean that you are settling for it, however when you allow 'what is' you stop fighting against it and you stop persisting it. Once you do that you can then begin to reinvest your focus, attention and awareness upon becoming a conscious creator of life, rather than an 'unconscious' spectator of it. You'll create from a place of power, rather than pain. Accept 'what is', be OK with it, without saying OK this is all that there is. When you can allow 'what is' and acknowledge it without letting it defeat or define you, it will often inspire within you a way out of it. Let 'what is' bring out and reveal the greatness that is already within you. If your current reality doesn't look the way that you prefer it to look, that's perfectly OK, please understand that you haven't done anything wrong, this is not the final destination, it is just a pit stop on the way to your blessings.

COURSE CORRECT

Don't let the autopilot of who you were or 'what was' keep you locked onto a certain direction. It doesn't matter how long you have been travelling in that direction for, you can always turn around and choose another way. Take back control of your life if you don't like where you are heading or how things are looking. It's never too late. Start today, make a subtle course correction. Decide to no longer give into your old ways of seeing and doing things, choose again. If you don't start implementing those new changes today, you'll only regret it tomorrow.

STOP EXPECTING YOUR DESIRES

There is no need to guess or expect when or how your desires will manifest, just knowing that they will is enough for the universe to do its job. When you're anxiously waiting for your desires to manifest the way that you expect them to, from those lower feelings of lack, limitation, wanting and needing, you'll not only rush your anxious energy towards every little opportunity (which will stop them from reaching their full potential and from revealing their real purpose) however you will also continue to persist those feelings and that experience of lack. You'll also tend to get annoyed or frustrated with how things currently look, all of which is resistant by nature. That type of expectation often stops the manifestation, or at the very least slows it down. Expect greatness, just not when, where or how that greatness has to come about.

EXAGGERATION

It is important that you reserve your excitement and enthusiasm only for those things which you desire to see and feel even more of. At times we tend to speak with a passionate energy about that which we don't want. We tend to speak with passion about our own problems, the problems in the world or the faults of others, all of which is highly creative. Exaggerating problems and talking about them at length with passion only makes them bigger and stronger. Exaggerate your blessings instead. Exaggerate the greatness that is within you, make it bigger, not from a place of your ego but from the faith in your own power and purpose. What you have passion for and speak passionately about most often, the universe will tend to give you even more of, whether it is 'good' or 'bad'. So use your enthusiasm wisely.

THIS MESSAGE IS MEANT FOR YOU

I know that recently you have asked the universe and your inner self for guidance and help, asking, "What is meant for me?" and "Is this all that is meant for me?". This message is here to remind you that your higher self hasn't given up on you or your dreams. Your time is coming, so are your blessings, just don't give up now, especially not in frustration or fear. Do you really understand that you can't miss what is meant for you? Really take that message to 'heart', let it sink in. There is so much that is meant for you. Soon you will look back and understand just how true that statement was. It's time to centre yourself now in feelings of love, peace and appreciation, and time to focus upon your own path. Choose you, let others be, it's time to refocus. Trust, have faith, and detach. Go with the flow. It is time to take action, knowing your worth, power and purpose. No more holding yourself back, take risks, be yourself authentically. You can do this.

YOU'RE NOT THE ONLY ONE

You are not the only one going through that or feeling that way. No matter how much your brain likes to tell you that you are the only one, you can guarantee that there have been endless amounts of people before you who have walked that path. Look to them for advice and support. They can help navigate the pitfalls ahead. You're only ever the only one going through something until you speak up. You would be surprised at how many people have gone through exactly what you are going through. In addition when you open up to others you not only heal yourself but you give others permission to do the same. Don't underestimate the power in speaking up.

SPEAK UP, STAND UP

There is nothing wrong with standing up for yourself and speaking out. Being spiritual doesn't mean that you don't have an opinion, or that you should let others 'walk all over you'. Being spiritual means that you can respond to negativity from a place of love, authentic power, clarity and a higher perspective, rather than reacting from a place of anger, hurt or pain. It allows you to become transparent to the harsh words of others and enables you to see through them to the real reason for their actions, it helps to allow in a solution too. Being spiritual will allow you to remain centred regardless of what you face or who you encounter.

YOU CAN'T BLOCK ONE AREA

It is important that you allow yourself to feel every emotion. Every feeling and emotion has purpose. The moment that you stop yourself from feeling one emotion, you will end up blocking all of your feelings. When you hold back one thing, be it anger or fear, you will unintentionally hold back everything, including your blessings and desires. You can't pick and choose which emotions to shut off and stop feeling. When you shut down and stop yourself from feeling sorrow or shame, you will also stop yourself from feeling joy and peace too. In addition when you stop yourself from receiving help, it will also affect every single area of your life. You'll stop receiving help in every area of your life. You can't focus upon one area of your life without it rippling through and being reflected throughout your entire life. Similarly when you feel good, it will affect every single area of your life too. Your joy will ripple through you and flow into all that you do and everywhere that you go. Therefore it is important to allow how you feel. No more compressing or suppressing your emotions, let them flow through you (and learn to express them in a healthy manner) so that you are then able to choose peace and joy again. Learn to let go of those shameful feelings and fear based perspectives that are attached to your emotions and attached to processing your feelings. When you have the courage to face your problems and how you are really feeling from a place of love (and not from a forceful feeling) they begin to fade away.

'KILLING' TIME

Instead of 'killing' time, learn to invest it. When you appreciate and value your own time, things begin to change. Your time and energy are some of your most valuable 'commodities'. Invest your energy and time in focussing your attention and awareness upon thoughts and feelings that empower and encourage you, and participating in activities and actions that lift you higher, rather than filling boredom or giving into thoughts that are encouraging you to do that. When you give into boredom, fear or pain, you are inviting more of the same into your life. Although it is easy to fill boredom (because it is so accessible to you, since it is on the same frequency that you are on when you are feeling down) it ultimately won't fulfil, inspire or energise you. Please don't confuse time of rest, recovery and recuperation with filling boredom. Rest is necessary. Use boredom as an indication to refocus upon your goals, to come up with new and exciting ideas, to go on an adventure and to have fun. Go up an octave and step into your best self.

PARENTS BELIEFS

Not everything that you learned growing up needs to be abided by. Not everything that you learned was necessary or helpful. Often our parents or those in our environment did what they could with what they had. However many of the lessons that they taught us were based on fear. It is often those beliefs that are still secretly controlling your life, your decisions and your actions. They are subtly stopping you from doing that which you desire to do simply out of fear. It is time to become aware and time to create new beliefs that support the person that you are becoming and already are at the highest level. If you find any beliefs from your childhood that aren't useful, instead of fighting against them or blaming your parents for what they taught you (or failed to teach you) claim back responsibility for changing things. Parent yourself.

HAPPY NOW

Please understand that happiness and peace are only ever available in the present moment. If you're not choosing it now, you won't feel it 'then'. You'll forever be chasing the ego's idea and version of happiness and peace. True happiness always begins with the decision to be happy right now. Choose to be happy right now not necessarily because of anyone or anything in particular, but because you know that it is who you really are and how you're supposed to feel at the core level. Often we only choose to be happy after years of allowing everything and everyone else to affect, determine or take away our joy. We choose joy after being fed up with feeling miserable and 'down' all of the time, but don't wait until then to feel happy, choose it now. It is truly draining to hold back your happiness and joy. Let it in. Make yourself this promise, that you are no longer waiting until 'then' to be happy. Give up needing something to happen in order for you to be genuinely and ecstatically happy. Happiness doesn't come to you, you go to it within yourself. You become it, you choose it, you encourage and support it. When you choose to look for reasons to be genuinely happy now, you will begin to allow in everything that feels like that joy to you. You will remove all of the blocks that were holding back everything that you have ever desired. Joy is the way forward and the answer that you are looking for.

WHY YOU'RE MADE THAT WAY

Be yourself authentically and unconditionally, show people who you really are, rather than trying to be someone else that you think that they will like or admire. Being yourself will always open doors, being someone else will only lead to unhappiness and unfulfilment. You are made the way that you are for a greater reason and purpose, the universe doesn't make mistakes. You're needed as you are and where you are. The universe specifically made you that way so that you could handle your purpose. Your character, and who you really are is supporting your purpose. It will be the vehicle that will take you towards your 'destiny'. Being yourself will help, heal and inspire others, being someone else won't. Use your past and gifts to create a better and brighter future for all.

"TO BE OR NOT TO BE"

To paraphrase what Shakespeare wrote: "To be or not to be, that is the question". That saying has a profound truth to it that often gets overlooked. Simply put, until you decide to be something or feel something you will never see it. It's up to you whether or not you decide to become or not become something, it is ultimately your own choice. If you don't become it 'now', you'll never become it 'then'. The quote doesn't say, to do or not to do, it says to be or not to be. It is the 'being' and the embodying of the feeling of that which you desire to be, that holds the power. It is the emotion within you that powers it and draws it to you. Remember emotion is energy in motion, feelings get things moving. Never forget that it is your 'being' that determines your reality, not just your actions. So no matter what you desire to be or see, tune into the frequency of it, find the feeling of it, embody it. Put your mind to it and your heart in it. When you do, you will begin to vibrate in harmony with that which you desire, which will begin to let in everything that is on the same frequency and spectrum as it. So ask yourself, "What am I conscious of consistently being, powerful or powerless?".

ACCEPT BEFORE TRYING TO CHANGE

Have you been pushing away fear or anxiety lately? Have you been trying to sweep the past under the rug? Maybe you have tried to 'bury your head' to the real issue or problem that you are currently facing and how all of that makes you feel? Please understand that when you run away from something, it always 'pops' back up somewhere else. Until you face the real issue (whether it is on the surface or 'buried' deep within you) it will keep coming back in another disguise for you to finally face it, move through it and find healing. Refusing to accept things and how they make you feel, only ever keeps them prominent in your life. They will continue to reappear elsewhere in your life until something changes. Once you acknowledge, accept and allow 'what is', you can then begin to change things, mainly because the momentum has slowed down and the resistance has stopped. You're no longer persisting that which you don't want (or that which you don't want to feel) by fighting against it or pushing it away. When you begin to let it be, it begins to let you go.

HOW ARE YOU BEING VALIDATED?

A difficult question that we need to ask ourselves at times is, How am I being validated? How am I seeking attention? Is it in healthy or harmful ways? Sadly there are those people who seek attention and validation in harmful ways, believing that any attention is better than none at all. There are those people who seek drama, pain and hurt in relationships because it is still attention and connection, and it is still allowing them to be seen, heard and validated in the easiest and quickest manner. It allows them to feel like they still matter or that they are still able to affect things. That is often the same reason why children misbehave (if they're not being seen or being validated in a loving manner, then they'll seek to be seen and noticed in those harmful ways). Take some time to become aware of how you are seeking attention and even how you are giving attention to others.

BEGIN WITHIN

No matter what you desire to be or do, begin within. Before you can see something on the outside you first need to feel, believe and be it on the inside. Trying to be a success on the outside before first feeling it on the inside will be a battle in vain, it won't change anything for long. When you begin within and create the inner state that you are seeking on the outside, it helps to create the outer change. Success is not a result, but a state of being, or more accurately a state of allowing. That inner feeling of success

27

and worthiness will not only inspire your actions, as well as where you go and who you will meet, but it will inevitably bring you into alignment with that which you desire at the highest level. Until you begin within, you'll always go without. Only once you believe it and feel it on the inside can you conceive it, achieve it and then receive it on the outside. Find the feeling of that which you desire to be or see, and embody it fully and consistently. When you do, you will begin to vibrate in harmony with it, which will begin to let in everything that is on the same spectrum as it.

SPIRITUALITY EQUALS SERIOUSNESS?

Once you have done the 'inner work' and healing, it is time to let go and have fun. Life isn't about being so serious all of the time. You're here to have fun and to create. Being 'spiritual' isn't about over thinking or over analysing everything and everyone, that is the ego's idea of being spiritual (which is just another identity for it to hide behind). Being 'spiritual' doesn't make you any better than anyone else, it does however allow you to see, at the core level, that you're just like everyone else. It's time to start having fun.

IS IT REALLY THE PATH OF LEAST RESISTANCE?

How does the 'path' that you're currently on feel to you? Empowering or exhausting? How do you know if the path that is unfolding in front of you right now is the 'right' path, also known as the path of least resistance (which is the path that will naturally lead you towards your joy and peace, and the path which is in alignment with your higher self) or if it is a path which is a manifestation of the wavelength that you're currently on, also known as the 'easiest' path? (which is a path that will take you around and around the same issues and perspectives, which will continue to lead you towards even more things and experiences that feel like how you're currently feeling right now, which is at its basis the 'wrong' path, because it is a reflection and a manifestation of the lower frequency that you're vibrating at, and not a reflection or a manifestation of your higher self). In essence, the perspective that you're looking at yourself and the world from tends to determine the path that will unfold in front of you. If you have been focussing upon lower feelings and perspectives, then the path that will unfold before you will likely be the 'wrong' path, which will lead you off course. It will be the easier path, but not the 'right' or the best path for you. It is too easy to choose that 'easier' path, simply because it's on the same frequency as you, it is in close proximity to you. Ultimately the path that unfolds depends on you and the frequency that you're currently and consistently vibrating at. To summarise it all, the 'right' path (which will tend to lead you towards your best self and your best life) always begins where you are, it will always unfold in front of you, however until you centre yourself and you begin to vibrate in harmony with your higher self, the path that unfolds before you will just be a reflection of the lower frequency that you're currently vibrating at which will likely lead you towards even more experiences, things and people that will make you feel like that, rather than the 'right' path that will take you higher and further. You will know the difference between both paths by how they feel. The 'right' path feels empowering, it satisfies you and ignites your inner joy and passion, the other paths won't. When you connect with your higher / inner self you will allow the 'easiest' path and the 'right' path (also known as the path of least resistance) to become the same path, and that is when everything will begin to have an effortless ease to it, in essence when you will begin to go with the flow.

BLESSINGS CAN'T FILTER THROUGH

Imagine this analogy for a moment, that the energy of the entire universe is just like a bag of flour, and your perception or your beliefs are the sieve or filter in which that flour (or power) flows through. The more broad that your point of focus and awareness is, the bigger that the holes will become and the more power (or flour) that can flow through. The narrower that it is, the smaller the holes are and the less flour (or power, blessings and miracles) that can get through and flow into your life. When you expand your perception and beliefs you'll immediately begin to filter out that which you don't want and naturally begin to allow in more.

DRAMA IN 'LOVE'
Those people who consistently fight, argue and find themselves in relationships that are focussed upon some sort of drama, you can guarantee at some level are still in pain. They are dealing with untreated and unhealed trauma. When you're in pain you can't see things clearly. So if you can't see yourself clearly, how can you see your partner clearly? When two hurt people come together and look to each other to heal the pain that they feel within themselves, and at some level need the other person to fix them or 'complete' them, the relationship is doomed to fail. They are unconsciously looking for the love and support that they never received in their childhood, in someone else who likely currently has no real love or respect to give, especially when they can't even love themselves. How can they love, assist or support anyone else when they can't even love, aid or support themselves? Until couples who are in pain find healing, they will continue to project their pain and issues onto each other, and fail to take accountability for how they really feel, for how they are reacting and fundamentally for getting better.

ONE LAST PUSH
The birthing process of your desires can be a long and tedious one at times. It can often take years of hard work, effort and consistency to finally reach the place that you desire to be at. Right now your desires are ready to be born into the world, however they need one last big 'push' to be birthed into your reality. However this isn't about pushing or forcing anything into being, but allowing it to happen naturally. This isn't the time to give up, it is the time to rest, recover and try again. Never give up in anger or frustration. Often we give up right before something 'big' is about to manifest. Right now you can't see what is right around the corner for you, especially all of those incredible opportunities and circumstances that are about to manifest and

change things for the better. You have come so far, too far to give up now. Take a deep breath, focus, centre yourself, do the necessary work and give this and yourself one last 'push'.

CRITICISING OTHERS?

Those who are often the most critical of others are in fact the most critical of themselves. Those who criticise other people for what they do or what they fail to do, are often in the need of self acceptance. Only someone who isn't content with themselves and who is critical of themselves has the time or energy to be so critical of others. The reason why they're so critical of everyone and everything is because they are on the same frequency as those critical thoughts or perspectives, that's why they can see everyone else's faults so easily, they have easy access to those type of thoughts. Those who judge and criticise others, judge and criticise themselves the most, or they were brought up in a vibrational environment of criticism and not feeling good enough. Always remember that pointing out other people's faults doesn't make you any better than them, and it doesn't distract others from your faults either. The real reason why some people can be so quick to be critical of another person's looks is often because they're so critical of their own appearance, they have easy access to those type of thoughts about others because they have them regularly about themselves. It's not what you judge you become, it is what you judge you already are. If they had compassion for themselves they wouldn't judge others so harshly or so easily. Those people who try and judge you, what you do and who you are, are just showing you who they are and how they feel, they're not showing you who you are. They can't see you without first seeing themselves. Pass no remarks on it. Let it be and let it go.

INSECURE PEOPLE?

It is often said that the most insecure person in the room will 'go after' the most secure person. They will often try and make their voice the loudest in the room (believing that that is how you get people to listen to, respect and admire them). They feel that if they can defeat, embarrass or 'take down' the secure person, then they will somehow gain that power within themselves, or have that power and control over other people. That insecure person wants the power and authority (and ultimately peace) that the secure person has. If you find someone doing that to you, rise above it, make your boundaries clear and remain unaffected by their projections of pain.

BOOMERANG DESIRES

Think of your desires as being a boomerang. Just like a boomerang your desires can't come back to you when you are still holding onto them, when you're still attached to them and especially when you haven't even let them go. In addition when your current happiness, peace and worth is dependant on getting what you desire, your desires can't come back to you. As soon as you want something, let it go. Don't let go of the desire for it, but release your attachment to your desires. Surrendering your desire is all about letting go of needing a certain result to feel good now, it's about deciding to just start embracing joy now, it's about letting go in the faith that you're being led to greatness. When you genuinely let go of the 'wanting' of something and you start embracing the 'having' of it and how that feels, you will begin to attract and allow in your desires. Imagine it like you finally let go of the 'boomerang' so that it can come back to you. Remember this doesn't mean that you should let go of the love that you have for what you desire, it is about releasing the wanting, needing and wishing for it, and start embracing how it would feel to have it, to be it or to see it. You aren't letting go of your desires, you're just letting them go so that they can come back to you.

THE BIGGEST DISCOVERIES

Most of the biggest and life changing discoveries that you will ever make in your life will come to you from staying in the present moment and from opening yourself up to more. The 'big' answers that we are all seeking are rarely found by those who are searching for the solutions, but by those people who are open to 'receiving' them. Answers are often found by those people who have opened up that space to allow in the ideas, perspectives and solutions that reside at the highest frequencies. When you continue to allow your assumptions (or your ego's assumptions) to guess what might happen, or what should happen, or the way that the miracle will appear, you unintentionally block it. Doing that would be approaching things from a place of lack (and therefore the vibration of not having it). Instead approach things from a place of peace and power, from a calm allowing. Anything that is done with force or fear, is doomed to fail. The answers always sneak in when you're not looking for them.

HAPP-in-ESS

Happiness isn't out there, it is already within you. It is called happ-IN-ess for a reason, it's found inside and within you. The word happiness has the word 'in' hidden within its spelling to remind you of that. Happiness isn't out there, it isn't hidden in a result. That type of happiness is fleeting, it doesn't last. We have got to stop visualising happiness as a result of getting something. Happiness is only ever a state of being, it isn't something that you have to achieve.

WHAT IS FEAR?

Your feelings are currently letting you know right now in real time whether or not you are on a frequency that would be able to let in the experience that you desire, and whether or not you are vibrating in harmony with your higher self. When you are not vibrating in harmony with that which you desire to have, to do or to be (and when you're not vibrating in harmony with that which you already are at the highest frequency) you will tend to have 'bad' or 'negative' feelings such as fear, to make you aware that you need to change how you are seeing things and seeing yourself if you are to experience things the way that you prefer to experience them. Fear is often that feeling of resistance between what you want to do or be, and what you currently think, feel and believe that you can do or be. Fear is what happens when you don't see yourself as your higher self sees you, when you are seeing things as either being too big or seeing yourself as being too small. Fear is a reminder to put things into perspective and proportion. Fear is the feeling of the misalignment between what you desire to do and be, and what you currently believe is possible for you. Once your desires, beliefs and definitions (of yourself and what you desire) are in alignment, fear disappears. Find peace rather than being 'in pieces'.

MOST ARGUMENTS

Most petty arguments that we find ourselves in daily, are often either an attempt to hurt another how we have been hurt (projecting our hurt onto them) or an attempt to get back the perceived power or control that we think that they, or the world has stolen from us. The truth is that you will only find yourself arguing consistently over something when you are in pain. A happy person doesn't fight. Arguments only occur when you are consistently vibrating at a lower level, or when you are on the same frequency as someone else who is on that lower frequency. Finding yourself in those situations is always an indication that something needs to change.

CLAIMING LACK

What are you actively accepting and associating yourself with, lack or abundance? What are you subtly accepting and settling for? If you don't actively accept wealth and abundance, you will tend to claim poverty and lack by default, often because it is what you experienced growing up, it feels familiar to you, almost expected. It is what you are still associating yourself with or identifying yourself as at the core level. When you are still at some level identifying yourself with the struggle or lack (even subtly by bonding with others over stories of having to struggle) you can't allow in your abundance of blessings. You may still be unknowingly claiming lack as a part of your identity and who you believe you are now, which determines who you will become 'then'. Give up justifying and excusing the limitation in your reality and your mindset. There is no glory nor praise in struggling or denying yourself of that which you desire. You don't have to struggle, you weren't supposed to. You are not meant to live a life of lack and limitation. It is time to choose more. You can't continue to associate yourself with lack, especially when you desire more. Remove all limits that you have placed upon yourself by aligning with your best self. You desire and deserve more, it's time to see beyond 'what is' to what will be. Dream bigger and know your worth, value and greatness. When you stop sustaining thoughts of limitation and any of those lack based beliefs with your focus and attention, the illusion and delusion stops. Let go of sustaining beliefs of struggle, pain and poverty and start sustaining empowering beliefs and thoughts of abundance. Support the life that you desire to see.

BE SELF CENTRED
One of the biggest misinterpretations is the term 'self centred'. Someone who is truly self centred, is someone who is centred within themselves. We often think that being 'self centred' is doing what we like without thought for anyone or anything, however that is actually selfishness (or lack of knowledge of 'the self'). Until you're centred within yourself you'll continue to allow yourself to be affected by 'what is', what was or that which you are observing or experiencing. When you're 'self centred' nothing or no one can affect you for long, and you'll no longer base or centre your joy, peace and success upon or within anything else but yourself.

YOU HAVEN'T PEAKED
You haven't peaked, you have only reached a hill, a hill that depending on the frequency that you're seeing things from will either inspire you to keep going or convince you to give up. I know that you're tired but don't give up. Rest and try again. Don't confuse this hill for the summit or the peak. Your story isn't over yet, there is still so much more in store for you. The journey so far may have been a tiring one, but look at how far you have come

(rather than worrying about how far you still have to go). You'll make it just as long as you have faith and you take it all step by step.

ADMIT FAULTS AND PROBLEMS

When you take the time to become aware of potential issues, faults, or negative patterns of behaviour within yourself (in the name of growth and healing) you can begin to acknowledge and then let them go without resisting or fighting against them. By acknowledging and admitting our own faults, without guilt or shame, we can commit ourselves to changing and overcoming them. Any negative trait or pattern of behaviour that you can see within yourself, you are able to change or let go of. Your inner being is making you aware of that 'fault' and is opening your eyes to that issue because it is no longer serving you, which is often why this process is called awakening.

YOUR BELIEFS

Be aware of your beliefs. If you are not aware of the beliefs that you are operating your life from, you won't be able to change them. It is important to find out whether or not your beliefs are having a positive or a 'negative' affect and impact on your life and the life that you desire to live. Be aware of those beliefs, or beware the affect that they will have on your life if you continue to give them free reign on the choices that you make and the actions that you take. Bring your beliefs to the surface. Ask yourself, 'What do I believe most to be true about X, Y, Z?'. Any response that you receive is often what you believe most to be true right now. Your reactions, including your unconscious beliefs and any lack, pain or fear based thoughts will make themselves known. If your reactions are 'positive', let them be, if they're 'negative', let them go. You can't afford to hold onto any belief that no longer serves you, especially any belief that places limits upon what you can do and who you can become. You can't allow your old beliefs to continue to hold you back from succeeding and allowing in your blessings. In time, once you choose to consciously respond to life as the person that you are becoming, that will begin to become your new natural response to life. A new empowering belief will have been formed.

THINKING IRRATIONALLY

A simple fact that often goes unnoticed is that you can't act rationally when you are thinking irrationally. It is only once you step back, calm down and centre yourself will you then be able to think clearly and make more informed decisions, and make decisions from a higher and more broader perspective. When you are in the midst of a problem the momentum is often too strong to see things clearly. Never make an important or life altering decision in a moment of anger, fear, anxiety or worry. When we are thinking irrationally we will tend to make situations much bigger than they need to be, and we will end up being more dramatic than is necessary. BREAKING NEWS!!!, your mind likes to be dramatic. Don't let the 'headlines' of your mind stop you from taking action, or allow them to stop you from seeing things clearly, and from finding peace or being happy. To change the size of the problem, try changing the perspective that you're seeing it from. See problems as they are, and not any worse than they need to be. See through them to the solutions that are hiding just beyond them.

IS IT REALLY GUIDANCE?

Please understand that the universe / God will respond to you where you are, every single time. That is where the path of least resistance begins, which is the path that will take you further and take you up and out of the current circumstance that you are facing. However don't confuse the divine guidance that the universe brings you with perspectives of your current lower frequency. When you are facing a tough or a difficult situation that you are unsure about, such as whether or not you should leave your current job, you might ask the universe a question such as, "Should I leave this job?", yet at the deepest level you fear that you can't do without it and you believe that you have no other options, therefore the 'advice' that you are open to receiving back will confirm that perspective and feeling to you, rather than being 'true' and divine guidance from the universe. If you ask for help and guidance, and you leave enough room to allow it in, you will receive it. However it is important that you vibrate higher in order to receive that real and divine guidance. Until then the 'advice' that you will receive won't be helpful. It will continue to confirm to you what you already believe and how you are currently already seeing things, rather than showing you what is ultimately best for you. In addition, when you find yourself feeling overwhelmed by a negative situation, it is often difficult to see a way forward, however the universe can. When the momentum has subsided ask the universe for guidance and for support. If you leave enough room it will light up the path ahead. Don't ask, "Why does this always happen to me?", as the universe will tend to highlight the problems rather than the solutions. Begin by first allowing how you feel, and then choose to completely detach. Intend for the solution to reveal itself to you, ask the universe or your higher self, "How can I move forward stronger from this?". That perspective will allow the answers and divine guidance to reveal itself to you and be highlighted in your consciousness and reality, you may even choose to pray for guidance. Prayer is in essence a form of visualisation, it is a form of communication and connection with your inner and higher self, it is a way to strengthen your faith in what you desire and prefer while also strengthening the connection that you have with that higher power. Ask for guidance and you will receive it every single time, just as long as you are open and able to allow it in.

UNHAPPY PEOPLE?
Unhappy people tend to spend more of their time and energy focussing upon and talking about people, things and events that they don't want or don't like more than the life, feelings and events that they do desire to have and experience. It is often said where your attention goes, energy flows. Unhappy people allow their undivided attention to be transfixed upon 'what is', what

was or what they don't like. When they do that they will have no time left to focus upon and envision all that they do prefer. Make yourself this promise, to only ever rest your undivided attention and awareness upon that which you desire to see or feel more of. Your attention is the basis of creation. Think of your time and energy as being precious commodities, just like money. They will run out fast if you invest them poorly. Only invest in those things that will add value, joy, love and peace to yourself and all others.

REACTIVE REACTIONS

Do you recognise and truly understand that your reactions are just like an automated system, a system that automatically engages and responds to your environment without much conscious thought or effort from you? That system will continue to react for you until you consciously respond for yourself. It will form its current reaction based on how you reacted to a particular (or similar) thing or situation in the past, using past analysis of that situation to make assumptions and predictions in the present moment. Therefore any time that you react to something, you're actually only ever reacting to the present situation or struggle as the person that you were, not as the person that you are right now. Until you 'turn off' the system, take back the 'controls' and begin to respond to life, things won't and can't change. Those reactions can be highly reactive and explosive if not kept in check. When you begin to step back (and no longer react to life) and you begin to consciously respond to your thoughts and experiences as the person that you're becoming, every single thing about your life will begin to improve dramatically and change for the better.

LIFE ISN'T FAIR, GET USED TO IT

When we grow up in an environment of lack (with limited amounts of money and opportunities) we are often told that 'life isn't fair' and that we should just accept it and get used to it. We are often told, at an early age, to stop asking for what we want because our parents (or those who raised us) couldn't afford it. Other things that we were told, often subtly, is that we won't get what we want, that life is always going to be a struggle or that things will never really get better. Although that perspective was intended to 'toughen us up' and protect us, it often causes great harm. More than likely you are at some level still living with those beliefs and still seeing yourself and life from that limited perspective. Maybe you even feel guilty for wanting more or for having more. We can't continue to pass down those fearful beliefs (which are based on lack and limitation) to the next generation, they aren't helping, a change is needed. Give something worth receiving to the next generation, instead of persisting that generational fear and the idea of lack and limitation. Your parents did what they could with what they had, forgive them, they didn't know any better, but you know better now, new beliefs are needed. Having that cynical, lack and fear based perspective is holding you back, it is ultimately preventing your blessings from flowing into your reality, it's stopping you from dreaming of better and visualising more, and preventing you from becoming your best self (all of which would allow in that which you desire). It doesn't matter what happened before, things are changing. No more giving into that old way of seeing things or fighting against that lack based perspective. It's time to update your beliefs. Start again, believing that anything is possible for you. It is time to release the fear and embrace the truth that life can be great if we give it enough room to be.

FORCING THINGS?
Give up trying to force things. The need to force things into being is often a sign of inner feelings of fear and lack. When you try and force things into being, you'll likely be trying to make something happen that just isn't in your highest good. Your higher self and the universe always knows better, so trust it. Please understand that at the highest level your higher self could be protecting you from something that you want, but isn't meant for you, ultimately because you are meant for even better and greater. Trust what unfolds. If you don't get what you desire it only ever means that you're meant for even more.

A CLEAR AND CONSISTENT VISION

Without a clear and consistent vision of who you desire to be and what you desire to see, the only thing that you will tend to perceive and focus upon is 'what is' or 'what was' (which is often what you don't want). A clear and empowering vision will allow you to gain a higher perspective, enabling you to see everything (including yourself) more clearly. It will allow you to see beyond 'what is' to what can be. Until then you'll tend to allow what was to determine the reality of what will be, or allow what happened to you to limit and shape what you can become. When you have a bigger and brighter vision for your life (that you can believe in and 'live into') it tends to pull you forward and lift you up and out of your current circumstance.

THE DOORS TO YOUR DESIRES

Like everything in life, there is a natural order to things. Things happen and unfold in a way that allows us to not only be able to handle them, but also enjoy them too, and the same goes for success and your desires. Think of there being numerous doors and gates that lead you to the success that you desire. The gates are there keeping you from your desires not because you don't deserve them, but because if you were to go from the first door to the last door of success you wouldn't be able to handle or enjoy your desires. Each door that you go through, leaves you with a valuable lesson and blessing (or a 'key' piece of information) that will allow you to be able to handle what's next. It is all necessary. The space between each gate is the training ground for success. Opening up the doors one by one allows you to thrive, not just merely survive. It's important that you don't try to jump the 'gates' to success. Take things step by step, there is no need to rush through the gates, ultimately they're not keeping you from success, they're only keeping you from harming yourself and from being overwhelmed. All of the gates and lessons are necessary, they're protecting you at the core level. Each closed door or gate you encounter is letting you know that there is still more to learn and lessons yet to be applied before you can reach the 'final' gate that opens up the door to your success. It is so important that you move towards the current opportunity or gate that has just opened up, rather than sticking around the door that you have already walked through. That won't keep you safe or fulfil you. If you continue to come across closed doors, bless them. Those doors were not meant for you. They're locked for a reason, essentially to keep you from what is not meant for you. Take a look around you for the door that is just about to open up in your immediate environment, one that your specific talents, skills and personality is a perfect fit for. Embracing who you really are is the key that will open up that door.

THAT'S YOUR JOB
How you feel is ultimately your own responsibility. It isn't up to someone else to make or keep you happy, fulfilled or safe. You have got to take back responsibility for looking after yourself. When we blame something or someone else for how we feel, we hand over our power to that situation. Also when you allow others to directly affect or determine how you feel you'll never find lasting peace. Your happiness will always be conditional, constantly dependent on another situation or person.

AFTER PAINFUL EVENTS
It is vital that you give yourself time, especially after a painful or unexpected event, to not only process your feelings, but also to step back, and centre or ground yourself again. Don't fall into the trap of reacting in the moment, you won't be able to see properly or think clearly from that lower frequency of pain and hurt. Give yourself enough time to come to terms with what has happened. Go through the motions, or the emotions. Acknowledge, allow and accept 'what is' and how you feel. Until you do, you'll continue to push against it, which will continue to persist it and resist your healing. Give things time, process things at your own speed. Please understand that no one ever sees the lesson

straight away, that only comes in time once you are able to step back and see things from another perspective.

GET YOUR HOPES UP
Are you afraid to get your hopes up just in case you'll be disappointed? We often think that not getting our hopes up will stop us from being upset, however doing that is likely stopping things from improving too. Regardless of how things look or 'what is' get your hopes up and keep them there, that is where they should be. Getting your hopes up is not about needing things to go a certain way in order for you to be happy, it is about being happy and allowing your hopes to be increased as a natural result of your increased frequency. Above all else, don't give up hope.

FEELING EMPTY?
Feeling 'empty' is often the result of centring yourself in 'what is' or what was. It's important to understand that you can't centre yourself within those things, you need something deeper and more stable. That is essentially why you feel so empty. Those feelings of emptiness are a result of not being centred within yourself, and when you have allowed an experience or a feeling to stop you from getting in touch with the love, peace and purpose that is within you. You can't centre yourself within a result or an opinion of someone else. You may also feel empty when you haven't given yourself the love, patience, care and support that you need, and when your inner 'cup' is empty. The moment that you begin to get in touch within, you'll begin to feel the fullness of who you really are.

YOUR SOUL ALWAYS KNOWS BEST
Your soul always knows better no matter how wise that you think you are. No one is beyond support or guidance. Ask your inner spirit or soul, for guidance and for support, it will listen and answer you every single time without fail. It will often speak to you in subtle little ways that you never even thought of before, such as overheard conversations, messages in songs, newspaper

articles etc, so be open and remain aware. Your soul will primarily speak to you via your feelings and your intuition or gut feeling / instinct. Your spirit is always there silently guiding and encouraging you, just open up and listen. Trust how it makes you feel about things.

THOSE 'BIG' PROBLEMS
When you focus upon the 'largeness' of your problems rather than the vastness of the power of the universe, problems seem to get bigger. In addition when you only focus upon the 'smallness' of you, you will also lose awareness of the power that is within you too. It is important that you don't let how you have been used to seeing your problems in the past determine how you see problems in the present, and especially determine the energy that you bring to them. How you see something is how it will appear. Acknowledge the problem, however rise above it to the frequency that the solutions reside at. Choose from now on to no longer make the problems in your life 'big', or at least bigger than they need to be, and make your faith in yourself and the universe bigger.

FEELING ALONE?
You're not alone, the universe is always with you. There is a hidden hand that is guiding all things, which is also protecting you every single step that you take. No matter where you are or where you go, that divine energy and love will be right there beside you. If you ever feel alone, lost or powerless, always remember that you have your ancestors too. Call upon them. Whether you know it or not, they are always there silently encouraging and protecting you every single step of the way. They're walking alongside you. They are all lined up right behind you, ready to help. Feel them speaking through you. Tap into that eternal energy that is always available to you. Feel that divine protection and love wrapping around you, feel it renewing and restoring your spirit. You have an army of ancestors that are ready

and willing to help. You're stronger than you could ever begin to imagine and even more loved than you know.

START WHERE YOU ARE

Start where you are and use what you have. You are here in this place, at this time, for a greater reason and purpose. Often one of the biggest excuses that we use to not take action upon our dreams and goals is saying that, "I'm not in the right place" or "There are no opportunities here". Many times the opportunity that you were looking for begins where you are right now. It is often said start where you are and use what you have, ultimately because the path of least resistance always starts where you are, which will eventually lead you to where you desire to be. However when you believe that there are no good opportunities where you are right now, they can't reveal themselves to you. You'll fail to use the present moment effectively and you will end up holding back the opportunities, experiences and thoughts that would allow things to improve. You stop the possibility of things getting any better. Doing that will cause you to focus upon the lack in your present environment or within yourself, which will allow and call in even more of that into your awareness, path and environment. You will cut yourself off from receiving those ideas that could take you out of that current environment. So always remember, start where you are right now and do what you can, and the universe will begin to respond in time. Don't give up. Dedicate yourself to making committed decisions rather than exaggerated excuses. Always remember that excuses are to be excused.

SAY NOTHING

It is often said that if you don't have anything positive or helpful to say, don't say anything at all. Sometimes saying nothing is the best solution and the best response. The reason why is because it would require you to go down to a lower frequency to say it. Although that sentence will keep you in good stead, sometimes you will need to say something. Sometimes it's necessary to make people aware of your boundaries and limits for your own peace of mind and safety. When you centre yourself and consciously respond (rather than reacting to what other people say or do, from a place of pain and hurt) you will know the difference between having something to say and having to say something.

LET GO OF PAIN

You don't have to do anything to heal, except let go of the pain. Although it sounds so simple when it is said like that, in reality it can often be a difficult process for many. At some level we tend to believe that letting go of the pain means that we are condoning what happened or what someone else has done, or that we are letting them 'get away with it', however that is not the case. We don't have to create a way to peace, healing and happiness, those feelings are who we really are, they're our natural state of being. However what we do create and continue to practise, are the blocks and limitations to our inner happiness and peace. All you need to do to heal is remove the blocks to your peace and happiness. So what is blocking it? What perspectives and beliefs are currently separating you from your inner peace and separating it from you? Remember you don't create the way to happiness through more action, you do it through more 'allowing'. You feel your way to peace. Holding onto the story of 'what was' and the pain associated with it, won't bring you healing or peace, it will only ever continue to drag you down and hold you back from becoming your best self. It ultimately stops you from acting upon your highest purpose. You can't keep allowing the actions and projections of someone else's pain, keep you from your healing and your purpose. Please give up the need to hear sorry or hear the reason why they did what they did (or why they failed to do something) it is just not worth it. No more letting that situation be in control of your healing and your peace, choose you. Although you may have been hurt badly by someone else in the past, you have unknowingly continued to hurt yourself even more since then by holding onto that pain, anger and hurt. You can't reach for healing when you are still holding onto and claiming that pain. By accepting that we are in pain, we can begin to accept back responsibility and accountability for getting better. Letting go is a steady and consistent process, it can't be rushed. Please don't go searching for stuff to let go of either, let what is ready to be healed within you come to the surface by itself. Healing is a natural process with a natural order to it. It is in essence a constant process of just letting things go, which in turn frees you. Don't rush it though, just keep on forgiving, 'allowing' and letting go when something that is ready to go raises its head. Anything that is currently in your awareness right now is ready to be acknowledged, understood, healed and released. Let it move on now, don't force it, allow it. You will begin to move on with your life the moment that you begin to allow the pain to move through you, rather than you moving away from it.

REDEFINE FAILURE

Failure is one of the most misunderstood experiences. We are often raised to believe that failure means that at some level we aren't good enough, or that we are a failure. However failing doesn't mean that you are a failure, it just means that there is another and an even better way forward for you, that you're getting closer to success, that you're meant for more, and that there is still work to be done before you can get the results that you desire and deserve. Failure is always an opportunity to better yourself (which you can often only see looking back). Redefine and reinterpret failure as an opportunity to refine what you're doing. Embrace it and what it's here to teach you, although it isn't always easy, it's critical to your overall success.

MONEY MAKING IDEAS

Every single moment of the day we are constantly being supplied with multi million dollar ideas, however we often cast them aside before they even have a chance to grow and develop. We think to ourselves (or we let others tell us) that it'll never work. It's vital that we see beyond our first reaction (which is often just a reflection of who we were or how we are used to seeing things).

However please understand that we aren't meant to see 'the way' to success straight away, that often comes in divine timing, that is the universe's job. It's your job to take those inspired ideas that fill you with passion and excitement to their highest potential. Holding onto an idea won't give it a chance to 'flower'. Plant those ideas in fertile ground, let them grow, follow through with them, water them, protect and nourish them, bring them to fruition. Be patient, give them time. Think of each thought that fills you with passion and excitement as being a seed, which given the right conditions, has the potential to grow into something incredible.

DON'T GIVE UP HOPE

When you don't have faith in the idea that 'It all works out in the end', you will tend to want to give up, or you will end up giving into your fears. You will inevitably start to focus upon where you are or where you are not, and start to get thoughts like, 'You're lost' or 'There is no hope'. You will get those type of thoughts not because they're the truth but because they're a reflection and a manifestation of the frequency that you're currently vibrating at. That which you focus upon, the universe will continue to provide you even more proof of. You can only ever see that which you believe to be true. It's time to start believing in your success rather than believing in your failure and your limitations. That is why it is wise to never give up hope. When you have hope left in your heart, you leave 'the door open' to allow in thoughts, people and situations that will take you higher and to that next level.

I'M TOO OLD NOW

Getting older isn't an excuse to not go after your dreams. You're never too old to become the person that you have always dreamed of becoming. If you're still here then you still have time. You still have so much to do and so much to offer. When you believe that you don't have enough time, then you won't. When you believe that you have no purpose now simply because you're older, then you won't. What you believe, you will become. Believing that you are too old is an excuse that will take away your gifts and keep you unhappy. The only thing that's stopping you is your current mindset.

APPROVE BEFORE IMPROVING

Any attempt to improve yourself without first approving of yourself will always be in vain. If you're not happy and you're not approving of yourself now, you won't be happy 'then', a result won't change that. You'll always be chasing happiness and worthiness. Is there any part of yourself that you're still secretly rejecting? Please accept yourself fully, as you are and where you are. You will ultimately become that which you accept or fail to accept about yourself. Your natural state of being is love. Trouble only occurs when you let something or someone get in the way of knowing, remembering and feeling that, and when you allow something to stop you from loving, respecting and valuing yourself. Embrace every single part of yourself. Make it a priority to love and approve of yourself unconditionally. The universe doesn't make mistakes, you're made the way that you are for a greater purpose and reason.

IT'S THE WAY THAT YOU DO IT

There is an old wise saying that states, "It is not what you do, it's the way that you do it, that is what gets results". That simple sentence has so much truth to it. It is not only the 'what' that you do (which is the actions that you take) but the 'how' that you do it that primarily creates your results. In addition it is not only the way that you do things that matters, but it is also the 'why' or the reason why you do it that has significant importance too. So ask yourself, what is the reason for my actions? What am I hoping to achieve? Why am I doing it that way? By asking why, you will help to reveal the intention or the energy beneath it. The intention for doing something always directly affects and helps to determine the result. The intention determines the energy that will flow into the task that you're doing. Before you do anything, set your intention first and plan your actions around that intention. That way your actions will be implemented from a place of power, and not from a place of pain or lack.

IT'S ALL FALLING APART

Things often only fall apart to allow even better things to come together. You asked the universe for change, for more, for greater, and this could be the first step in the process of that happening. Opportunities are often first disguised as a disaster, however if that is how you define it (a disaster) then that's how it will appear to you and how you will experience it. Please understand that the universe often brings you peace from the pieces of your old life. If you are only focussing upon what you are letting go of and leaving behind, you won't be able to see what you are about to let in. You'll continue to block your blessings. This is the time to have faith. Don't panic and most importantly don't be afraid to let go and go with the flow. You aren't being tested or punished by the universe, you are simply being reminded of your own inner strength and power. Your prayers are being heard and are being answered. Let go and let yourself be led to greater.

PANIC EASILY?

Feelings of panic are never a reason to be afraid, they are in fact always an indication to relax. When you feel panic regarding anything, first of all let it be (which helps to let it go) just let it move through you. Relax, don't fight against those thoughts or feelings, or analyse them or try to push them away, or give into them. Please understand that what you are actually doing when you are panicking is you are making that situation or thing bigger than you. You are giving away your power to that which you're observing or that current situation. You are saying that it is bigger than you, when it isn't. That is exactly the reason why it feels panic inducing, not because of what is happening, but because of how you are interpreting it and how you are seeing things. You believe at some level that it has the power to defeat you, when it doesn't. That is when your body will give you those feelings of panic to make you aware that how you're seeing things isn't how your higher self sees it. It is a reminder to relax and remember that all is well. Don't fall into the trap of fighting against those feelings, understand that they are just passing through you. They always do. Relax into the thought or feeling of something else that feels better to you, or another perspective or point of focus. Whenever you do that you'll be able to release the momentum of that 'panicky' feeling, and the resistance against feeling better. You'll be able to choose again, from your new higher frequency and higher perspective. Realise panic is just a 'wrong' and distorted perception. There is nothing to fear. Panic is always an indication to remove your attention from how you're currently seeing yourself and how you're currently seeing things. Now that you are beginning to change how you are seeing feelings such as fear and panic, you have begun to change the power that they once had over you forever. Remember that you are more powerful than you could ever begin to imagine.

IT IS TIME
This message is appearing before you today because you're ready. You've done the inner work, you've worked on those plans long enough, it's time to turn them into a reality. It is time to start believing in yourself and your dreams. It is time to rise above your limitations and fears. No more talking yourself out of taking action. It is time to reveal your talents to the world. No more living a sheltered life, it's time to step out of the shadows and into the spotlight. Stop denying your magnificence to yourself and others. Rise up. Claim your greatness and power. Everything that you're seeking right now will begin to unfold the moment that you start believing in yourself and you start taking action.

WHAT IS PERFECT TIMING?
'Perfect timing' is more than just coincidence, luck or chance, it is the result of being on a higher frequency. When you're vibrating at that frequency you're allowing in that which you're seeking at the highest level. You'll find that people, answers and opportunities just seem to magically appear in your consciousness

and environment, you'll always find yourself in the right place at the right time, which we interpret as being 'perfect timing'. In essence, 'perfect timing' is the time that it takes for you to come into vibrational harmony with that which you desire, which would begin to allow it into your reality.

WHY SO SERIOUS?

Seriousness always leads to serious situations. There is no need to be so serious and professional about everything all of the time. Those who are the most 'uptight' tend to find themselves in those serious situations the most often. Being serious isn't a reflection of your power, self control or strength, it's often just a sign of your own fear. Lighten up. When you do, you'll rise up to a higher frequency. There is no need to be so serious all of the time to achieve greatness or be respected. So relax and go with the flow. Let joy create the path ahead rather than your serious nature. A delicate balance between both sides is key to living your best life.

THIS HAPPENS BEFORE CHANGE

Before all great change your mind will often resist. Your mind may be flooded with thoughts like "I'm not good enough", "I'm not ready", or, "I can't do this", however please don't give into those thoughts. Those thoughts are just who you were and what you used to think, feel and believe regarding that which you're currently observing or doing. Use those thoughts as a reminder and invitation to view yourself, and that which you desire in a way that feels better to you. From that place of power, move forward with purpose, positivity, courage and confidence. You have work to do, you're needed, you can do this!

THEY'RE TEACHING YOU SOMETHING

Every single person in your life has purpose. Not one single person who comes into your life has nothing to teach you. We are all teachers for each other, all teaching in different ways. Some will teach you through pain and others through love. Sometimes they may not even consciously or verbally teach you anything, but in hindsight you'll see the lesson that they taught and the blessing that they brought you. Everyone has at least one vital and valuable lesson to teach you. Learn from their mistakes too. You will often find yourself drawn to those people who have something 'big' to teach you (whether 'positive' or 'negative'). They are here to teach you something that will alter your current life course.

DRESS REHEARSING FEAR?

Do you ever find yourself dress rehearsing fear? Maybe you are consistently imagining the worst and preparing for it now just in case it happens? Maybe you're trying to get all of the anxiety out of the way before it happens and you're 'dress rehearsing' the situation so that you would know how to handle it if it should happen to occur? It is vital that you stop doing this. It is wise to be prepared for the worst, but expecting it will continue to hold back your blessings. The moment that you start to imagine failure in your mind (imagined or not) you will start to get into the feeling place and frequency of it, which helps to call it into your reality. When you anticipate how you're going to feel in regards to anything, you will begin to call that into your awareness and environment. Your anticipation is helping to create it and allow it into your reality. You're telling your mind that this upcoming situation is something to be fearful of, which your brain saves as a memory so that any time that you think of it again, your mind will supply you with those fearful thoughts, perspectives and feelings to save you time. Every time that you encounter that situation again you'll just pick the subject and its vibration back up where you left it off last time. All of which will cause you to feel that way any time that you think of it. In addition you'll start to define yourself as being an anxious person, which the universe will respond to and reflect back. You'll end up calling and allowing into your reality even more situations which will make you feel anxious. However the real reason why you feel anxious is not because you should be scared of that which you're doing or that which you're observing, but because your higher self is reminding you to relax and change how you're seeing things. It feels bad to you because it's not how your higher self sees things. Having that 'negative' expectation regarding yourself and your desires will continue to block the best result and experience from unfolding. It's time to respond to life rather than just unconsciously reacting to it. Instead of imagining the worst and having faith in failure, trust in greater. Trust that your inner or higher self is taking care of it and that it will all unfold in perfect and divine timing (which always takes longer than your ego expects it to take). In the meantime just connect to the best outcome. Please remember that you don't need to prepare for failure, you already have within you the ability and the knowledge of how to react in the moment if things should happen to go 'wrong'. Those solutions reside at higher frequencies, and not the frequency and perspective of fear and dress rehearsing failure. Vibrate higher.

FORCING IT?

Although effort is required in life, if you feel like you have to 'make' something happen or force something into being, that is often a sign from the universe that it isn't meant for you, or that it either isn't meant to happen right now, that you're meant for more and for even better. Now this doesn't mean that you shouldn't put in the work. You have got to take action and at times 'push' yourself to do that which you're capable of doing. However give up trying to force things to go your way only. Leave room for better and for greater. Let the universe do its job, let it decide the way that it should appear and how it will manifest, let it determine the 'right' time. It can see the best route. Trust that the 'way' will reveal itself to you, and that you can't miss it. Be patient. Your job is to decide what you want and why you want it, and let the universe work out when and how you will receive it. That need to force things into being is often just a reflection of your own fear and doubt, rather than a reflection of your faith in the belief that things will all work out for your highest good. Remember that what you push against, always pushes back harder. Just let go and go with the flow.

ANCESTORS

Consider this for a moment, just imagine if your parents (or your grandparents) didn't meet at that precise moment in time, you wouldn't be here. Go back 100 generations and marvel at that perfect timing and divine guidance. An invisible hand and higher power led them through every single struggle and hardship, protecting your family from disease, famines and wars just so that you could be here today. That higher power knew that you were needed. Do you finally realise just how special and how loved you are? That higher power is protecting and guiding your life too. To carry on feeling unworthy and unloved, knowing what you now know, would be an insult to your ancestors and the entire universe.

TALENT OPENS DOORS

Think of your unique set of talents and gifts as being a key. A key that will open up a very specific door that is meant just for you. Too often in life we get caught up looking at everyone else's open doors or we allow ourselves to get distracted looking at all those closed doors that we have encountered. However those doors were never meant for us. Just like the key to your home will only ever open up your door, your talents will do the same for you. Your talents will only open up those doors that are meant for you, doors that will lead you to where you belong and what is right for you. Someday soon you're going to come across the door that is meant for you, and it will open up and reveal to you all of those blessings that have been residing at a vibrational level until now, which have been patiently waiting for you to rise up and allow them in. Please understand that there are many different doors to your purpose and blessings. Don't worry if you miss that window of opportunity. As one window or door closes, the universe will open up another one just for you. The universe always leaves an open door in close proximity to you that will eventually lead you to where you're meant to be. Don't give up, look again, and keep going.

THE PEOPLE THAT CHANGE THE WORLD

The greatest success stories often come from those people who have faced the greatest struggles and failures in life, those people who have survived the greatest pain and suffering. They turned those trials into the making of them, rather than the breaking of them. They refused to allow 'what was' to determine who they are, or define what was possible for them, they chose to rise above it all. They focussed their attention upon what will be rather than fighting against, focussing upon or giving into 'what was', which in time began to allow in their blessings instead of cutting themselves off from them. It is often those exact people that will change the world for the better.

VALUE YOURSELF

We often learn growing up what our worth and value is by how other people treat us or fail to treat us. If our parents, or those around us, didn't value or respect us, then that is often the value, use and worth that we will tend to claim and bring with us throughout our life, that is until we become aware and we change within. When we grow up in an environment in which we don't feel validated or feel like we were seen or heard, then what tends to happen is we either shrink back or we rebel. At the core level we often treat ourselves how others have treated us, or we end up treating others that way. When we treat ourselves poorly we allow others to treat us that way too. They will begin to treat us how we have been treating ourselves. We will allow others to hurt or disrespect us to the level and degree that we have been hurting and disrespecting ourselves. It often becomes a never ending pattern and cycle of hurt and pain until we choose more. It is not until we decide to see, recognise and claim the value and power that is within ourselves are we then able to acknowledge, face and then forgive the past and choose again. Often the truth is that our parents didn't know any better. They could only give to us what others had given to them. They may have unintentionally hurt us because they were in pain, they didn't know how to handle their pain or know how to go about healing it. It is all that they knew. In order for things to change, you have got to start seeing the value and worth that is within yourself, which was there all along, but was hidden beyond the disillusion of unworthiness. Start by accepting and loving yourself unconditionally now, and start doing it today. Choose love as the filter in which you see yourself and the world from.

BLAMING

When you continue to blame someone or something else for where you are or how you're currently feeling, you'll continue to be stuck on a lower frequency, which will take you off course and prevent you from being your best self. When you're on that lower frequency you'll continue to be supplied with thoughts like, 'Look at what they did to me' or ' This isn't fair', which the universe will respond to and reflect back. You will continue to allow into your life even more events, people and things that will make you feel like that. Blaming someone or something else will cause you to be stuck in a cycle of self destruction, it will also remove from you the opportunity and the power to change your life for the better. No more 'wallowing', it is time to claim back responsibility for your own life and for what happens next. Once you stop blaming, you can start claiming back responsibility and accountability for how you feel, for what happens next and for determining your own future. You will then be able to vibrate higher and allow in those solutions that you have been seeking.

WHAT IS COINCIDENCE?

There is no such thing as 'coincidence', luck or chance. That which we perceive as being coincidence is often the result of a much greater power at play. Coincidence can often be the beginning stages of your desires manifesting into your life, and also be part of the process of the universe answering your prayers.
Coincidence can also keep you safe. It is that force that will place you in the right place at the right time, especially when the conditions are right. Coincidence isn't the result of mere chance, it

is the result of being in alignment with who you really are and that which you desire at the highest level. Coincidence is what happens when vibrations coincide and align, and when beliefs and frequencies are in harmony with each other. When your vibration is in harmony with the frequency that your desires reside at, coincidences occur.

WHAT ARE YOU SENDING AHEAD?

What you do now affects what is next, whether 'positive' or 'negative'. What you do now is pre-sent ahead into your 'future' (which is just an updated version of now). It is important to understand that any pain or emotions that are not fully felt, processed, healed and released in the present moment are literally being pre-sent into your future in order for you to see and face them again (which will often be in a more difficult scenario and disguise) for you to see the lesson that it was there to teach you, and for you to start applying it in your own life and find healing. Only once you allow that pain based energy to move through you, will you then be able to consciously create your reality from a place of peace and power, rather than a place of pain and fear. When you embrace your inner self, and the power, strength and love that is within you, you will start to send that energy ahead allowing a path that feels like that to unfold in front of you. Your 'yellow brick road' will start to unravel and begin to take you in an even better direction. You will begin to allow love, joy and peace to lead you to roads and avenues that will bring you to your destiny and highest blessings, rather than roads and avenues which would take you away from them.

KEEPING EVERYONE HAPPY?

When you make it your job and responsibility to keep everyone else happy, what you are really saying to yourself and the universe is that your happiness doesn't matter and that it is not a priority, which is what the universe will respond to and reflect back. Every situation, experience and person that you will encounter will confirm that to you and leave you feeling that way, they'll all confirm to you that your happiness isn't important. When you make your happiness a priority, everything begins to come together.

ONLY AN EGO FEELS UNWORTHY
Please believe in yourself. Believe in your worth, talents, message, purpose and your value. Until you do, no one else can. The universe wants you to succeed, however it can only ever respond to you, it can't choose for you. The universe can only ever give you back even more of what you are currently focussing upon and what you feel and believe you already have or that which you're worthy of receiving. Please understand that only an ego feels unworthy and not good enough. Go deeper, get in touch with who you really are. You really are enough as you are, and where you are. In addition, give up seeking the confirmation and the validation of another successful person (or even someone that you love) to make you feel like you are enough and to know that you have 'made it'. Give up needing to make someone else proud too, it's unnecessary. When you seek any of those things, you make that the goal, which holds back (to some degree) the success that was meant for you.

CONTROL
Give up trying to control circumstances, situations, things or people to feel happy, safe and strong. The need to control everything is the most common symptom of fear. Trying to control everything is truly exhausting. It was never your job to control things. Let the universe do its job. Surrender your fears. Trust, let go and go with the flow. Trust that you'll be protected and guided. Surrender the stress, and embrace the best.

GROWING TOGETHER OR GROWING APART?
In most relationships you will either grow together or grow apart. Not everyone grows at the same rate or at the same pace, some people outgrow each other and that's perfectly OK. Too often you see those people who hold onto a toxic relationship in fear, and

try and force their partner to grow with them, or grow for them. Deep down their request for growth is because they are afraid that they won't love again if they let this current relationship go, believing that things won't get any better than 'what is'. Yet at the core level they are both desperately unhappy and are ready to move on. They both know but maybe don't want to face the fact that there is no more room to grow in that relationship. Any thought that says, 'I'll never love again', is just a reflection of the lower frequency that they are viewing love, themselves and life from. It is not the ultimate truth. The truth is that not every relationship is supposed to last, and it is not your job to try and force things to work either, especially if you are doing it all alone. It's not your job to push your partner to grow with you. You can of course encourage them to grow (and assist them when they're ready to grow and once they begin to grow) however you can't force them to grow with you for the sake of a relationship or for the sake of your happiness. It has to be their choice. It isn't your job to pray for someone else to change either, or your responsibility to make sure that they reach that breakthrough. Focus upon your own growth, and know that if the relationship comes to an end that you can let go in the faith that you are both being led to more. Take with you the lessons that you both learned from that relationship and from each other. Your soul knows when it's time to let go and move on. Problems only occur when you don't listen to it the first time.

DIVINE TIMING
I know that you are tired of waiting for your desires to show up, you have kept yourself thinking positively and feeling good for so long now, and you just want success to arrive. However very often we haven't learned the spiritual lessons that would allow us to not only fully enjoy what we desire, but handle it too. The universe will only ever give us what we can handle when we can handle it, all at a pace that we can enjoy. Everything that you experience and go through, or more accurately grow through, leaves you with a lesson, a lesson which will allow you to be able

to handle what is next. Therefore any moment that you find yourself feeling frustrated, annoyed or angry at the universe for not giving you what you want, be thankful. Recognise that the universe is only protecting you. Right now the universe is currently organising situations and events that will lead you to your success. Just have faith that it is all arriving in divine timing.

MADE TO FEEL GUILTY FOR YOUR FEELINGS?

An environment in which everyone feels comfortable speaking openly and honestly about how they really feel is necessary in order for us to heal and become our best selves. When you are made to feel guilty about how you feel, you'll never be able to open up and heal. In addition when you're afraid to speak about how you're really feeling in the moment or in regards to the past, in fear of the repercussions or in fear that it might upset someone else, you won't be able to heal or grow. It is important to leave guilt, shame and blame behind when it comes to creating a safe environment for healing. Let everyone express their experience and their perspective. Give them enough room to express how you too may have unconsciously affected them. Be able to hear how you can heal and improve too. Don't just listen to them, but make them feel heard, acknowledged and understood. You would be surprised at how much that can assist in someone else's healing and growth.

REJECTION BRINGS DIRECTION

From rejection comes direction. A closed door is always a blessing. Rejection is always protection from the universe. Rejection keeps you from what is not meant for you. If you don't get what you desire it only ever means that you are meant for more. Rejection is a blessing that will guide you towards your purpose.

WHO BENEFITS WHEN YOU WIN?

When you succeed and win, who wins too? Who is your success helping? Who and what is your work promoting, saving, supporting and encouraging? That simple question will keep you in alignment with your core values and morals. Success truly is all about service and giving back (not just financially giving back too). The more successful and 'bigger' that you get, the bigger that your responsibility to help and give back becomes. What you get, give to others. Educate, inspire and encourage them. A truly successful person lifts others up and shares their success. Share what you have. What you hold back from others, the universe ultimately holds back from you.

TRYING TO CHANGE SOMEONE?
It is important to understand that you can't change anyone else but yourself. You can of course lead by example and inspire other people to improve and better themselves, however when you try and change others they will tend to see you, your help and your actions from their limited perspective and they'll end up resisting your help, especially when that help and advice is uninvited. When you try to change them they will often push against you and reject any real wisdom and guidance that you could offer them. They can't see, hear or understand the advice that you're offering them from the wavelength that they're at. They can't see what you see, their outlook and frequency will continue to confirm to them what they already feel and believe to be true, they are bound by and limited to what their perspective tells them is currently possible for them. Until they decide to commit themselves to changing for the better and for themselves, nothing changes. Without the desire to change, and until they have opened up and broadened their perspective and increased their frequency, nothing changes.

SETBACKS
Every single 'setback' that you face has purpose. They are all unfolding in a very particular sequence in order for you to grow into your best self. Every single setback is an opportunity for you to know and claim your inner power, purpose and peace. You can rarely see this when it is happening though, however it is often crystal clear looking back that it all had purpose, and that if one

thing had happened out of order or had gone any differently you wouldn't be where you are right now, and you wouldn't know yourself to the degree that you do now. In essence it's all happening for you, not to you.

SELF TALK

How do you talk to yourself? In what tone? Critical or kind? What language do you use? It is vital that you speak to yourself in a loving, compassionate, empathetic and optimistic tone. Practise seeing yourself through the eyes of love, not through a filter from your past. Don't allow how others have talked to you in the past to determine the way that you talk to yourself in the present. Don't use their harsh and critical words to punish yourself with. Rise above it.

DON'T HATE REALITY, SHAPE IT

Instead of hating the reality that you don't want, shape the reality that you prefer. Allow 'what is', and welcome in what's next. Embody your highest self and step into the reality that you prefer now. In addition, if you don't consciously create and shape your reality, you'll tend to be shaped by it. Until you know your power you'll tend to misuse it, allowing your past and everyone or everything else around you to define and decide your future, or you'll allow them to use you for their own needs. Be a product of your present choices, not your past mistakes. It is up to you to define your worth, value and purpose.

LOVE YOURSELF

Our parents did what they could with what they had. They couldn't give us something that they didn't have to give. They were just using what their parents gave to them. You have got to give yourself everything now that you never got but needed growing up. Give yourself the love, education, support and encouragement that you never got. Until you do you'll end up seeking it from others and looking for it in your results, or end up over-compensating for it in your future. Change begins by updating your definitions, especially updating your sense of self which you have been carrying with you since childhood. You have outgrown it. Understand that from here on out it is your job to love, support and encourage yourself fully and to the degree that you need. No more waiting around for someone else to give you the love that you should be giving to yourself. Parent yourself.

TRY AGAIN
Just because you haven't 'made it' yet, doesn't mean that you won't 'make it'. Give up using past failures as proof of what is possible for you, or using it as an excuse or reason to not try again. Let go of those limitations. Just because you failed in the past, doesn't mean that you aren't able to succeed in the present or the future. Think and look again, try again. You know more now, you're even stronger and wiser than ever before, you're truly a different person now. It's time to try again.

LETTING GO DOESN'T MEAN GIVING UP
Often when you find yourself pushing against reality and trying to make things happen, that is an indication that it's time to step back. Forcefulness is always a reminder to let go and go with the flow. Letting go doesn't mean giving up, nor is it about giving up your desires either, it just means give up trying to do everything all by yourself. Surrender the struggle, release the need for things to go your way only. Let the best version of things unfold, don't cheat yourself out of even better. When you allow God / the universe / your higher self to unfold the highest version of things, life begins to have a natural flow to it. Let go in faith, trusting, believing and knowing without a doubt that you're being led to greater.

PROVING OTHERS WRONG?
You can't prove anyone 'wrong'. Often the real 'truth', your 'truth' and their 'truth' are all on different frequencies. When you argue with someone else, they can't see what you see. They experienced something very different to you according to the

wavelength that they were on. They can't see your 'truth' from there, it is literately not even on the same wavelength as them. The more that you try and convince someone else that they're wrong, the more that they will tend to stick to their 'truth'. The frequency of truth that they're operating from will supply them with even more thoughts, opinions or feelings that will convince them even more that they're right and that you're wrong. Please understand that arguments aren't meant to be won. The 'real truth' of what really happened always reveals itself in time, it doesn't need someone else to prove it. That is often why a mediator is necessary in disagreements, a mediator can access the frequency of 'truth' because they have no bias attached to what was or the outcome. They're able to tap into and reveal the truth that was there all along.

LISTEN
It's vital that we learn to listen with empathy to those people who speak openly about how they feel, rather than trying to immediately offer a solution. If you offer a solution instantly they rarely feel listened to or heard. Only once you listen to them fully in the present moment with your 'awareness' and 'consciousness' are you then able to truly hear them and help offer any real support or assistance. When you do that you will give them a safe space to speak openly about how they really feel (and also release any resistance that they have going on in regards to it). Only once they let out the pain, can they open up and allow in the answer.

LET YOURSELF RECEIVE
When we are so used to being independent and relying upon ourselves for everything we often think that receiving something is a sign of weakness, that it would be 'charity' at some level to receive something back, so we often unknowingly end up pushing away and blocking that which we want the most. However please understand that no one is beyond receiving, be it receiving money, support, love or opportunities. Only an ego feels unworthy of receiving something, or feels like it has to do everything by itself.

There is no need to prove your independence or strength. Make peace with the fact that no one helped you before, however it's important to see the actions and the steps that you took to protect yourself from feeling or facing the pain of not being supported, encouraged or cared for, actions which you're likely still taking today. Understand that the real reason why you currently continue to push people away and pretend that you don't need them is because of that which you dealt with in the past. However please understand that it is not a weakness to let people in and to work with them as part of a team. You aren't here to work alone. There is no need to try and do everything all by yourself. You're here to create with other souls. When you're so determined that you're going to do it all by yourself you'll unconsciously lock yourself out of receiving help and support that the universe is sending your way. You'll ultimately block or limit your own success. It's not weak to accept support or strong to reject help, it's actually the other way around.

YOUR REPUTATION
Don't worry about trying to defend yourself to others, the truth always comes out in the end, however don't be afraid to let people know that you won't tolerate their lies any longer. Don't be afraid to set the record straight. However there is no need to defend yourself against every bad word that someone says about you. Some things just aren't that important. Your focus and undivided attention is a highly creative tool, only rest it upon that which you desire to grow and show in your reality. There is no need to explain yourself (or that which you do or who you are) to someone who has committed themselves to misunderstand you, and especially to those people who are using your life as a distraction from their own pain and their own lack of happiness or purpose. Always remember that your reputation is only who others think that you are, it is not who you really are. Your higher self and inner being is who you really are. Your reputation takes years to build and only seconds to break, however your character and who you really are stands firm throughout it all. Focus upon

building your character rather than building a reputation for the ego to thrive upon. Only the ego needs a reputation to feel enough, to feel powerful and to feel important, your inner self knows that you already are.

IN EXPRESS TIME

The word 'express' has multiple meanings. To 'express' something means to convey something, however it also means to push something out, and it also means doing something at a high speed. So what are you expressing? Are you expressing thoughts, feelings and perspectives that empower you, or that which is holding you back? What you continue to express, will not only be expressed out and into your reality, however it will all come back to you in express time. Be aware of what thoughts and feelings you are consistently expressing. Only express at length those things that you desire to see expressed into your reality.

ACCEPT COMPLIMENTS AND CRITICISM

It is important that you are open to accepting and receiving not only compliments in life, however some criticism too. Allow what others say, however don't allow it to affect who you are and how you see yourself. Criticism can be helpful at times, especially when it comes from those people who are on a higher frequency. Listen to any criticism that is encouraging, especially any feedback that allows you to better yourself or that which you do. Listen only to criticism that comes from a place of love and peace, that says 'you did this wrong' and not that 'you're wrong for doing that'. Don't take any criticism to heart, especially any criticism that is aimed towards who you are, as that is unnecessary. That is someone else's opinion of you, and not criticism. It is so important that you are open to the advice and support of others. Only someone who has low self esteem, low self worth or a distorted image of themselves will reject a compliment or fight criticism. When people compliment you, listen to them from a higher perspective. In addition, when people offer criticism listen to it from a higher perspective too. Take what is useful and let the rest go. Don't cast off the compliments that other people give you or your work either, especially when someone says something like, 'You're so talented'. Learn to humbly accept, appreciate and honour your compliments. Stop rejecting them saying, "Oh I'm not that great". Affirm your greatness, but not from the ego. Accept those compliments without allowing them to become a part of your identity. However learn to not define yourself in relation to your compliments or criticism either.

DOES FEAR MOTIVATE YOU?

The universe will always use the path of least resistance to get you 'moving'. If you're easily and quickly motivated by fear and pain to make the necessary changes in your life, then the universe will consistently supply you with fearful situations in order to get you to make those changes that you have been putting off, those changes that you ultimately desire to make. Learn instead to be motivated by happiness and peace. When you learn to do that, you will no longer need 'negative' situations to occur in order to get you to evolve and make those changes that you have been putting off.

ONLY ADD TO YOUR HAPPINESS

It is important that you only allow external things to add to the happiness and peace that is already within you. If your happiness is dependant upon 'what is' or what you have, you will never be genuinely happy. That type of happiness is conditional, it is dependant upon something beyond your control. Happiness that comes from results is only ever fleeting, it is not genuine or lasting. If you believe that you need to do, to have or to be something before you can be happy, then you will always be chasing the illusion of happiness. In addition one of the biggest blocks to your desires is needing them now to be happy. Until you're happy now, with or without your desires, a result that feels like that happiness can't show up 'then', since our reality and results are only reflections on the outside of what and how we already feel within. In addition when you need your desires in order for you to be happy, what you're telling the universe is that you're unhappy now which is what the universe will respond to, which will ultimately continue to block your desires, results and blessings. Unconditional happiness is ultimately a choice and it is wise to choose it before you try and achieve any external result.

RUNNING AWAY YET AGAIN?

Often in life it's necessary to face the uncomfortable truth of our actions or our lack of actions, especially our habit of running away. Are you still running away in fear? Running away from uncomfortable situations? From the past? From your own feelings? We can't keep running away, doing that won't solve or improve anything. What you run from will be waiting for you when you get there, it always catches up. You can't outrun your own frequency or run away from yourself. Things only improve once you stop running, once you become 'still', once you tune in within and once you begin to face (and also acknowledge, accept and allow) 'what is' and how you're feeling.

WHO CARES WHAT OTHER PEOPLE THINK

There is no need to fear what other people might think, feel or believe about you. They can't see you without first seeing themselves. The only reason why we fear what others might be thinking about us is when we base who we are on the opinions of other people. It's time to think for and also define ourselves. You can't let another person's thoughts and opinions about you affect or define how you think of yourself and how you see yourself. The real reason why you feel fear when you believe that other people won't and don't like you (and the real reason why it feels so bad to you) is because your higher self is making you aware through those awful feelings that how you're currently seeing yourself isn't how your higher self sees you and how things really are at the highest level. Fearing that other people won't like you is always a reminder to step back and see things clearly. Remember, what you think, you will become, so use your thoughts wisely. See yourself from the eyes of greatness and not from the eyes of fear, the past or someone else. Think of yourself now as the person that you're becoming, the person that your higher self knows you to be, and not as the person that your fear tells you that you are. When you're at peace, the opinions of other people will no longer be able to affect you for long. You will begin to understand that being upset at what someone else has said to you (or about you) would in essence be one 'ego' being upset over the opinion of another 'ego', both of which are false identity's. They aren't who either of you really are. When you begin to no longer make other people's approval, acceptance or validation the goal, you can begin to make your happiness, peace and purpose the priority.

THE PROJECTOR
Your mind, feelings and beliefs are just like a projector, projecting the path ahead, creating it in the image of that which you focus upon most often within yourself, others or the world. Life always unfolds from within. Think of your beliefs, feelings and thoughts as being a hologram that will appear on the outside for you to see it and then change it if it is not in alignment with that which you desire to experience. When you change that which you are putting out, and that which you expect to see, the image that you project changes and so does the reality that you will experience. Until you go within and make those necessary changes, you'll always go without that which you desire.

JUST IMAGINE IF THEY HAD GIVEN UP
I know that it can feel incredibly disheartening to fail after all of the hard work and effort that you have been putting in, however don't give up. Every great person who has ever made a lasting and positive impact on the world (be it through what they did, what they said or what they created) faced moments of doubt, failure, criticism, uncertainty, sorrow, frustration and pain. However they didn't give up. They kept going. They believed in themselves and their higher purpose. If they had allowed 'what is' to determine what will be, look at all of those incredible things that we would've had to go without. Knowing this, just imagine what the

world would have to go without if you gave up today. You're needed more than you could ever begin to imagine.

SULKING & SILENCE SOLVES NOTHING
When you're upset with someone it's so important that you learn to speak up and express your true feelings, rather than 'sulking' or giving them the 'silent treatment'. Sulking won't magically improve or change things, it will in fact just prevent things from getting any better. It will prevent you from facing, understanding and releasing how you're really feeling, and stop you from recognising the root cause of your actions and feelings. It will keep you on a lower frequency. When you find yourself about to give someone the silent treatment, recognise that as an indication to be open and honest about how you're really feeling. Regardless of what someone else has done, said or implied, be accountable and be responsible for your own emotions and reactions, that's how you heal and grow. Finally, it is important to understand and make it clear that the 'silent treatment' mentioned here isn't in regards to those situations where you're choosing to be silent whenever you encounter those people who taunt you, who make fun of your reactions or even belittle you, no reaction is always better in those situations. It is best to make your boundaries clear and remove yourself from that situation as soon as possible instead of giving them the emotional reaction that they want. However it's important to understand that when you're choosing that course of action (to be silent and to remove yourself from that environment or situation) you ultimately know why you're choosing to not respond, it comes from a higher awareness, however whenever we sulk and give others the 'silent treatment' (whenever we're hurt) we often don't have a valid reason for doing it, we don't have any clarity for why we're choosing that reaction. So to clarify it, sulking and giving others the 'silent treatment' is always a reaction from pain or a lower vibration, whereas the lack of a response when confronted by those hurtful people is a response from a higher perspective. One is reactive in

nature (which will persist your pain) and the other is a response from a place of peace and purpose (which will assist your healing).

I CAN'T HELP MYSELF
Who is the one person in your life who always helps and supports you? The one person that you can always rely upon? The person who is always there when you need them? The person who checks in on you or inspires you to be great? What if there is no one that you can think off? Maybe that's because you're too busy being that person for everyone else, or you're too busy proving your own independence and strength that you fail to allow anyone else to help you. Make sure that you're not helping everyone else at the cost of you not helping yourself. Give yourself the same love, support and care that you're giving away to others. Give it to yourself first. You can't afford to give it all away. Don't fall into the trap of putting yourself last for the sake of the 'greater good', or feeling that you have to be strong for everyone else. That helps no one. You too need support and help from time to time. No one is beyond help and support. Embrace vulnerability, let other people in, let them help you too from time to time, you matter. We all have our own struggles and problems regardless of how wise, strong or spiritual that we are. It doesn't make you any better of a person to pretend that you don't have struggles. We are not meant to go through life alone, or meant to have a problem free life either, only an ego believes that.

LET YOUR TALENTS DEVELOP
Like all things in life, our talents often need time to grow and develop. It often takes a while for the work that we have been putting out to match the expectation and vision that we have in our own imagination. When you first start something, it rarely feels good enough. However don't let how it currently looks determine how it will always look. When you believe that it (or you) will never be good enough, you inadvertently prevent things from improving. Like the traditional printing process of photography, let your talents, skills and work develop. It often

takes a period of darkness and uncertainty for the image that you have in your mind to develop into its highest form. Don't give up until the bigger picture reveals itself.

MEDITATE INSTEAD OF SELF MEDICATING

The more that you meditate the less that you will tend to self medicate. You will no longer need to soothe your pain with drugs, alcohol or other destructive habits. When you meditate you will be able to acknowledge, accept and allow your pain (and 'what is') and then allow it to move on. When you meditate you open up that space which will allow the pain out and also let the resistance go, which in turn allows you to reconnect with your inner peace and happiness again. When you meditate you will begin to see yourself how your higher self sees you. You will also begin to release the resistance that is holding back 'positive' and empowering thoughts and joyful experiences from coming into your conciousness and into your reality. You will no longer feel like you have to control what is happening on the outside to have peace, power and happiness within yourself. You will be able to start seeing things clearly, and more than likely you will start to see yourself clearly too, maybe even for the first time in your life.

YOU ARE NEVER THE ONLY ONE

It can often feel like we're the only one feeling that way, or the only one going through something, and the only person who had that past. Although it might not feel like it, you're never the only one. You're only ever the only one until you speak up. Once you open up and speak openly about how you're feeling and about what you've been through, you'll soon realise that there are countless people who have the same story as you. We often think that we're the only one struggling, or the only one with those worries, fears, uncertainties and insecurities, however rest assured that you're not alone. Take comfort knowing that others have been through it, and got through it. They're proof that it gets better, never forget that.

HIGHLY CRITICAL PEOPLE
Learn to let the cruel words of others go, stop holding onto them, replaying them and turning them into affirmations to hurt yourself with. Those people who consistently find fault with your appearance or your actions, and who humiliate, embarrass or belittle you for having them (as an attempt to instil guilt or shame, rather than pointing them out from a helpful place which would encourage you to grow, evolve or improve) are often highly critical of themselves. They're just showing you who they are and how they treat themselves. They're not showing you who you are. Only someone who doesn't love or respect themselves fully will hurt others in that way. If putting others down makes them feel better about themselves at some level, or makes them feel superior or more powerful, that's an indication that they're in pain. Instead of putting others down, they need to learn how to love themselves more.

YOU DON'T HAVE TO PROVE YOURSELF
It's so important that you give up trying to prove your worth, power, beauty, ability, intelligence, value and greatness to others, and instead just focus upon feeling it within yourself. Often the only reason why we seek other people's approval and acceptance now is because we have allowed the people in our past to determine or define who we are and how we see ourselves, so we wrongly believe that others have the power or ability to determine who we will become. Only you can define yourself. When you start picking yourself apart (using the words that others have used to hurt you with) choose to step back and build yourself back up, but this time with a more stable foundation.

THEY CAN'T STOP YOU
What other people use to try and hold you back or stop you, the universe will use to propel you further and take you higher. No person or thing has the power to stop you from becoming your best self and living your best life. They can't stop what the universe has planned for you. The only thing that can stop you, is

you. Stop giving other people the power or ability to decide who you are or what you can become. Keep moving forward. Ultimately what others use to cause you pain and harm, the universe will use to bring you closer to who you really are, and closer to your highest purpose. Always remember this, no matter what they say or what they do, they haven't got the power to stop you.

CONSISTENT DESIRES

Only when you have specific and consistent desires are you then able to set your frequency and vibration to the tone of the reality where your desires are actualised, which would begin to call forth that reality. When you step into how that reality feels now, you are not only calling in a reality that feels like that, however you are choosing that from all of the possibilities of what can be, as the reality that you desire to experience now. Choose to support the reality that is a reflection of who you desire to be, and who you know yourself to be at the highest level. Until you have a clear idea of what you desire to do, and what you desire to have or be, you can't live into the experience and the feeling place of it or live life from the 'end result' which would help to allow it in. It is time to start thinking from that reality rather than just thinking of it. Tune into that frequency, frequently. It is your job to guide and focus your attention, awareness, thoughts, feelings, conciousness and emotions upon how it would feel to be, to see, to have, and to do that which you desire.

THEY DON'T LIKE ME

If you think that others won't like you or like what you do, then they won't. You'll either become a person that others won't like or you'll draw onto your path and into your life those people who won't like who you are and those people who won't respect what you do, essentially those people who aren't meant for you. You'll become the person that you think that they believe you are, rather than the person that you really are. You'll be living within their limits and your own fears. You won't be able to allow in who and what is meant for you when you rate and place other people's opinions above your own. When you give 'weight' to their opinions you won't be able to live up to your highest potential. Pass no remarks on what they're saying about you, it literally doesn't matter (it doesn't create matter).

GOING TOO FAST?
What speed are you going through life at? Too fast or too slow? If you're going too slow, the universe will often place something in your path that will wake you up and get you moving. Something that will shock or inspire you into changing or taking action, something that will get you to make those big changes that you have been putting off in order for you to become your best self. However if you're going too fast (especially if you are doing too much and not taking enough time for yourself) then the universe will often place something in your path to slow you down, something that will cause you to step back, heal and take things at a slower pace from a much more centred place. Pay attention to what the universe is communicating to you, and learn to listen the first time, so that you don't need something 'big' to shake you awake.

RECEIVE BACK SUPPORT
It is incredible that you are able to give so much love, support and compassion to others, however are you able to accept and receive that love and support back? Can you receive and accept support without feeling like you are lowering yourself, letting yourself down or that it is a weakness at some level? Your definition of receiving is key to your overall success. When you're unable to accept help, it ultimately affects every single area of your life. When you reject help, you are also rejecting your blessings too. When you are feeling 'down' (which is really when you are vibrating at a lower frequency) the momentum is often too strong to see things clearly, which is why we need help and support too. Be willing to receive back the same amount of help that you are giving to others.

JUST PRETENDING TO BE HAPPY?

Forget feeling or faking joy just to make things happen, that is always the work and the perspective of the ego. Only an ego thinks that it can trick the universe into giving it what it wants. When you are conditional in your happiness you will often just pretend to be happy for a short period of time, you will tend to subtly take a peak at your reality to see if it is working, and when you can't see any obvious changes you will likely get annoyed and the 'joy' will abruptly end and you will then begin to view life from a 'told you it wouldn't work' mentality. Only genuine feelings of joy are highly creative. It is important that we stop letting our joy, happiness and appreciation be conditional, and being determined by a result of getting something or being something. Let your joy be unconditional, not in comparison to another person or thing. Let yourself be happy now, rather than only imagining and visualising yourself being happy when you get something or when you achieve something. Choose joy simply because you know that it is who you really are at the deepest level. Let that be the intention for feeling it, simply choosing to feel joy now because of how it feels and because it is how you're supposed to feel. There is no power in faking joy and pretending that you are happy when you are very clearly not. All that does is resist how you are really feeling, which tends to perpetuate it even more.

NO ONE SUPPORTED ME

Are you still waiting for permission to be great? Don't need someone else to push you to achieve greatness, if you're waiting for their support or to be told that you're good enough, then you'll be waiting forever. Let go of the story that 'no one supported me' or that 'no one cared'. That story is exactly what is stopping you from growing and reaching your highest potential now. Allow yourself to be great, challenge and encourage yourself, remind yourself daily of your worth, talent and greatness. It's no one else's responsibility but yours.

EASILY OFFENDED

Any time that you are easily offended by the words or the actions of another person that is always an opportunity to look within (to find out what exactly it is that someone else has done or said, or primarily what you assumed that they meant, that has affected you so deeply). You wouldn't take it so personally if you didn't believe it was the truth. This doesn't mean that you shouldn't stand up for yourself or educate others when you face ignorance, this is in regards to constantly being offended by the smallest of things. Being easily offended is often the result of being on the offence and defence, when you feel like you have to protect or prove yourself, and primarily when you're operating from the level of fear and pain. Being easily offended is also a sign that you still see yourself as a victim. It's our assumptions and rarely the actions or ignorance of others that is the cause of most of the problems in our life.

THIS IS WHY YOU MUST TAKE RISKS

What looks like a risk to you (from the wavelength that you are seeing things from) isn't a risk to your higher self. Going from 'here' to 'there' always feels like a risk when you're viewing life from a lower frequency of fear, unworthiness or doubt. In order for things to change, you're going to have to take creative risks. Living cautiously never fulfilled anyone, or ever supported someone in becoming their best self. You have got to follow that call within you, that is your higher self calling you to more. Rise up and take a leap of faith towards your dreams. The staircase only appears to those people who have the courage to jump, and to those people who believe that it will appear.

WALK AWAY

Being strong isn't always about how much you can take, tolerate, accept or handle. Sometimes being strong is having the power and ability to walk away from certain situations, and saying enough is enough. Please understand that being strong isn't about showing how long you can hold onto that broken relationship or 'dead end' job for either. It is necessary for us all to re-define strength and especially how we see giving up or walking away. It isn't a sign of weakness nor is it a failure to walk away, it is often the ultimate strength. It requires embracing the unknown and being vulnerable. Walking away isn't always about giving up either, it often entails letting go of that which is no longer serving you, and letting go of that which is holding you down and holding you back, and that which is stealing your peace and joy. Have the courage to make those tough decisions long before you need to. Know when enough is enough, don't need it to happen a few more times to make sure that it is. Walk away from that person, place, thing or thought, but before you leave it behind, take with you the lessons that you have learned from that experience and apply them in your own life.

DO THIS BEFORE YOU SAY 'NO'
If you say 'no' to this current opportunity, who knows what else you're turning down and missing out on. The biggest success stories and breakthroughs often evolve from the smallest of opportunities. How that opportunity currently looks now isn't a reflection of what it can become, it could just be a stepping stone that will help to bring you to the place where the universe can intervene and bring you to your purpose. Before you say 'no' to something, find out if you're simply saying no because you're afraid. Don't let fear consume you and your dream. In addition, instead of imagining how it would feel to fail, imagine that you have already won, train yourself to embody that feeling.

SET THE TONE
Too often in life we allow those 'negative' people who cross our path to determine, affect or alter our mood and set the tone (or frequency) for the entire day (or we allow a 'negative' situation to do the same). If you allow someone else's 'negative' energy to do that, you'll end up taking that pain with you and end up giving it to everyone else that you meet. When you encounter that which causes you to lower your frequency, make the conscious choice to

rise above it. Let it move through you and past you. Give up analysing or replaying it. You have a responsibility to set (and protect) your own frequency and tone, until you do you'll continue to allow yourself to be too easily affected by everyone and everything.

HOW TO FIND 'THE WAY'

The answer, 'way' and opportunity that you're currently looking for will appear when you're not looking for it. What you are seeking always sneaks in. In essence it manifests into your reality and your consciousness when you are in a place of 'non resistance' and complete allowing. So relax, let go and you'll begin to let it in. Essentially you can only ever allow in that which you are currently on the same frequency as. Until you're on the same frequency as the abundance of that which you desire, you can't allow it in. You can only allow in that which you're seeking once you have moved beyond the vibration of lack (which is viewing the absence of that which you desire, viewing yourself as being a person without it, and looking at it from a place of needing or wanting it) to the frequency of how it feels to have it and be it (which is the frequency of its abundance). In time you'll come to recognise that what you were seeking was there all along at the highest vibrational level, however it was only once you came into harmony with how it felt, were you then able to see it and allow it in.

FACING A DISASTER? DON'T FORGET THIS

When you are facing a disaster or a troubling situation it is so important that you take a few moments to step back, rise up and see things from a higher perspective. Now this doesn't mean that you should ignore 'what is' or how you really feel about it, however in order for things to go any differently you need to respond to life with a higher awareness. Don't let how things currently look solely determine how you feel and what you believe. Doing that won't help, it will in fact prevent things from getting any better, and continue to remove you from the frequency that solutions reside at. In those moments of uncertainty, place your faith in greater, rather than in what is.

IT WILL ALL COME TOGETHER SOON
Often in life we can feel like things aren't happening at a speed that we would like them to, and that no matter how hard we work things never really seem to change, however don't give up hope. Keep going. Every small change and improvement is accumulating into something incredible. Whether you can see it or not, things are changing at a frequency level. Please understand that there often isn't an exact moment where everything finally 'clicks', but a moment where you realise that it already has clicked. The only reason why things won't come together for you is when you give up before the bigger picture has a chance to reveal itself to you. Until then, focus upon doing your best and being your best self.

REAL LOVE IS CONSISTENT
In relationships the single biggest thing that you must look for is consistency. So is your partner being consistent with you? With how they treat you? With how they speak to you? If not, then there isn't love or a stable relationship there. When you consistently make excuses for them, things can't and won't change. Every time that you 'forgive' them you're giving them permission to hurt you again but even worse next time. Ultimately one good moment or one good thing in a relationship shouldn't be able to make up for all of the numerous ways and times that they have hurt you. Simply put, you don't have to tolerate love.

DON'T GIVE UP WHEN THIS HAPPENS
It is often only once we step out of our comfort zone, do we realise all of the ways that we were subtly holding ourselves back. The moment that you step out of your 'comfort zone' these are some of the things that will tend to happen. That which needs healing within you will come rushing to the surface to be

acknowledged and released. Everything within you will tell you to give up or run away. You'll be flooded with thoughts that will tell you that you're not good enough and that you can't handle it, but stick with it, let those thoughts and feelings move through you. Those thoughts are not a reflection of the truth or what you're capable of, they're only echoes of who you were and how you are used to seeing things. Lean into those uncomfortable feelings, don't fight against them or fear them. You're more than capable of doing this. You're stronger than your current perspective will let you see.

IS YOUR SELF TALK A LIFE SENTENCE?

How you talk to yourself is key to your overall well being and success. Ask yourself, "Do I speak to myself in a supportive, encouraging, empowering and positive way?". Too often we allow our inner dialogue to be determined solely by 'what was' or what we're currently observing or experiencing (whether real or not) rather than allowing our inner dialogue to support the life that we desire. Your inner dialogue needs to be more than just a running commentary on how things currently look or how you're currently feeling. If things are to be any different we are going to have to respond to life rather than just reacting to it. The sentences that you speak to yourself is what you are sentencing yourself to.

HOW TO MOVE BEYOND MISTAKES

It can often feel difficult to move on after a 'big' mistake. Guilt and shame tends to stop us from forgiving ourselves, improving and then moving forward. However it's important to understand that more than likely you made that mistake at a point in your life when you didn't know any better. You didn't know what you know now, this insight was on a completely different frequency to you back then. Even if you did know better, you may have been in pain, which distorted your ability to think and act logically. You've got to step back and view that mistake with a higher awareness and from a higher perspective. Observing and analysing the same mistake numerous times won't help, nor will it change anything. Turn that guilt into growth.

YOU'RE MORE THAN THAT PAST
Just because you had that dark past, doesn't mean that you can't have a bright future. Often the only reason why you can't see that bright future is when you're still viewing yourself and life from a lower frequency of pain and hurt. From that
perspective everything will look and feel like that darkness. It will cast its shadow upon everything that you do and see, that is until you heal. I know it's often difficult to see the possibility of things getting any better when you're feeling that way and when you're used to things going wrong, but have faith. You still have an incredible future that's waiting on you to heal. Remember your future isn't determined by the past, but by the present. What happens next is up to you.

YOUR IN-TUITION
Are you listening to your intuition? Think of your intuition as being your inner tuition. It is teaching you from the inside out. That is where the answers that you're seeking can be found. It's called intuition because it is found by looking and tuning in within. Fundamentally your intuition is tuned to the frequency of your higher self. Your intuition is the voice of your higher self. However please don't confuse your intuition for thoughts which are a reflection of your current doubts and fears. Your intuition will speak to you clearly when you're at peace, and leave you feeling empowered, it won't speak to you when you're over analysing things, and it most definitely won't speak to you in fearful 'what ifs'.

COMMIT YOURSELF TO SOMETHING
Until we commit and dedicate ourselves to our ideas and our projects we will often end up going from idea to idea without ever really achieving anything. Only once we make the decision to finally commit ourselves to achieving something can things really

change. Consistently commit yourself to something, really invest yourself in your ideas. You have got to give up abandoning your ideas at the first setback or struggle or when fear arises. Grow into the person who can do it. It doesn't matter what age you are, where you are or how things currently look, it is never too late to start, or to start again.

STILL HOLDING YOURSELF BACK?
Instead of counting, focussing upon and pondering all of the times and all of the ways that you held yourself back (or limited, betrayed and sabotaged yourself) and all of those things that you missed out on, start counting all of the ways that you're going to encourage yourself to do your best and be your best self. It is time to release that guilt, shame and resentment that you have been holding onto regarding your past, it's subtly spoiling your future. Make yourself this promise, that you're going to start saying 'yes' to life, that you are not going to let fear make your decisions for you any longer, and that you're not going to hide away from life any more. There is still so much more in store for you.

ARE YOU COURAGEOUS?
How do you see courage? How do you define it? We often think that courage is all about overcoming the big challenges in life, when in reality it can be as simple yet as powerful as apologising for your previous 'unconscious' actions, asking for help after previously rejecting it or trying again even though you failed before. Without courage nothing worthwhile can be achieved. Practise courage, strengthen your 'courage muscle'. Don't underestimate the power in courage. Once purposefully practised and applied, it will dramatically change your life for the better.

MEDITATE
Don't meditate to 'quieten' the mind, meditate to connect to your inner spirit. The intention always determines the result. Don't meditate to stop your thoughts, but to connect to the essence which is beyond and beneath your thoughts, which is who you

really are. When you meditate guide and focus your attention and awareness. Don't force your thoughts away or try and force peace in. Let it all unfold naturally. There is no need to try and work out your thoughts either. Give up trying to sort out your thoughts too. There is no need to 'police' your mind to see if you're thinking negatively either. Just allow every thought with a silent non judgemental perspective and an unconditional loving presence. In time those 'negative' thoughts will move on, until then hold a space for them to reveal and free themselves.

I NEED TO BE STRONG

You don't have to be strong all of the time, give up the idea that strength is somehow about proving how tough or how ruthless you are. Toughness is often just fear and anxiety in disguise. True inner strength has nothing to prove, it doesn't need to prove or convince others of its power. Someone who has tapped into their own inner strength and peace won't seek control or feel the need to show others how unaffected they are by everything and everyone, nor will they reject help and support or pretend that they're OK when they aren't. True strength is about being honest and vulnerable, it comes from within, it doesn't come from manipulating or controlling things on the outside. True strength allows you to speak openly and honestly about how you are really feeling from a place of peace, and it will encourage you to reach out for and accept help when you need it.

HELP YOURSELF

Repeat this to yourself, I don't have to do everything for everyone, it is not my job to keep everyone else happy and at peace, it's not my responsibility to make sure that everyone else is OK, it is not my job to walk everyone through life, and finally, there is no need for me to feel guilty for living my own life and finding peace and happiness. When you read those sentences, did you feel anything release from within you? If you did, more than likely you just gave yourself permission to finally find and focus upon your own inner happiness, peace and purpose, maybe for the first time. That feeling was the release of all the pressure and stress that has been building up within you to help everyone, a purpose that you weren't built for. It's time for you to support, honour, encourage, empower, motivate and help yourself.

NO CHANGE?

Some honest reflection time is necessary in order for you to become your best self. Many of us are going through life on autopilot, blinkered to what we are 'unconsciously' doing or failing to do. We unknowingly repeat the same day on a loop and we call it a life. Only years later do we look back and wonder where all of the time went and wonder why things never really changed. The real reason why things never changed is because we never changed, or because we never stuck to the changes that we implemented. Things can't change until we change. Only once we take the time to really see what we are doing (or in other words until we are completely aware and honest with ourselves in regards to what is working and what is not working) can we then dedicate ourselves to making the necessary amends which would allow in the changes that we desire. Make yourself this promise, that from here on out you are going to release what is not working and let go of that which isn't helping or lifting you or other people higher, and that you're going to consistently incorporate and support new practises that support the person that you're becoming and the life that you desire to live.

THEY'RE STOPPING ME

You will never find authentic peace and happiness when you perceive yourself to be the victim of someone else's anger and hate, or some other circumstance. When you believe that others are looking down on you or holding you back, then that is the type of experiences, interactions and people that you will call into your reality. Everything and everyone will confirm that belief to you. Although you may have faced very real prejudice or injustice in the past, that isn't who you are right now, and it has nothing to do with who you really are and what is meant for you. You can't let that mindset or someone else's pain or ignorance define you, or define what is possible for you, or define how you see others and your future. There comes a time when you have got to make the conscious decision to rise above it all if you're going to grow and become your best self. Freedom begins in your own mind first. When you change how you see yourself, you will begin to remove yourself from that lower frequency that those ignorant people resonate at most frequently, which will allow you to no longer encounter them as often.

FEELING LOST?

Only the 'mind' feels lost. Any time that you feel 'lost' that is always an indication that you are currently not in touch with your inner being or higher self. Your soul, inner being and higher self (or however you choose to define it) knows exactly what it is supposed to be doing and when it is supposed to be doing it. When you let go and go with the flow, you allow things to unfold naturally and you allow things to go as they should. The next step will naturally reveal itself to you and appear on your path just as long as you are aligned with your higher self and you are taking action from that space. As long as you're moving in the direction of what you desire, and from the feeling of (and the faith in) who you really are, you will always find your way back. You will never be lost for long.

NOT EVERY RELATIONSHIP IS SUPPOSED TO LAST…

Not every relationship or friendship is supposed to last and that is OK, people change. We all grow at different rates, someone who was once on your frequency 'then' may no longer be right for you now. It's important therefore that we don't allow a relationship or the length of that relationship to define us or define our worth. The purpose of a relationship is to assist you in seeing yourself clearly in relation to another, to show you clearly what you accept, expect, tolerate, allow, encourage and excuse. They are learning tools. If you hold onto a broken relationship, you do so at the expense of your happiness, blessings and future.

YOU'RE NEEDED

You have a vital part and role to play in this world. Your gifts and presence are needed. Don't underestimate your power. You have so much to offer, so much to give, but first you have to believe that. Until you do, you can't access, recognise, claim or use the power that is within you. Do you truly understand that you have an affect on more people than you could ever begin to imagine? Every single act of love has a ripple effect on the entire universe, your kindness spreads far and wide affecting everyone in its path. When you change how you treat yourself and others, you change the world. The greatest untold truth is that you change the world by changing how you see it, by changing how you see yourself and by changing how you see others.

STRUGGLING

Those people who have big dreams, and an even bigger purpose, will often face the biggest challenges and struggles in life. The universe will tend to supply those people with challenges and struggles in order for them to become the person that they need to be to handle the life that they desire. Every single struggle that you encounter has purpose, everything that you go through is an opportunity for growth. Challenges are often the training ground for greatness.

HOW TO START A NEW CHAPTER IN YOUR LIFE

The first step in starting a new chapter in your life is often recognising that the old story has nothing new to teach you. It is time to find closure and time to start a new chapter, one that supports the person that you are becoming, one that doesn't just repeat the dialogue of who you were or repeat the script of who you were with. When the internal dialogue and story that you have been listening to and following changes, surprising changes start occurring in your life. The old story needed your attention and participation to survive, but once you step back it begins to lose its power and control over you. If the old story starts up again, leave it, don't fight it or fear it, just write a new ending.

TIRED OF HELPING THEM?

Do you see yourself as the helper? As the person who is responsible for helping everyone? When you define yourself as that, that is all that you'll ever be to people. You'll 'attract' and allow into your life people who will use you, which will eventually steal away your peace and happiness. You'll end up doing for them that which they fail to do for themselves, which is often something that they never even asked you to do. That isn't your job or purpose. You are much more than just a support system for people. Any definition of yourself that isn't a powerful conscious creator, will ultimately stop you from reaching your highest potential.

MAKE YOUR OWN CHOICES

It's so important that you leave guilt and shame behind when it comes to living your own life. You've got to make your own choices and decisions based on what is in alignment with your highest self, not based on what other people want from you or what they'll be happy with. Ultimately at the deepest level they don't know what is right or best for you, only your inner self knows that. Not everyone needs to have a say in your life and your choices. Although they often mean well, you'll end up feeling unfulfilled if you let them (and their opinions) make all of your choices and decisions for you. They ultimately can't define who you are or determine your destiny. Sometimes you need to stand alone in order for you to know, feel and claim your own power, only then can you begin to believe in yourself and begin to find out who you really are and what you're really capable of.

EXPRESS APPRECIATION

The single biggest thing that you could do today to change your life is to start expressing genuine gratitude or appreciation. When you begin to consistently express genuine feelings of appreciation (which could be described as love and gratitude combined) for what you have, where you are and even for what you desire to have (before you see it, from a place of faith and certainty in its arrival) the universe rewards you. Expressing appreciation has a profound affect on your being and your reality. When practised consistently it will change your life for the better. When you express appreciation, it comes back to you in express time.

LOVE, NOT HATE

Those who hurt others are projecting their own pain. They're making others feel how they feel within. We can't expect them to love another when they can't even begin to love themselves. They often don't even know what it is to love and be loved. Hate is often their attempt at recognition, validation, power, control or what they perceive to be love. Our ability to love in the presence of hate is one of the greatest strengths that we can cultivate. Don't underestimate just how powerful your love is, it will transform hate.

LET THEM SUPPORT YOU TOO

Be willing to let yourself receive help, support and guidance. No one is ever beyond help. We all still need guidance and support from time to time. There is no power nor praise in trying to do everything all by yourself. It's not weak to accept help nor is it strong to reject support. Right now the universe is inspiring and using other people to help you, it is placing people, messages and situations on your path to help you, so in essence when you reject support from others, you're really only ever rejecting the support from the universe that you have been praying for and dreaming of. Open yourself up and let them in.

DO WHAT WORKS

Life truly flows with ease when you practise this simple sentence, do more of what works, and do less of what doesn't. It sounds simple, but it is rarely understood and applied. When it is put into practise and applied consistently it truly has a profound affect on your reality. So ask yourself this, "What has been working in my life?", "Which decisions that I have made and actions that I have taken have inspired me to be better and to do better?", "Which choices have added to my peace, well being and happiness, and which have taken away from them?". Also ask yourself, "Which decisions and choices (or lack of them) have been holding me back?". When you make the conscious decision to review your life from time to time, in the name of growth and healing, you can start to see which choices are supporting you and which are hurting you. You can start to respond to life, rather than just 'unconsciously' reacting to it. You can commit yourself to doing more of what works and less of what doesn't. Having the clarity of mind to know the difference between both is key to your overall success and well being. Be honest yet strict with yourself without being cruel. Commit yourself to making those difficult decisions and to keep up with the changes that you have made. There is an unseen power in making a decision. Ultimately always remember this, do what works, rather than just doing what is easy to do.

CONFIDENCE
Confidence isn't something that only a select few people have, it's not something that you have to earn either, it is a choice. Confidence is a consistent choice, commitment and decision to believe in yourself, your power, your abilities, worth, value and purpose. It takes practise though. Confidence is a positive thing, it is knowing that you are just as good as everyone else. Only 'cockiness' or arrogance is thinking that you're better than everyone else. Confidence is loving yourself continuously and unconditionally, and never needing another person to like you or what you do, so that you can like yourself. Once you believe in yourself and know that what you do and who you are makes a difference, everything changes.

WHY YOU NEED TO BE YOURSELF...
Show people who you really are, be yourself fully. You're made the way that you are for a greater reason and a higher purpose. Allow your personality to help support your purpose, your goals and your vision. People seek realness, they want authenticity. Be who you are, not who you think others need you to be, or

someone that you think that they'll like, admire or respect. When you pretend to be someone else you will tend to 'attract' into your life people who aren't meant for you. You will hold back 'who' and 'what' is meant for you at the highest level. When you work on approving of yourself before seeking the approval of others, you'll have no issue in being yourself fully.

DON'T FEEL GOOD ENOUGH?

Are you suffering from not good 'enough-i-tis'? Do you constantly feel not good enough or not worthy enough of receiving that which you desire? If you do, that means that you're still primarily operating from the level of the ego. Only an ego feels unworthy. We often think that having an ego means that you believe that you are better than everyone else, however that is not always the case. Any time that you feel that you're better or less than someone else, you're operating from the level of the ego. This doesn't mean that having confidence in your own abilities is the ego. 'Cockiness' is the ego. 'Cockiness' is believing that you're better than everyone else, however confidence, which comes from your higher self and inner being, is knowing that deep down you're good enough as you are and that you're just as good as everyone else, that is self belief. In addition feeling that you need to prove to the world or to someone else that you are better, or more powerful or even smarter than others, is always a sign to centre yourself and to vibrate higher. Any time that you operate from the level of the ego, you cut off the ease of access that you once had to your higher self and blessings.

SELF LOATHING

Self loathing is one of the most misunderstood feelings. It is felt by those people who continue to see themselves through the lens of the past or the lens of pain. That self loathing feeling often occurs when you continue to see yourself as who you were and not as who you really are at the highest level. However it is important to understand that your current reality is rarely up to speed with who you have become and who you really are. Those self loathing feelings are often felt when you focus upon feeling the frustration and disappointment of not being up to speed with who you want to be and when you don't have the life that you desire to have. Those self loathing feelings are often felt when someone allows their ego to tell them that they are not 'enough' as they are, and that they'll somehow only be enough once they look a particular way, or when they have that particular job or relationship, which isn't the truth. Self loathing is also felt (to a lesser degree) when you feel that how you currently look isn't in harmony with the image that you hold of yourself within, and how you know yourself to be at the highest level. That is why you tend to dislike yourself, because you feel like you are not living up to your highest potential. It is also felt when you're seeing yourself from the level of the ego rather than the perspective of your higher self. In summary, self loathing is often the frustration of feeling the difference between who you perceive yourself to be (which is just a reflection of the frequency that you're currently vibrating at) and the person that you know yourself to be at the highest level (which is your best self). Take self loathing always as an indication that you're not seeing yourself in your full light. A self loathing perspective is telling you that it is time to start seeing yourself fully, and to take it easy on yourself. Self loathing is always a call for more self love, compassion and self acceptance. Only from that place of self love can you become the person that you know yourself to be at the highest level. Your inner self is saying although you might not be the person that you want to be right now, who you are right now is enough.

NOT IF, WHEN
It is not a question of 'if' you'll receive your desires and blessings, it is just a matter of 'when'. You can't miss what is meant for you. The universe has a funny way of bringing things back around for you even if you have missed it a hundred times before. If you have missed your desires the universe will immediately begin to rearrange another method of delivery for you. Right now your desires might be invisible to the naked eye (just like the

wavelengths of radio and wireless signals) however they are there, they are very real and with enough focus and faith those desires that are currently only on a frequency level will evolve into a physical manifestation that you will be able to recognise. When you relax, have fun and focus upon genuine feelings of love and happiness you will begin to allow your inner being to naturally rise back up to the frequency that your desires reside at, which will begin to open up the 'door' and allow in the way, opportunity or those people that will bring you to your desires or even help bring your desires to you. However the process requires faith, consistency and focus. It's all about relaxing into your inner joy and peace, and letting the universe do its job.

PRESSURE TO BE PERFECT ALL OF THE TIME?

It is so important that we release all pressure, strain and stress to be 'perfect', and to have it all together at all times. No one is perfect, it is impossible to be happy all of the time, only the ego believes that it. Spirituality isn't about being happy and 'strong' all of the time, it is about acknowledging and allowing how we really feel and having the clarity of mind to understand why we feel that way, and then having the ability to do something about it to help change or improve it. Give yourself permission to be OK with 'what is' and how you're feeling. It is often the resistance against how you really feel that causes the most pain. Release the guilt and shame associated with feeling 'down' too. Only once we acknowledge, allow and accept how we really feel can we begin to choose again. Until then we will tend to resist how we feel or define it as bad and continue to persist that pain. Only once we acknowledge, allow and accept how we really feel, can we access our natural state of being (which is peace and joy).

HOW TO BE THANKFUL

Feelings of gratitude and appreciation are some of the most powerful and creative feelings. However it is often hard to feel thankful for something when you have no 'real' or current reason to be thankful. Especially when things are going wrong. It is always best to start small to generate the feeling of appreciation in those moments (which the universe will begin to respond to and reflect back). The more that you focus upon something that you are genuinely thankful for, the more that you are open to receive additional things to be thankful for, and even more thoughts of appreciation. Make it your duty to actively look for and accentuate any and every positive thing and experience, be it 'big' or small. The more that you look for things to be appreciative of, the more that they will tend to reveal themselves to you. If you still can't generate the feeling of gratitude or appreciation, look back at things that you were genuinely thankful for in your past (it doesn't matter when it happened just as long as you feel that appreciation now). When you do that the universe will begin to respond to those feelings. You'll begin to vibrate in harmony with everything that feel likes gratitude. In addition when you think that you have nothing to be thankful for the universe will begin to respond to that feeling, and you'll continue to go without.

AFFIRMATIONS?
Affirmations are a great tool that can help you to become the person that you desire to be, however if you are just repeating the words without intention, emotion or faith, they're useless. Only the ego thinks that they're working. If you're just repeating something that you have no real belief in or no real feeling for, then what you're really doing is resisting 'what is' and how you are really feeling. Of course the thought counts, however it's the feeling beyond the thought that will help to support you in creating the changes that you're seeking, not just the words that you speak or repeat. Your thoughts and feelings about the words that you are saying and the actions that you are taking are critical to your overall success too. Your emotions hold real power. The universe is always responding to that inner feeling and bringing you everything that feels like that on the outside. The thought will help to summon the emotion (that will help to change things) when you believe in what you are saying. Affirmations shouldn't feel like hard work or feel like you're just lying to yourself or that

you're trying to convince yourself or the universe of something. They should feel like you're affirming the person that you already know and believe yourself to be, and the person that you are becoming. So with every affirmation that you speak, ask yourself, "Do I believe in the possibility of what I'm saying?". Find out if there is any real emotion or feeling released within you when you repeat those affirmations. What you feel matters. If you are not feeling anything deeply when you repeat those affirmations, instead use your imagination to imagine the thought of being all that you desire to be now. Create the feeling rather than just repeating a sentence. That will help you much more than just repeating a few 'empty' words.

COLD HEARTED?

Being 'cold hearted' isn't a strength, it isn't a sign or proof of your inner power. Only the ego thinks and believes that being 'cold hearted' is a sign of strength. Being rude, ruthless or 'cold hearted' won't make people respect you either, and it won't keep you safe or stop people from having the opportunity to hurt you or love you. Being brutally honest isn't a quality of your strength either, nor is it something that causes other people to admire or respect you. Only the ego believes that it does. True strength is being vulnerable yet remaining centred. That which your inner self knows to be true strength is often the exact opposite of what your ego thinks that it is. It isn't strong or noble to shout at others, to embarrass them, or to belittle or undermine them. 'Winning' an argument always comes at a cost. 'Beating' someone in an argument or hurting them to the degree that they have hurt you (or someone that you love) doesn't make you strong or powerful. That isn't real power or real strength. You are still in the same position if you put others down, except now you are just looking down on them. Putting others down won't take you any higher or make you feel any better in the long term. Rise above it all. Proving that you're unaffected by things isn't strength either, nor is looking 'down your nose' at those people who are emotional or easily affected by their environment, all of that is a sign that you need to vibrate higher.

SAY AND FEEL IT UNTIL YOU SEE IT
All successful people know that you have got to feel like a success and speak of success before you can see it. There is no need to feel embarrassed or guilty for speaking about the life that you want, even when you can't see it. Regardless of how things look, continue to speak positively about that which you desire (without resisting 'what is' or pushing it away). Continue to feel it and believe in it, even when you can't see it. Speak it into existence. There is no need to feel like you're lying to yourself either for speaking about things as you prefer them to be. You're not lying, you're simply living into the reality that you prefer. You're making it real now so that it can become your reality 'then'.

HONESTY BRINGS FREEDOM
You can't recover if you are still lying, still holding onto secrets and still hiding how you really feel or still pretending that you're OK. Honesty brings freedom and healing. Being open and honest about how you feel will let out the pain and allow in the peace, healing and love. Secrets keep you sick, they keep you in fear and in pain, and separate you from all that is meant for you. Honesty isn't to be feared. Things are never as bad as your fear likes to make them out to be, just remember that those thoughts are just a reflection of the wavelength that you are currently seeing things from. You'll see clearer soon.

GROW OR LET IT GO
If you take everything that other people say about you to heart, you will never be able to connect to the best version of yourself. Learn to no longer take the criticism and the harsh opinions of others to your 'heart'. Until you do, you will likely feel the need to 'close off' your heart to protect yourself, which will also at the same time unintentionally block your heart from receiving and giving love too. Start taking other people's criticism only to the

mind and not to the heart. Learn from their criticism and feedback, consciously choose to either grow because of it or choose to let it go. Ask yourself, "Can I use this experience to grow? Or should I just let it go?". Don't analyse it for too long, if you do you will begin to vibrate at a lower frequency and begin to allow in perspectives and thoughts which will confirm their criticism to you, even if it's not the truth. Meditate upon it, centre yourself and view it all from a higher perspective.

YOUR GREATEST TOOL AND ASSET

Your feelings are your greatest asset, they are translators of your frequency. When you think of that which you desire your higher self and inner being will automatically show you how you have been viewing it and viewing yourself in relation to it, translating your thoughts regarding that subject into emotion which will allow you to feel (in real-time) what you have been putting out vibrationally (essentially what frequency you have been vibrating at and seeing things from) in regards to that particular subject, person, place or thing. Your feelings will then allow you to retune, refocus and guide your thoughts in the direction of that which you prefer, which will begin to retune your frequency (or feelings) allowing you to come into harmony with that which you desire which will begin to allow it into your conciousness and reality.

GOING OFF TRACK

The moment that you try to get other people's approval or validation, you will often start going off course. You will begin to move away from your highest purpose and joy. Your once unconditional, genuine and lasting sense of peace, purpose and inner joy will now start to become fleeting and dependant on your exterior environment and results. You will slowly start to lose all sense of direction and all sense of who you are and what you are here to do. When you make pleasing others the goal, you won't be able to achieve or allow yourself to receive your highest blessings. In addition, it is vital that you don't lose yourself trying to achieve a particular result either. If you find yourself consistently trying to please others, that is always an indication to step back, centre yourself and connect to your own inner joy.

HAPPENING FOR YOU, NOT TO YOU
Please understand that everything that is happening in your life is happening for you, not to you. Everything that happens in your life is necessary. You aren't being punished, it is here to help and heal you. Everything that you experience is an opportunity for you to grow, and to practise what you know, it may also be an opportunity to let something go. There is always a lesson and a blessing within everything that you encounter, experience or observe. What you learn will ultimately help you (and also everyone else that you know) to heal, grow and become the best version of yourself.

ALL ACTING ON THE UNIVERSE'S BEHALF
Every single day we are all helping each other in ways that we can't even begin to imagine. The universe is using you right now to help others, inspiring meetings and encounters that will allow you to provide them with the guidance that they have been looking and praying for. We are all interconnected, with interweaving purposes. The universe is flowing through you, it is using you for a higher purpose. We're all acting on behalf of the universe. Please understand that right now others are being inspired to help, guide and assist you too. If you reject another person's support you're only ever rejecting the universe and yourself. Be willing to not only give help but accept it too.

PLEASING OTHERS?
Do you suffer from the 'disease to please'? Are you constantly putting others above and before yourself? Are you consistently doing everything that others ask of you and doing more for them than they need? Are you putting their happiness and peace above your own? It is often called the 'disease to please' because only someone who is not at ease with themselves needs to do that. It is great that you desire to help and support others, however at a

certain point it can manifest into the 'disease to please', especially when you're putting other people's needs, happiness and peace above your own, and when you are helping other people primarily to feel needed or wanted. When you don't know your own inner worth and value, you will often think that it needs to be earned. You will at some level need and want others to like you or that which you do, so that you can like yourself. All of that is a distraction from your own lack of self worth. Give up needing other people to like you so that you can like yourself, give up feeling like you have to convince everyone that you're a nice person, and especially give up doing everything that other people ask of you just so that they won't have a reason or an opportunity to dislike you or have a reason to point out your faults. Rise above it all, know and claim your own worth. Of course this doesn't mean that you shouldn't help others any more, however choose to only help others from a self-full place. Give to them what 'overflows' from your already full cup.

HOW DO YOU SEE THE WORLD?

When you look out into the world, what do you see? What are you most aware of in others and in those around you? How you see the world says more about you than the state of the world. The wavelength that you are on determines not only how you see the world but what you see. We ultimately see things the way that we are, not necessarily the way that things are. What you see most often is usually what you're on the same frequency as. Do you see the positivity and the good qualities in others and those around you? Or just the negativity? Of course this doesn't mean that you won't see, acknowledge or become aware of the pain, problems and suffering in the world, however it is important that we don't allow our frequency to be determined solely by the problems or the pain that we observe in others and in the world. You will never find lasting or genuine peace and happiness when you do that. What you continue to see and focus upon you will inevitably experience even more of, or even more of how that thing feels. It's our duty to see things from a higher perspective, until we do our lower vibration will stop us from seeing things that way and continue to keep us from our desires. See things from a place of love and peace rather than pain and fear. In addition how do you see yourself? When you think of yourself as being powerful, successful, creative and as a 'good' person, you will see proof of that everywhere in your reality. However when you think, feel and believe that you are a 'bad' person, you will tend to allow in even more thoughts, feelings, perspectives and events that will confirm that to you. When you change how you see yourself, how you see the world and how you see your position in the world, everything changes.

SATISFIED WITH FAILURE?

Are you satisfied with and accustomed to failure? When you face failure on a regular basis, it can start to feel familiar at times, almost normal or expected, which calls it into your reality. Settling for something may feel normal but it never feels good (even though it often feels easier to give up and so much easier to not even try in the first place, than to try and fail). Please don't settle, it's too easy to do that. It doesn't feel good or fulfilling to settle, simply because you weren't meant to, that's why it ultimately feels so uneasy to you. That unsettling feeling within you is calling you to more, encouraging you to improve and to try again, so don't give up.

MAKE ROOM FOR MORE

It is vital that you don't let one apparent failure, setback or painful event cut you off from allowing in the abundance of blessings that are available to you. If you are still observing, fighting against or complaining about that one situation that went wrong, you will continue to 'attract' and allow in even more things that feel like that to you, which will continue to hold back the blessings that are trying to get to you. When you release all of the shame and guilt associated with your past mistakes and failures, you will automatically make room for everything that you desire and deserve. The space in which you let out the pain, allows in the blessing.

WHY LIMITS ARE CRITICAL
Don't be afraid to stand up for yourself, to have limits and to set boundaries. When you don't have limits that's when people will tend to take advantage of you. Anyone who makes you feel guilty for having limits, for saying no, for speaking your truth, or for voicing your opinion or feelings is to be avoided at all costs. Never ever apologise for having boundaries, for putting your peace and your happiness first or for expressing your own feelings. The golden rule to remember is that those people who are meant to be in your life and those people who are for you, won't be embarrassed nor ashamed of who you really are, and especially won't use guilt, shame or blame as tactics to control you.

GENERATE THE STATE
A great tool that will help you to come into alignment with that which you desire to be or see, is to generate the mood or state of that which you desire. When you generate the state and create the mood or feeling of your desires (by asking yourself how would it feel to have it or be it right now) you will begin to reveal the feeling and summon the emotion of that thing, which will allow you to vibrate higher. That feeling will begin to lift you up to a higher frequency which will naturally begin to allow in the thoughts, people and opportunities that will help to bring you to your desires, or allow your desires to manifest into your environment. Make it your duty and responsibility to choose your moods carefully, and to no longer allow 'what is' to primarily affect or determine your current state of being. If you don't set your own vibration, you'll tend to allow everything and everyone else to do it for you, you will often continue to create even more of what you don't want since you will continue to focus your attention and awareness entirely upon 'what is' or 'what was' or how all of that feels. Above all else, be responsible for setting your own tone and emotional state. Remember that it's your state

of being that will either bring your desires to you, or hold them back from you.

PERIPHERAL GREATNESS
You are capable of so much more than you can even begin to comprehend. The more centred yet expansive that your point of view is, the more that you will begin to get a glimpse of the depth and the width of your own greatness and power. Those people who suffer from a chronic lack of self confidence and who have poor self worth or very little self esteem, are always, every single time, viewing themselves from a narrow point of view. They're not seeing the fullness of who they are now, or who they really are at the highest level. They can't see the greatness in their peripheral vision. They can't see or feel the fullness of who they really are. If we go through life with that limited perspective about ourselves, we are unintentionally cutting ourselves off from our own magnificence, abundance and blessings. When you centre yourself you will begin to feel the fullness of who you really are and start to see, feel and become aware of the greatness that is in your peripheral vision.

USE WHAT YOU KNOW BEFORE LEARNING MORE
Are you looking for that 'perfect' quote or piece of advice to motivate you to greatness and success? Instead of doing that, use and apply the knowledge that you already have before trying to learn even more. Quotes often manifest from applied lessons. They read differently according to what you have gone through. The power of the quote is not in the words, but what those words awaken and inspire within you. In addition quotes read differently according to the frequency that they were spoken from and the wavelength that you are reading them from. Therefore before seeking to learn more, use what you already know, but haven't fully applied yet. It is the application of knowledge that makes you wise, and not the knowing of it. Knowing something and using it are two very different things entirely on an energetic level. It's not what you know but what you do with what you know that truly

matters, that is what makes the difference. Too often we know the lessons that life has taught us and we know that we should learn from them, but we often haven't truly or consciously practised or applied those lessons in our own life. Procrastinating on applying a lesson will continue to keep the same issue coming back around in another disguise in order for you to see it and apply it in your own life, so apply those lessons now that you've been putting off. Start today, apply what you know on an intellectual level and start practising it in your own life.

POSITIVITY IRRITATING?
Don't be embarrassed of your positive nature. A positive and optimistic outlook is your natural state of being, it is who you really are. Make a promise to yourself to no longer shrink back your positive nature in the face of 'negative' people. If your positive perspective upsets or annoys others, that is an indication of their own unhappiness, it has nothing to do with you. Positivity feels uncomfortable and even irritating to them because they are so used to how 'negativity' and pessimism feels, it's how they're used to seeing things, they believe that they're just being realistic. Positivity is unrealistic to them, they can't see what you see. However just let them be, see through it and rise above it.

LOOKING FOR AND NEEDING A SIGN?
Signs and symbols will appear to you when and how you least expect them to, however they often appear as aligned time, such as 11:11, 2:22, 3:33 etc (also known as reflection time). When you go looking for those signs, they won't and can't show up. Your frequency of needing and wanting them actually keeps them from you and keeps them out of reach. The moment that you look for a sign, it won't be there. They appear when you are not on the frequency of needing them (or on the frequency of lack) essentially when your current point of focus isn't preventing them from revealing themselves to you or you being made aware of them. When you're trying to find a sign, and when you expect it to be there (in order to make you feel better) it won't be there. This

is the exact same principle for your desires too. Trying to force anything into your reality won't make anything happen. Your desires often sneak in when you are not looking for them, essentially when you haven't got a contradictory vibration or thought that is blocking them from manifesting, the same goes for those signs that you are looking for. The signs that you're looking for will naturally appear to you when you are moving in the right direction. They are there to say 'keep going', they're a reminder that you're loved and that you're being divinely protected and that you are being supported in whatever you are currently doing. However you choose to define those signs, such as angels, your inner self, your ancestors, the universe, God or even the soul of a departed loved one, it is a sign that the divine energy that created the entire universe is with you.

THE UNIVERSE'S HIDDEN PROTECTION
The universe is always protecting you from the life that you say you want, until you're able to handle it. The universe will continue to keep success and your desires from you until the strength and skills that are necessary to succeed at the highest level have been instilled within you. You already have all of those skills within you, you just need to tap into them. In essence, the universe will never give you something that you're not vibrationally ready for or aligned with.

JEALOUSLY IN A RELATIONSHIP
Jealousy in regards to a relationship and a partner, such as being jealous of your partner's closeness with other people (especially when it is unfounded, wherein your partner hasn't done anything to warrant or explain the jealously that you feel) often stems from, at the core level, fear and also the feeling of not being good enough. The root cause is often a lack of self acceptance, self worth or a lack of self love. In addition when you feel like you can't trust your partner (and they haven't done anything to explain why you are feeling and reacting that way) that is often a reflection of your own past, fear, hurt and pain, and also a lack of

trust in yourself. Maybe you are seeing this current relationship through the lens of the past, or the relationships that you have seen growing up. Maybe you're trying to prevent a re-run of history. It is vital that you love yourself first, until you do you will seek love, attention and validation from your partner in order to make you feel fulfilled, whole and complete. Your jealously is ultimately fear that they might leave you or that someone else might be better than you (which comes from your own lack of self worth). If you fear that your partner will leave you then you will often seek to control love or your partner in subtle little ways so that you won't have an opportunity to lose that relationship and in turn lose the love that you have for yourself too. That's why it is vital that you practise loving yourself first, above and before everything else, so that if your partner happened to leave you they won't be able to take with them the love and worth that you had for yourself too. In addition, please understand that someone else's beauty, talent and success can't take away from yours, only the ego believes that it can. That is always a reminder to go deeper within yourself. Jealously is ultimately a reminder to step back, centre yourself and practise self love and self acceptance.

NEW BELIEF UPDATE AVAILABLE

We update our phones and our electronic devices regularly, however we rarely update ourselves and our own beliefs. More than likely, until you consciously change your beliefs you will still be running on your childhood beliefs, even though you're an adult now. It is vital that you update and continue to update your sense of self, and that you update the beliefs that you have active regarding yourself, others, that which you desire and the world around you. You can't keep seeing things the way that you have always seen them, especially if those beliefs aren't helping you or bringing you peace. Your beliefs flow through everything that you do and everywhere that you go, however when your beliefs change, everything changes. You can begin to change your beliefs by choosing right now which thoughts you are going to continue to focus upon and power through your attention, awareness and faith. Start seeing yourself now as who you are and the person that you are becoming, rather than still seeing yourself and the world around you from the eyes of that hurt and scared child that is within you. How you perceive the world helps to determine what you're able to achieve and receive back. Make sure that you update your inner beliefs before updating anything else. What you feel and believe to be true about yourself and other people is what you will perceive in the world, however please understand that what you perceive is only the effect. What you imagine, feel and believe is the cause. However when you update your beliefs everything changes.

DISTRACTED?

If you're still being distracted by small inconveniences, and you find yourself getting angry over the little things in life, you'll never be truly happy. You will always have a reason to be upset, which will continue to hold back your peace, purpose and power. The more that you talk about and focus upon problems the greater that they will tend to become. Only when you're not focussing upon your true power and purpose will you have the time and energy to be distracted by those small things. Give your mind focus, direction and purpose.

BE PROUD OF YOURSELF

Take a moment today to just look at how far you have come. Issues that once seemed impossible to get out of are now no longer controlling your life or determining your state of being. You have gone through some of the hardest struggles and darkest days possible and yet you are still here, you're still trying, still learning, still growing, still bettering yourself, and still ready for more. Be proud of yourself, you've made so many improvements. You're a different person now, your current frequency is closer in vibration to who you really are than ever before. Every single day you are getting closer in alignment with your higher self, and you're centring yourself even faster than ever before. Do you realise just how many people you have helped and touched?

Don't underestimate the power in you still being here. You're changing the world for the better whether or not you even realise it or see it. Your positivity echoes and radiates throughout the entire universe.

I'LL NEVER GET THERE
At times it can feel like we are never going to see the results that we're seeking, that those big changes that we desire will never manifest, especially when we continue to face so many setbacks. Please understand that you can't miss what is meant for you. You'll always get where you are going and what is meant for you no matter how many times you fall down or get lost, just as long as you don't give up or give in. Keep going. Someday very soon those changes that you desire are going to sneak into your reality and before you even know it, you'll begin to see the changes that you have been visualising and praying for.

LOVELESS RELATIONSHIP
Don't fall into the trap of having a relationship with someone who only wants you when they're lonely or bored. Until you have boundaries people will continue to take advantage of you and violate your lack of limits. When you know and determine your own worth and value, you won't tolerate anyone else treating you less than the king / queen that you are. Only from that vibrational place will you then be able to 'attract' and allow into your life 'true' love. Remember, all relationships begin with you. Before seeking a relationship with someone, work on the relationship that you have with yourself.

POTENTIAL
There is nothing more exhausting than not living up to your full potential. Holding back your blessings and greatness is an exhausting task. You will know that you're resisting the 'call' when you constantly feel exhausted. So what's stopping you from being yourself? What's stopping you from taking action? What's stopping you from doing that which your heart and soul knows is

in your highest good? What needs to happen for you to finally go after your dreams and give it your all? You have got to try, at least give it a shot. You'll never know if you never try. The regret of not trying is much more difficult to live with than the embarrassment of one small failure.

WHY YOU KEEP GOING BACK TO THEM

If you find yourself going back to the same person, even when they continue to hurt you or disrespect you, it's time to think and look again. The reason why you are drawn to that person is not because you're necessarily meant to be with them, or because they're right for you, but because you are on the same frequency as them emotionally and mentally. That is why you feel so comfortable with them and why they feel so familiar to you. Your current lower vibration is in harmony with theirs. One of the main reasons why they keep coming back into your life is because they will continue to treat you how you have been treating yourself. However the main reason why they keep coming back into your life is because they have something to learn from you, and the reason why you keep going back to them is because you still haven't learned or applied the lesson (or lessons) that they're here to teach you. Ask yourself, 'Are they teaching me that I deserve better?', if they are, then listen and learn.

MANIFESTING BAD ADVICE?

If you're asking the universe for a sign whether or not you should do something, don't ask it from the vibrational place that you're at (of frustration and lack) vibrate higher. If you don't, that lower frequency (that you're currently seeing things from) will supply you with advice that might say 'give up'. The advice that you will receive won't be helpful or a sign that you should or shouldn't do something, it's just a reflection of the lower frequency that you're currently residing at. The path that unfolds will be a manifestation of that perspective too. Please understand that the path that is currently unfolding underneath you (and everything that you encounter on that path) is a direct reflection and confirmation of the frequency that you're currently and consistently vibrating at. The path that unfolds will always lead you to even more of the same (or how that feels) until you change. To know the difference whether the advice that you receive is helpful or not, find the space or vibrational place that it was asked from.

LEARN THE LESSON NOW

Where you are right now has purpose, including this situation that you're currently dealing with. Nothing happens out of order, everything has purpose. Even if you are not where you desire to be, you're here for a reason. There is purpose and lessons to be learned where you are. If you don't learn the lessons now, they will inevitably come back around in another disguise until you finally 'get it' and apply those lessons in your own life.

Be-LIE-fs

Not everything that you believe is necessarily the truth or is helpful to you. The word belief has a word hidden within its spelling which will help you to see this more clearly. Belief is spelt be-LIE-f, with the word 'lie' hidden within the spelling of it. The word 'lie' is there to remind us that what we tend to have the most belief in, is in fact a lie, or an illusion. What beliefs about yourself and that which you desire have been based on a lie or an illusion? The belief that you are not good enough, that you have no power or control over your life, and that you can't do something, are some of the biggest lies that you are likely still believing and making real (which is helping to form your reality / real-ity). It's time to change your beliefs, and time to start responding to life rather than just reacting to it. There is no need to stick to a belief and a particular way of seeing yourself and the world just because you have always seen things that way. If a belief or a perspective isn't making you happy, change it. Start by reminding yourself that you can do anything that you put your mind to. Believe that you're destined for greatness, that things are getting better, that blessings are reserved for you. 'Lie' to yourself if you need to. It is not necessarily lying to yourself, it is reminding yourself that it is who you are and how things really are at the highest level. Soon enough those thoughts, or 'lies', will become very real be-LIE-fs which will help to 'attract' and allow in everything that is already yours at the highest vibrational level.

YOU CAN'T HEAL ALL IN ONE GO

The healing process can at times be a long, tiring and tedious process. Please understand that there are multiple layers to pain, and multiple layers to your healing. Go easy on yourself. You can't heal all at once, there are often unseen depths and levels to pain. Don't allow yourself to fall into the trap of feeling guilty or ashamed whenever the same issue from your past awakens once more, just recognise it as another layer of your healing. Knowing this, understand that anything that is currently ready to be healed will make itself known to you and it may even appear in your awareness today. So if you're facing the same issue yet again today, that is a reminder to let those feelings and memories move through you. When those feelings arise, step back, centre yourself, view it all from another perspective, acknowledge what is moving through you and choose peace and joy again.

ACKNOWLEDGE WHEN THINGS ARE GOING RIGHT

Too often the only time that we acknowledge, give our undivided attention to and focus upon something in our current reality is when things go wrong. Which is calling in even more of how that looks and feels into our reality. It is important that we look for and acknowledge things that are going 'right' too, instead of only fixating upon those things that are going 'wrong'. The more that you look for things that are going right, the more that they will tend to appear in your current reality (the same could be said for when you are focussing upon things that aren't going well). When you accentuate the positives, you will become a person who good things continue to happen to, and the more that you define yourself as that and the more that you consciously see and affirm all of those good things that are happening in your life, the more that you will allow them into your reality. What you are appreciate of, appreciates in value.

IT IS GOOD TO MAKE MONEY

What is your perception and outlook regarding what is 'positive'? On the surface level that which we feel is positive for us (e.g. money) and that which we desire most of all, we can also at some level unknowingly fear it. We may have a negative belief or expectation going on in regards to our desires lingering in our awareness due to our past experiences with them. Many times those people who want to be rich (yet who have been brought up in poverty) were taught to fear money or they at the very least misunderstand money and those people who have it. Maybe they were taught that money was the 'root of all evil', or that rich people are ruthless and unkind, yet they still desire money at the deepest level. There is this constant battle and resistance going on within them in regards to money. Until their desire for money and their beliefs about it are in alignment, things can't change. You can't continue to define yourself as being a good person and at the same time believe that money is bad, and still expect and hope to receive money. Those two beliefs aren't resonating at the same level, they aren't in alignment with each other. You won't be able to experience having money and being happy with it until you change your outlook and beliefs regarding money. Your desire for something and your beliefs and expectations about it and your definitions regarding yourself, must all be aligned in order for you to allow in the experience that you desire and prefer to have with money. Please release your fears. Your fear regarding money is just an indication that you have got to change how you're seeing money, not that money is not meant for you, or that money is bad. Understand that money, like all things, just reveals who you already are. Money won't change someone who is kind and loving, it will only make them an even better and more loving person who is able to help even more people. There is nothing to fear regarding that which you desire at the deepest level. Start collecting positive perspectives regarding money and everything that you desire, e.g. that it is good to make money, that it is great to have enough money to help the world, and that it is positive to make money doing what you love, and fundamentally believe that you are good enough to make money.

FIGHTING FEAR, ANXIETY OR NERVOUSNESS?
You can't think feelings of fear and anxiety away, when you try to do that what you will end up doing is adding momentum to those feelings. You will unintentionally give them your attention and awareness, which powers them. Over thinking will only ever keep you on the same frequency as your fears and anxieties and continue to allow in even more thoughts that feel like that. When fearful or anxiety based feelings arise, allow and acknowledge them, and begin to see them for what they are (which is a reminder to relax and see things from a higher perspective). Don't get caught up in what fear is telling you, instead see it as a reminder to relax and let go. Let it be, see through it. From that place you will be able to see clearly again.

LET THEM GROW
The moment that you write someone off as being a certain thing, you will begin to lose sight of who they really are and who they have become. We are often so busy looking for and justifying who we believe someone to be that we will miss who they really are now. See people for who they are right now, and not as who they were. See them from the present, not the past. It's unfair to not allow them to grow. Just like you were a different person a year ago, be willing to see others in that same light too.

BE HONEST WITH YOURSELF
When you can't tell the truth about yourself, you won't be able to tell the truth about anyone else. The frequency that you are viewing yourself from will also distort how you see and interpret others and their actions too. It is so important that you are honest with yourself, with how you are feeling and with who you really are. Only once you do that will you then be able to see things and

others clearly. So what are you being dishonest about in regards to yourself? Are you still holding onto shame and guilt at some level regarding yourself, regarding how you look or who you are? If you are, you will end up blocking your highest desires from unfolding and manifesting in your life. Please understand that there is nothing wrong with being yourself and being who you authentically are. Guilt and shame in living authentically and being yourself isn't allowed. Let it go. As long as your true intention is one of peace, love, expansion and compassion for all, live your best life, be yourself fully. Only once you are being yourself fully will you then be able to help others and see others clearly. Being yourself is necessary in order for you to live on purpose and for you to make the impact on the world that you are capable of making.

USE FEAR PROPERLY

All feelings have purpose, including fear and anxiety. However when you misunderstand and misinterpret those feelings, and you get distracted focussing upon or fighting against them (rather than understanding what they are there to awaken within you) you will not only lose the message and purpose that they held, however you'll also lose the opportunity to change things for the better. That's when problems will start to arise. In essence those negative feelings are there to make you aware that what you're currently focussing upon or how you're currently seeing things isn't how your higher self sees them. Fear is a reminder to step back, allow how you feel, understand why you're really feeling that way and to start seeing things from a higher perspective.

AFFECT AND CREATE YOUR OWN REALITY

It is vital that we learn to affect our own reality, rather than consistently being affected by it. Too often in life we allow the outer circumstances of the world to primarily determine or affect our inner state of being, which in turn creates our reality and our results. Once you learn to respond to life rather than unconsciously reacting to what 'already is', you can then begin to reinvest your energy, re-guide your attention and awareness and change your reality in all of the ways that you desire to. Your reality begins with you.

RIPE AND READY

Your desires need time to fully develop and grow. I know that you want your desires right now, however you truly wouldn't want them to arrive a moment before they're ripe and ready. Trust that everything has its own season and time. Feel the peace of knowing that your desires are growing, ripening and arriving in divine timing. Relax, there is no need to force anything, trust that everything is unfolding perfectly, as and when it should. Learn to see 'what is' through that lens of perfect and diving timing too, knowing that 'what is' is also here in divine timing too. Think of it this way, everything is here for a reason, and it is all arriving in its own season.

HOW TO REACH HIGHER FREQUENCIES

There is no one specific way to increase your frequency (also known as your vibration) to the spectrum that your higher self and your highest desires naturally reside at. Some of the ways that you can increase your vibration is by focussing upon that which makes you feel good, by meditating, by doing yoga, by connecting with nature and by finding things to appreciate either in the past or the present (as long as you feel the appreciation now that is all that matters). There are many different ways to increase your frequency and whatever method you choose just make sure that you're having fun while you're doing it. Allow it to energise and empower you. Anything that centres you or brings you peace will also allow you to rise back up to the highest frequencies that you naturally reside at. In essence it is not about doing more, it is often about doing less. It is about learning to take your attention of any perspective, person or thing that is keeping you on a lower frequency.

A BREAK DOWN

Don't confuse a 'break down' for a breaking through and a breaking away of that which is no longer serving you and from that which isn't in your highest good. If you define something as being a 'break down' or a disaster then that is how it will appear. A break down is often just a break through and a blessing in disguise, it is a breaking away from everything that is holding you back and from that which is stopping you from becoming your best self or preventing you from accessing the genuine and lasting peace and happiness that is within you. A break down always comes before a major break through, so keep going.

BE KIND AND PATIENT WITH YOURSELF

Please be patient with yourself, especially when it comes to your own healing. There is no rush. In addition please release the pressure that you have placed upon yourself (or that society has placed upon you) to be perfect all of the time. The way in which you speak to yourself is so important too, especially the tone of voice that you use. How you see yourself helps to not only determine how the world treats you, but what you will tolerate too. Please respect yourself. Be kind, gentle and compassionate with yourself. Be as nice to yourself as you are being with others. In order for others to treat you better and for them to consistently respect you, you must first respect yourself. When you love and respect yourself and you honour that which you do, you will not only no longer tolerate it when other people treat you badly, however you won't be in a vibrational space that would allow those type of people into your life so easily. Please be patient with your growth, you can't rush it. Patience is necessary in order for you to achieve anything worthwhile. Start by talking to yourself as you would talk to a young vulnerable child. Give up using those harsh words that others have said to you to hurt yourself with again, those harsh words won't motivate or inspire you to change. Before putting yourself down and being so hard on yourself, remember that there is a small, vulnerable and often scared or hurt child within you that still needs love, affection and acceptance. Speak to that inner child with a kind, gentle and loving tone of voice. Encourage and support them as they flourish into an empowered, compassionate and loving adult.

'SPELLINGS'

Your words, both written and spoken, have profound creative power. Your written words, or your 'spellings', have an unseen almost 'magical' affect on your reality. Words spoken with faith and feeling are highly creative, and words written with intention have undeniable power. Use your words to speak things into existence. Rather than only talking about and seeing things as they are, see beyond them to the possibilities of what they can become and how you prefer them to be. It is also important that you write down your desires by hand (not using technology) as there seems to be an unseen power in the written word. When you write down your desires and read them aloud daily, you will automatically begin to focus your attention, and actively show the universe your commitment and willingness to act upon your goals and desires. Writing down clear and specific desires also activates the highest feelings of faith. It helps to set a clear intention and vision, and helps to remove any inconsistent desires. All of which helps to ease any subtle resistance that you have going on, you begin to allow the universe to flow its energy freely towards your desires. Focussed desire, helps to release power.

EFFORT, ENTHUSIASM AND ENDURANCE

Some of the most important ingredients for success are effort, enthusiasm and endurance. When you're unwilling to put in the time and effort to better yourself, to do your best, and to put yourself 'out there', and especially when you're unwilling to push yourself to be better and do better, things can't and won't change. In addition without enthusiasm in yourself, your work, your message, your ideas and those people that you interact with, things can't change. The energy that fuels your work and creates the path ahead always comes from the intention or the reason why you do things and the frequency that you're on. When you do anything with enthusiasm you energise and fill it up with the highest potential of what it can be (you won't do it from a place of doubt, lack or fear, but from a place of confidence and faith that you are capable of doing it well and that you're capable of receiving the result that you desire). Continuing to undermine and underestimate yourself will continue to hold back your desires. Finally endurance is also critical to your overall success. It will be the glue that will bring it all together, it'll allow you to be able to endure 'what is' and allow you to see through it to 'what will be', all of which is critical to your overall success. Endurance will also inspire you to try again even after you fail, it will encourage you to keep on stepping into your higher self. It will keep you moving towards your highest goals and purpose in spite of all those failures and setbacks that you have faced. Those 3 ingredients will take you a long way when it comes to your overall success. Other ways of wording this would be having consistency, confidence and commitment in all that you do and all that you are. However you choose to phrase it, those three core principles are key to your overall success, and they will help you to become your best self.

FIND FORGIVENESS
Instead of trying to change the past or 'what was', focus upon changing how it affects you now in the present moment. When you continue to focus upon or fight against that which has caused you pain, and you continue to have hate in your heart for those people and things that have hurt you (or hurt someone that you love) you won't be able to refocus upon loving and accepting yourself fully in the present moment. It is vital that you change your point of focus if things are to be any different for you. When you forgive, you will begin to live for yourself again, it is not selfish to find peace. It is important that you refocus and reinvest all of that wasted energy in empowering yourself rather than powering the feeling and the experience of hurt and pain, all of which would continue to make the affects of it even bigger in your life. Only then will you be able to create the life that you desire from a place of peace and power, rather than pushing away the past or

the present from a place of fear. When you bring an awareness to the affect that pain and hurt has had on your life (and the affect that your lack of forgiveness has had on your life thus far too) you will begin to see clearly all of the times that you allowed the past and that pain to steal your happiness and peace. When you clearly understand the impact that your refusal to heal has had on your present and the affect that it will continue to have on your future, you will choose forgiveness every single time. It's never too late to forgive and move on. As long as you are still here, you still have time to forgive and time to live your best life.

LISTEN TO EVERYONE

Be willing to hear everyone's point of view without letting it affect you. Listen to what they say, not because it is necessarily useful or the truth, but because it has purpose. Listen intently with your awareness but not your ego. The moment that someone opens their mouth they can't help but show you their frequency. Their thoughts and beliefs are a reflection of the frequency that they reside at, the same way that what you see in others and what you hear shows you the frequency that you reside at. So how does their words feel? If they speak from a higher frequency of love, peace and clarity, listen and allow it to inspire and empower you. If they're on a lower frequency, listen too. However don't fall into the trap of defending your truth to someone who is on a lower frequency. They can't see what you see from down there. Educate them if they're willing to listen, if not, let them be.

FIGHTING AGAINST YOURSELF?

Do you find yourself feeling exhausted most of the day? Maybe you are unknowingly fighting against yourself. When you spend the majority of your time, energy and effort fighting against your own thoughts and your current reality, you will have no energy or time left to focus upon thoughts, feelings or perspectives that will empower you and make you feel good, which would ultimately change things for the better. There is no need to fight against, fear or analyse your negative thoughts, or any need to try and replace them by forcing positive thoughts in their place. Instead of fighting against 'what is', help to create what will be by gently focussing your attention and awareness upon thoughts and feelings that would lift you up and empower you, especially those thoughts and feelings which are closer in alignment with who you really are and what you desire and deserve.

VIEW IT BY ITSELF
Learn to focus upon what you do want, rather than fighting against what you don't want. Focus your attention, thoughts and feelings upon that which you prefer. Power that perspective and align yourself with how that feels. You don't have to push away or beat that which you don't want in order to achieve that which you do want. Give up the idea that you can receive that which you do want by pushing against, 'beating' or focussing upon that which you don't want. It doesn't work that way. Nothing really changes when you do that. When you do that you are only ever powering that which you don't want, your focus is giving it your energy and power which is bringing it to life (which will also bring it into your life and onto your 'path'). Start to see what you do want by itself, and not in comparison or relation to anything or anyone else. Naturally allow what you don't want to give birth to the desire of that which you do want, and immediately begin to focus your attention and awareness upon that and how that looks and feels to you. Be 'pro' the solution, rather than 'anti' the problem. You can't change anything by focussing upon it from feelings of hatred and anger, only unconditional love can change things, and change them for the better. Be 'for' things, rather than against them.

I'M PROUD OF YOU
Do you realise just how far you've come? You're still here, still growing and still trying. Take a moment now to acknowledge and affirm all of the positive changes that you have made and have committed yourself to. When you do, they will become stronger. What you focus upon grows. Often in life we tend to just confirm and focus upon things when they are going wrong, however it is

important that we focus upon things when they are going right too. When you take the time to appreciate and accentuate the positive changes in your life, you will begin to open up and allow in even more events that will make you feel like that again. Actively acknowledge those things that are going right. Acknowledge the new found peace and happiness that is within you now. You prayed for this one day not too long ago. Some day soon you are going to look back (when you have that which you are currently visualising and praying for) and realise just how powerful you are. Trust me, there is nothing to worry about.

STILL RUNNING AWAY FROM IT?
Running away from your feelings, mistakes and that which causes you to 'look within', won't solve or change anything. That which you push away or push against, always pushes back harder. Move through things rather than moving away from them. Remember that your frequency is creating the path ahead and until you heal and vibrate higher, you will continue to call onto your path and into your life everything that feels like that pain or that which you're avoiding. The only reason why those uncomfortable and painful situations continue to happen to you in the first place is because of what's going on within and what you're failing to set free. Until that changes you'll continue to encounter situations and people that will awaken that pain and hurt within you (in order for you to see it, face it, allow it and then choose again). What you acknowledge and face, you will ultimately let go of. Always remember that you can't outrun or outsmart your own frequency. When you change on the inside, those changes that you have been seeking on the outside will begin to appear.

VENTING VERSUS COMPLAINING
It's OK to be annoyed by things in life, however continuing to complain about problems won't make them any better. You have no right to complain about a problem or a situation that you don't like, if you are not willing to commit yourself to change it or change how you are seeing it. It's how you see a 'problem' and

what you do about that problem that really matters. Ultimately things won't change until you change. If you don't make any amends, the problem will continue, as will your unhappiness and frustration regarding it, all of which will continue to power the problem. Venting briefly about a problem will certainly help to let out the pain and the resistance, however constantly focussing upon and 'moaning' about it will only ever allow into your reality even more thoughts, feelings and things which will feel like that problem.

KNOW YOUR VALUE

It is terrible what people will settle for and do to themselves and others when they don't love, respect or know themselves fully. In addition when you don't know what you have of worth and value within you, you will more than likely end up just giving it all away to everyone and anyone, and ultimately allow yourself to be continuously mistreated and taken advantage of. When you know your own worth and value, you won't accept, tolerate or settle for anything less than what you desire and deserve. You won't let other people mistreat you, because you won't be mistreating yourself any more. When you change how you see yourself and how you treat yourself, you will lead the way for others to treat you better too. It always begins with you.

THE PRE-SENT MOMENT

Your current reality is just a reflection of who you were and what you thought was possible for you. It's the pre-sent, it is never up to date or up to speed with who you are right now. So stop looking to the outside world to confirm the recent changes that you've made within. They will come in time. When you automatically believe that your present and future are going to look and feel like the past, then they will. Your expectation and your attention upon that perspective creates it. In addition when you fight, judge or resist 'what is' or you focus upon 'what was', you will not only persist it but you will also block and deflect the blessing that was just about to unfold in your life. It often takes a while for those desired changes to come into focus and into fruition, but until they do, have patience. Detach, relax and have faith that the changes that you are seeking are currently unfolding, even when you can't see definitive proof of it. Make your faith bigger than what you can currently see.

FOCUS, NOT FORCE

You create the life that you desire by focussing your attention and awareness, not by forcing your thoughts or faking your feelings. Use focus, not force. Your attention and presence is your real power. When you focus your attention and awareness upon anything that feels good, your frequency will automatically begin to rise up, which will 'attract' and allow in everything that feels like that to you, which often includes your desires.

HOW DO YOU AFFECT THEM?

How do you make others feel? How are your actions (or lack of actions) affecting others? Often we're too busy blaming others or holding them accountable for how they have affected us, to even recognise the affect that we have had on them and everyone else too. Reflect on that responsibility. Be accountable and responsible for not only how you feel (and for changing it) but for how you're unintentionally or intentionally making others feel too. In addition, give up blaming others or giving them the power to determine how you ultimately feel. Be responsible and accountable for your own mood. Be accountable for how you're ultimately affecting others and for making the necessary changes. It will be one of the greatest things that you will ever do.

THAT ISN'T YOUR JOB

It is so important that we allow other people to make their own decisions and at times their own mistakes. Be there to gently guide, support and help others when they ask, but please understand that it's not your duty, job or responsibility to make their choices for them or to protect them from everything. You can't do their learning for them. Let them live their own life and give them enough room to make their own mistakes and then learn from them. As hard as it is to watch at times, it's necessary for their overall growth. You don't know the lesson that they'll learn from that experience, and how it will help to change them for the better. It all has purpose.

IT ALL WORKS OUT

Don't worry, it all works out in the end for you, it truly does. You might not be able to see, feel or even believe that from your current perspective, however it truly does. When you hold onto that belief it will get you through the darkest days. Your faith in the positive end result stops you from focussing upon or getting lost in thoughts and feelings such as, 'Why is this happening to me' or 'I can't do this'. Your faith in better days, allows them in. When you know that you 'make it', it becomes a self fulfilling prophesy. In your darkest moments, allow 'what is', acknowledge and accept how you feel, and centre yourself in the faith that it all works out in the end, and just watch how the universe responds.

DEVELOP YOURSELF FIRST

It is vital that you develop yourself before you try to develop a career or a relationship. Until you know, love, respect, accept and work on yourself, life will constantly feel like a battle in vain. Once you know who you are, no relationship, person or thing will have the power or ability to hurt you or take away your power, peace, worthiness or happiness. People will only ever be able to add to who you are, rather than being able to take away from it.

JUDGING OTHERS

It can often be difficult to give 'second chances', especially to those people who have hurt you or hurt someone that you love and care about. However when someone changes it is important that we also change how we see them too. Now this doesn't mean that you have to give second chances to those people who have hurt you badly in the past. You don't need to give anyone a second chance or let them back into your life if you don't want to.

However this message is not meant for those situations, it is more in regards to those people who have caused minor problems in your life, which were mainly due to their lack of knowledge or a lack of awareness, or more accurately their own unprocessed pain. People can and often do change over time and it is important that we open up that vibrational space to see them as the person that they are now, and not just who they were or what they did. People grow and change, just like you have grown and changed over the years. Just as you now know yourself to a higher degree, they too may know themselves to a higher degree also (including that which they did to themselves and to others when they were in pain). You would be surprised at the mistakes that people make when they don't know (or love) themselves fully. However don't be a fool either. Remember what they did, however don't judge them for it and continue to view them from that lower perspective. Doing that will 'draw' that type of behaviour out from them when they are around you. Give up 'judging' someone based on where they've been or what they've done, especially when they're consistently making an effort to change and to better themselves. See them as the person that they are becoming. Don't judge someone based on what they have done, but what they are still doing. It is important that you find a middle ground between not being 'gullible' while still being reasonable.

RACISM AND SEXISM

At times in life you will encounter individuals who are on a lower frequency. Those individuals who are filled with prejudice and hatred, who are sexist, homophobic and racist amongst other things. However please don't let those people affect you. Please understand that they are just showing you who they are, not who you are. They often don't even know themselves fully, so how can they know you or even begin to tell you what or who you are? They are just projecting their own pain, fear, ignorance, inadequacies and insecurities onto you. They're operating from the level of fear, they can't see you or see themselves clearly from there. When they are lost in those feelings of anger or pain, they can't hear or see anyone clearly. Fundamentally the root cause of that type of behaviour is a lack of knowledge, and they can't get that knowledge from the frequency that they currently - and frequently reside at. Educate them if they are willing to listen, however if they're not then let them be. Refocus and turn up the volume on the solution, rather than the problem. Ultimately only an ignorant person needs someone inferior than them to feel their own power or strength.

USE YOUR PAST
Use your past to brighten another person's future, be a light in their darkness. Use what you've been through to help someone else, give purpose to that pain. When you share your story in an open, honest and purposeful way it will undoubtedly save lives. Sharing your story will unconsciously give someone else the permission to do the same. When you share your story you will help someone else to release the guilt, shame and resistance that they have going on in regards to how they really feel. You will help to remove any blocks to their happiness, peace and healing, all of which will allow them to release their past and reach their future. There is no greater gift that you could give to another person than to let them know that they're not alone, and that they're not the only one going through something.

LET GO OF THE PROBLEM
Getting annoyed and frustrated at a problem won't help you to solve it, it will in fact only ever perpetuate it. The moment that you see a problem either within yourself or within your current reality, the solution that you require is born within you. All that you have to do is allow it in. When you believe that the answer will come to you, it will. However when you feel and believe that you're helpless and that nothing can be done about that particular problem, then it won't. It always begins and ends with you. When you have faith in the solution and you focus upon how that solution feels, you will allow the information that you need (and when you need it) to appear in your life. You will leave

enough room for the best version of things to unfold in your reality. Problems can often help us to better ourselves and to know ourselves better. They're opportunities for us to change and grow, and for us to get a clearer idea of what we do want. They're not meant to be pushed away, they're meant to be used as a reminder to start focussing upon and letting in that which we do want. Release the problem and let yourself receive the solution.

YOUR ANCESTORS ARE STANDING IN THE WAY
Did you know that any time that you have a desire to have, do or be something, your ancestors know. They will either stand by your side (directing and guiding you, in essence leading the way) or they will stand in the way (protecting you) if that which you desire isn't in your highest good (or in the highest good for your future ancestors too). They won't allow something that would undo all of the hard work that they have done. Of course you will still have free will and free choice over what you do and where you go, however they won't allow you to go astray. They will however allow that which will encourage you to grow and that which will awaken you (no matter how difficult or how painful it might be for you). They ultimately want the best for you, they reside at the highest frequencies alongside your highest self. They can see the purpose of everything, they know what lays ahead for you. Feel the peace within you of knowing that at the highest level you can't get it 'wrong', and that you can't get lost for long. Rejoice in the faith that it is all taken care of, that you're being divinely protected, and that no matter how bad things might look right now, or how far down the 'wrong' path you might go, that it is all going to be OK.

THESE 3 THINGS ARE KEY
In life I have found that there are three core elements to a happy, fulfilled and peaceful life, they are as follows. Number 1, a connection to and an understanding or awareness of that unconditional loving presence that is deep within you, and an awareness of that higher power which you're a part of (not apart

from). Number 2, a complete allowing or total surrendering to 'what is' with an unwavering and unconditional faith in greater and what will be. Finally number 3, an unconditional loving acceptance and appreciation for all things, especially who you are, what you have, and what you're here to do. Those three core elements will have an undeniable affect on your life. They will ultimately allow the path of least resistance to unfold and allow you to go with the flow. Life isn't supposed to be hard, it is supposed to be 'effortless'. Focus upon less effort and more upon allowing. When you consciously practise those three elements you will undoubtedly begin to see for yourself the power that they contain.

VERY EASILY IRRITATED?

If we are to be truly happy, we can't keep allowing small issues and inconveniences to cause us great upset. Only someone who is in pain has the time or desire to hold onto grievances, or will allow themselves to be irritated or outraged by every little thing. A happy person won't waste their time and energy doing that. They understand that nothing is worth sacrificing their joy and blessings for. If you are still holding onto those small grievances you won't be able to let in your biggest blessings. Choose wisely what you give your attention and awareness to. Centre yourself and rise above it all without looking down upon it.

WHAT ARE YOU GIVING UP ON?

Every single person who has ever accomplished anything worthwhile stood exactly where you are standing right now. They felt at times lost, hopeless, overwhelmed, frustrated and were often on the verge of giving up numerous times. However just look at them now. If they gave up in those moments of uncertainty and darkness, they would have never been able to achieve or receive their highest blessings. Knowing this, just imagine what you are about to give up on. You've come too far to give up now. You can't afford to give up, you're almost there. Soon you'll look back and wonder why you ever worried.

CLAIM YOUR DESIRES

Declare that your desires are already yours now, knowing that at a vibrational level the moment that you ask, the creation process is complete. Accept and claim that new reality as the reality that you choose to experience right now. Intend and expect for your desires to manifest, knowing that they already have at the highest vibrational level. All that you have to do to begin to allow them in is increase your vibration to the frequency that they reside at.

BELIEFS ARE ONLY HABITS

Beliefs are just habits. They are just thoughts that you have practised into being your current and consistent way of seeing and doing things. More than likely you have been listening to your thoughts and beliefs for years. You have practised them into becoming who you feel and believe you are or how you feel and believe that things are. If you practised a 'negative' belief into being then you can practise a positive belief into being too. You can change your beliefs by first becoming aware of your current thoughts (which are a reflection of your current frequency) and from that space you can then begin to remove the power from them and then let them go. You can do this by first allowing them and then refocussing upon feelings and thoughts that empower and lift you up higher. Beliefs will begin to form in time which will begin to support the person that you desire to be, and allow you to see things how you prefer them to be. Just give it time, be consistent. Choose to consistently see beyond your first reaction (which is just how you are used to seeing things) let those thoughts 'be' and choose to respond to life from a higher perspective. Power positive perspectives rather than fighting against 'negative' ones. All of this requires you to become aware. For any real progress to be made you have got to start responding to life rather than just reacting to it (as reacting is only ever a re-enactment of who you were and how you are used to seeing things). Responding to life will allow you to view things from a higher frequency, which will in time begin to 'attract' and allow in consistent positive and supportive thoughts regarding everything, which will then in time, create empowering beliefs. It does take practise but it's worth it.

ACT-ION
Once you have done the 'inner' work (by stepping into your highest self and preferred reality) follow the call. Action is what must occur after you act the part. Imagine the word 'action' consists of the words 'act', 'inspiration' and 'motion', act-ion. One part doesn't work without the others. It's so important that you meet the universe half way and that you act upon those inspired ideas that you have received. Stop talking yourself out of taking action. It doesn't matter what happened before, this is a brand new opportunity so please stop viewing it through the lens of the past. That tiny voice within you that says that you can't do it, is only ever a reflection and an echo of who you were and what you used to believe, don't listen to it. Believe in yourself, have faith and take action.

ARE YOU APPRECIATIVE?
Until you're truly thankful and appreciative of what you already have, you won't be able to allow in more. When you're genuinely thankful and grateful for what you have the universe tends to give you even more. Genuine feelings such as love and appreciation are non resistant, they are not holding onto or pushing against anything. They are feelings of complete allowing. The vibration of appreciation effortlessly allows in even more things, people and circumstances to be thankful for. The universe will in time respond to that feeling of appreciation and will bring even more things that feel like that to you. Genuine 'thank you's' and honest 'I loves you's' are so powerful. When you continue to focus upon that which you don't have from a place of bitterness and anger, instead of focussing upon and feeling appreciation for what you already do have, you will unintentionally block that which you want most of all. The more thankful that you are, the more that you will be thankful for. When you genuinely appreciate and feel

heartfelt gratitude for all that you have and all that you are, miracles will begin to happen.

'SPIRITUAL'

Spirituality doesn't mean that you have to be strong all of the time. That is a dangerous concept. Forcing yourself to be happy and strong is not only exhausting but dangerous too. Spirituality is about allowing how you really feel, it's not about ignoring your feelings or pretending to be happy, it's about recognising that you're unhappy, understanding why you feel that way and then having the tools to allow you to move towards a perspective that will allow in your joy again. It most definitely is not about plastering positivity over negativity. Ignoring your feelings and emotions isn't helpful. Please understand that your feelings are there to help you, not to hurt you. It's OK to feel down, it is only the belief that it's bad to feel down that causes us problems. Ultimately 'negative' feelings aren't supposed to be ignored, they're meant to be understood and then used to inspire change. Don't be in a rush to push them away, they have use, and being in touch with your inner being will allow you to see that.

INTUITION

Learn to listen to and trust your own gut, rather than relying upon others for their advice, support and guidance. Your 'gut' instinct and your feelings are there to tell you how close or how far away you are from what is meant for you. Other people can't help you with that. Your gut instinct is primarily for you. Your intuition is guiding you step by step, saying "Go here" or "Do that". It is fixed upon your highest purpose and your higher self, it will subtly let you know when you're 'on track' and when you're not, and it will do that through your feelings. How you feel now and how you feel when you think of your desires is letting you know when you're on the right track and when you're not, so learn to be still and listen. You'll often find that problems only occur when you don't trust or listen to your gut.

YOU CHOSE THIS GENERATION FOR A REASON

Humanity is currently going through a time of great change. We are beginning to see the dawn of a new era of connection, empowerment, love and unity. Anything that is not a part of that, and any actions or belief systems that aren't based on love, are making their way to the surface to be seen, felt and released. The presence of pain in our environment is therefore here to help and heal us, rather than hurt us. Don't be afraid of it. Regardless of how things currently look, they are always steadily improving and getting better. You chose to be alive during this generation, simply because you wanted to be a part of the solution, you wanted to see and experience change and the old way of doing things fall apart to reveal a better way forward.

YOU NEED TO READ THIS

There is no glory in making yourself small and timid. Build yourself up. What and who you believe you are, you will become. Know that you're destined for greatness. Believe in your abilities, be vulnerable, show the world who you really are. Know your worth and value. Care for yourself, love yourself fully as you are and where you are. Turn your dreams into goals and plans, and take action with courage and enthusiasm. Inspire, motivate and encourage yourself. No more hiding away, holding yourself back or putting things off. No more being apologetic or trying to please and impress everyone. Give up pushing away that which you want. This is your life, and your time, don't waste it.

ACCEPT YOURSELF

Your life is a reflection of your own self acceptance and self worth, it is a mirror image of what you're able to accept and receive. When you accept, claim and recognise your own greatness, the universe does too. Until you accept yourself, you can't accept your blessings. If you don't set your own self worth and value, you will tend to allow everyone else to do it for you. Without boundaries and limits you will tend to let people mistreat you and violate your space and peace. Only you have the privilege of setting and determining your own worth. When you stop all the resistance that is holding back your blessings (by accepting and loving yourself fully now) you will begin to allow in everything that feels good to you, everything that you have always wanted yet didn't feel worthy of receiving or having. Your blessings are always trying to get to you, but they can't reach you when you feel unworthy or not good enough.

YOUR NEEDS ARE VALID

Your needs are valid, as are your desires. Stop undermining them and casting them aside. Your inner needs and highest desires are a reflection of your best self, you can't keep ignoring them. They have purpose. It's time to make yourself a priority and time to prioritise your needs. It's reckless to put yourself and your needs last. You're good enough to be put first. You deserve the best. You've got to stop accepting and tolerating less than what you desire and deserve. No more betraying yourself. When you start prioritising your needs and goals, the universe starts prioritising you.

WHEN HELPING OTHERS IS RECKLESS

It is important to understand that what you don't give to yourself first, you inevitability withhold from others too. When you don't give yourself 'real' love, you withhold love from others too. You can't give to another what you don't have to give. If you're not giving something from a place of love, peace and power, then it's not worth it, it has no real value. You have got to stop giving away the love to others that you haven't even given to yourself first. Give up the idea of giving love to receive love. If you don't love and care for yourself fully now, then you won't be able to care for others fully either, or be able to allow in a result that feels like that love. Before you help others, help yourself first. It's not selfish, nor is it a credit to help everyone else except yourself, it is reckless to do that. It is time for you to be self-full. Self care is key.

WHY DO I DO THAT?!

Bring an awareness to your actions. What you do out of ignorance will continue to happen to you until you bring an awareness to it. Remember until you change, nothing changes. Take back responsibility for getting better and doing better. Bring an awareness to your reactions, impulses and decisions. Find out what you are doing or what you are failing to do. Doing something out of ignorance isn't a lasting excuse nor a valid reason to keep on doing it either. Step back, centre yourself and ask, 'Why do I do that?' and 'How can I improve?'. Asking the question in a positive context and from a higher perspective leaves enough room for clarity and insight to come up with an answer. That's why it's called insight, because it comes from looking and tuning in within.

HOW DO YOU FEEL ABOUT IT?

How you feel about things is so important, those feelings are a reflection and an indication of the frequency that you are seeing them from. How you feel most often from day to day and moment to moment is what you are allowing into your reality. How you feel regarding things is more important than what you initially think of them. Your feelings are making you aware of what you have been consistently putting out and getting back in regards to everything. It helps you to see your expectations regarding everything, including your desires, so that you can change it if it is not in alignment with the experience that you desire to have with it. In order for you to allow in that which you desire, the energies or frequencies need to be vibrating in harmony with each other. You can't allow in an abundance of money, when you think of yourself as being poor, or when you are focussing upon lack and when you continue to expect to struggle in regards to your finances. Your desire for something and your beliefs about it need to be aligned in order to allow in the experience and reality that you desire and prefer. Your feelings allow you to feel if you're currently in alignment with what you desire and who you are at the highest level. It is not just the thought that counts, but the feeling too. When you begin to come into alignment with what you desire consistently, by viewing it and viewing yourself from a higher perspective, you will first begin to have positive thoughts regarding it which will eventually lead to a positive expectation and in time positive feelings regarding it, all of which will begin to allow it in.

REAL-ITY

The spelling of the word reality, contains a hidden secret, it is spelt real-ity. Reality has the word 'real' hidden within its spelling. So contemplate this, what are you making real and making into your reality? Whatever you feel and know to be true now about yourself, the world, others and that which you desire, you will make real which will in time be reflected back into your reality, whether imagined or not. Whatever you feel, believe and do, always returns to you. Choose to make real those things that empower you, those things that lift you up and elevate you, not that which holds you back. Feel the realness of that which you desire to be and see, and soon enough it will become your reality.

REJECTING YOUR BLESSINGS

Often when we don't get that which we desire we stop ourselves wanting it. We often reject that which we want the most in an attempt to numb, soothe or control the pain of not receiving it. We tend to unconsciously decide that if it doesn't 'want us', then we don't want it or we don't need it, all of which causes us to push it away even more. We end up blocking that which was trying to get to us. Let yourself love that which you desire, instead of rejecting it and rejecting yourself in fear. Fundamentally, stop talking yourself out of that which is meant for you.

IT IS LACKING LOVE

What you lack in your material based reality, is often a direct reflection of what you fail to feel love for. When you show your desires unconditional love, you will receive love (and experiences that feel like that love) back from them. However it is important that you show yourself unconditional love first. You can't 'attract'

135

that which you love and desire when you don't even love yourself. The two vibrations aren't lined up. It is only once the two perspectives are vibrating in harmony with each other consistently can you begin to allow in that which you desire, or that which would lead you to your desires. So remember until you show your desires unconditional love, they can't reflect that love back to you. The situations and circumstances that you will have with that which you desire will reflect back to you the feeling that you have been fuelling it with. It will appear how you have been seeing it, and how you expect to see it or experience it. Please understand that you have got to love that which you desire before you can see or receive it. Love it where you see it and love those people who have it. Find love in all of the perspectives and experiences regarding it. When you begin to show yourself and your desires unconditional love, that which you love often turns up in the most miraculous ways.

FEELING GOOD DOESN'T CHANGE THINGS
Feeling good doesn't necessarily create the changes in the present moment, it does however help to create the path ahead and open up the avenue in the present moment that will take you further. Too often when we start to feel good, we will begin to look around for proof that it is working (or that it is changing things) and we will tend to get angry when there are no obvious changes, all of which will often cause us to go back to our old way of seeing and doing things. We will end up feeling angry, 'hard done by' or pessimistic about our desires and our current reality. When you do that you are placing your faith in the belief that your positivity hasn't worked or that it won't work, which the universe will begin to respond to. When you consistently expect the worst and marinate in those lower frequency feelings, you will continue to project that lack and 'negativity' forward, which will create even more of how that lack feels in your near 'future'. Rest assured that being in alignment with who you really are now and being in touch with your inner joy really is changing things, however please understand that those changes are happening below the

surface, and they will reveal themselves and come into focus in divine timing (which is often longer than we expect). Until then detach and focus upon becoming your best self.

DISAPPOINTMENTS DON'T LAST

Things won't always turn out the way that you have planned and envisioned and that is OK, it all has purpose though. Don't let yourself get caught up in a 'this isn't fair' mentality. Of course it's OK to be disappointed, frustrated and upset, but don't let those feelings take you off course, and stop you from seeing what is really going on. Don't let a few moments of disappointment stop you from a lifetime of becoming the best version of yourself (it will if you let it). Remember that failure is only ever direction and guidance in disguise. Failure will help to nudge you down a path that is better suited to you. It will help to guide you towards the path that was made just for you, the one that was intended and intentionally created for you by the power that created the entire universe. Ease up on needing things to go your way only, always leave enough room for another way and an even better way. When you think that something can only happen for you some particular way, you will tend to close off and shut down all of the other possible ways that it can happen for you. Understand that every 'failure' that you encounter has purpose. It's directing you towards even better, protecting you from what is not meant for you, and pointing you towards what is. Don't give up or fall for the illusion that things didn't work out. Feelings of disappointment don't last. Centre yourself, dust yourself off and try again.

PAINFUL GROWING PAINS

The process of growing can either be a painful or a pleasant one. We can either choose to listen to those little 'warning' signs that the universe is giving us, and look within, learn from our past mistakes and apply those lessons that we've learned, which is a much more pleasant way to grow rather than needing something 'big' to get us to finally listen and learn. We can either listen and learn now, or continue to ignore the signs. If we don't want to grow on our own, then the universe will often bring us the lessons in a more painful and abrupt way. That is often when those big unexpected events occur which shake us to the core. It is always best to listen now to the 'whispers' before they need to turn into a roar to get our attention. Maybe the universe is whispering 'slow down', if it is, it is best that you listen now and slow down before you need some 'big' event to cause you to slow down and take life at a much more slower pace from a much more centred place. When we notice and learn to listen to the little 'pebbles' of support and guidance that the universe is placing on our path (in order to get our attention and for us to grow) we won't need a wall to collapse down upon us in order for us to finally listen, learn, let go and grow.

TALL TREES GROW FROM SMALL SEEDS

Imagine that every single inspired idea that you receive from your higher self or the universe is a seed. Those seeds can only ever grow when you plant them. Holding onto an idea won't make anything happen. All ideas, like seeds, need to be nurtured, watered and given a chance to grow. Shine a light on them. Don't discount any idea (or seed) as being impossible or too hard before you even plant them. Give all divinely inspired ideas an opportunity to evolve into something great. Just like a forest won't grow overnight, have the patience and the wisdom to know that all great things take time. As long as you keep planting those seeds / ideas, they will continue to grow. Don't allow yourself to get distracted by the height of everyone else's trees that you fail to notice just how tall your own seeds and trees have grown. In addition give up trying to plant your seeds in the shadow of someone else's forest. There is no need to do what others have done to be successful. Walk your own path, plant your own ideas and seeds and give them plenty of room to grow into something beautiful. Let them grow at their own pace. Don't get disheartened if some seeds don't survive, in time those seeds and ideas that were meant to bare fruit will.

THEY'RE OUT TO HURT ME

Not everyone is out to hurt you, however when you are so used to being hurt you'll tend to start seeing things that aren't there. Your vision of the world will be blurred and distorted. You'll only see that which you already believe to be true about yourself and others, and in time you'll begin to protect yourself from perceived pain. You'll ultimately operate from a level of defensiveness, and fight an unnecessary fight. It's just not worth it. Decide to reinvest that wasted energy and time in knowing, growing and seeing yourself and others clearly. Choose what adds value to you and all others, and that which is in alignment with your highest good, not just that which is the easiest and 'safer' option. Don't choose the easy option by default. Although fulfilling boredom is easier to do, it won't bring you lasting peace, fulfilment or happiness. Priorities are needed. It is time to redefine yourself and time to start expecting better.

HATE ISN'T HELPFUL

When acts of hate are so prevalent in today's society it is often normal to get swept away with the anger, fear and chaos of those atrocities. Of course fear and anger are normal stops on the way to healing from such hate, however they are not the final destination. Don't retaliate with hate when confronted with evil. Their hatred is just a projection of their pain, rise above it, become invisible to it. We can't let the hatred of another person take away our peace too, that is exactly what they want. The very reason for those horrific attacks is because of fear and hate. Fear and anger solves nothing and destroys everything. A person who is connected to the peace within themselves won't need to carry out those hate filled and heinous acts to finally feel worthy of love, peace and acceptance. All fear, anger and hate stems from a lack of love. Anger and fear won't bring us the peace that we are seeking. There will only be peace on earth when there is peace in the minds and the hearts of those people who live in it. Hate won't heal us, love will.

NO MORE NEEDING PROOF

Let go of needing to see proof of your desires to believe in them. In reality, until you believe in them, you won't be able to see them. Give up looking for proof of your desires arrival too. When you do that from a lower perspective, you'll tend to reaffirm and confirm the absence of your desires, instead of anticipating their arrival from a place of faith. You will affirm the 'lack' in your current reality and confirm to yourself and the universe that you are a person that is without their desires. You'll end up blocking and resisting your desires even more. You allow in that which you desire by consistently being a match to how it feels energetically, not by forcing it in. Until you vibrate in harmony with your desires, the strongest vibrational offering regarding your desires or your current reality will often be lack, which is what you will get back.

REJECTING WHAT YOU WANT THE MOST?

When you grow up in an environment that didn't (or couldn't) support or encourage your dreams and development, and didn't acknowledge your gifts or purpose, you can often be left with the belief and feeling that at some level you are just not worth supporting, constantly feeling that you're somehow never quite good enough. Often until we have healed and taken back responsibility for helping and supporting ourselves we will often spend a lifetime subtlety rejecting that which we want most of all, feeling at some level a deep lack of purpose, value or use. If you have experienced a past like that you will tend to either have a 'defeatist' attitude (which causes you to give up at the slightest setback or you will sabotage yourself by not giving things your 'all') or you will end up becoming overly self reliant to compensate, rejecting support or constantly feeling the need to prove that you don't need anything from anyone, even though it is necessary in order for you to succeed at the highest level. To accept any help or support from that mindset and perspective would feel like you're admitting that you're not 'strong enough', so you'll often end up rejecting it all. It is time to centre yourself, open up your eyes and start seeing yourself clearly, see what you're capable of being and doing now. Remember that only an ego feels unworthy.

ACTIONS DO SPEAK LOUDER

Actions really do speak louder than words. Taking inspired action is greater than any and every affirmation that is said without faith or feeling. Until you act upon your inspired ideas, they will always only ever remain a possibility. What you act upon is showing the universe what you believe most to be true. The universe takes that which you act upon very seriously. It will begin to align you with even more of that which you act upon and how all of that feels. It will take that as your preference. If you act upon fear, you'll inevitably receive back from the universe even more things to be fearful of, and if you continue to act upon or give into boredom you'll receive back even more thoughts and experiences that will make you feel bored, and the same goes for giving into procrastination. In summary, the question that you need to ask yourself is, 'How do I expect to succeed when I won't commit myself to doing that which I desire and when I am not taking consistent action towards that which would lead to my success?'.

BELIEVE IN A HIGHER POWER

Believing in a higher power has purpose. Believing in a power greater than ourselves (or a power that we are a part of) can help us to believe in ourselves. It gives us focus and inspiration, especially when we find it difficult to trust, believe in or even love ourselves. Believing in a higher power allows us to know and claim our own power too. When you know that you're a part of (rather than apart from) a loving and powerful energy, you will naturally begin to believe in yourself and believe in the possibility of more. You will have a reason to believe in better, a reason to keep going, a reason to love yourself and a reason to remain hopeful, all of which would help to pull you forward. Although believing in a higher power is not necessary, it most definitely can help you to become your best self and encourage you to claim and tap into your own inner peace, power and purpose. When you believe that a higher power is looking out for you, that it knows your name, that it loves you and that it is always protecting you, you will begin to make room for the universe to support you in all of those ways. When you think that the universe or God hates you, that you're unworthy of its love and that it is punishing you, and when you don't believe in a higher power in the first place, the universe has no positive belief, thought or feeling to respond to and reflect back. The universe will continue to give you even more proof that the universe / God doesn't exist or that it won't help you. In addition when you don't believe in your own power, the universe will continue to respond to that belief and give you even more proof and confirmation that you're powerless. Please understand that the universe is a mirror which can only ever respond to and reflect back your most consistent thoughts and beliefs regarding everything. Until you believe in something, you'll achieve nothing.

DON'T FOCUS UPON NEGATIVE FEELINGS

The more that you focus upon 'negative feelings' and those things which take you 'off track', the harder that it will feel from your current perspective to let them go and to refocus upon positive or empowering feelings, thoughts and perspectives that would lift you up. The reason why it feels so difficult to refocus your attention upon that which is in alignment with who you really are, is often because of your current lower frequency. Your current thoughts and perspectives (which are only a reflection and a manifestation of the frequency that you are vibrating at and seeing things from) will continue to convince you to carry on seeing things the way that you currently already see them (that is until you change your perspective and change which thoughts you're giving into). When you are feeling down or angry, thoughts that feel like that are on the same frequency as you, they take little to no effort to appear in your awareness. They manifest and reveal themselves effortlessly to you. The real reason why we tend to get so lost in those patterns of 'negative' thoughts is because we have given them our undivided attention for so long, which makes them even stronger, all of which begins to 'solidify' us on that lower frequency. Every perspective and thought that we receive tends to confirm to us what we already know and believe to be true, they are reflections of our current feelings or more accurately our current frequency. We tend to think that those pain or fear based thoughts are who we are or how things really are, so we give into them yet again, all of which keeps us where we are. We allow that lower perspective and frequency to determine the way that we will begin to see everything including ourselves. We have unconsciously added momentum to that original 'negative' outlook. The ability to think clearly is much more harder for us to do from down there, especially in comparison to giving into those old thoughts that have so much momentum behind them. The momentum and power is often so strong that we just get carried away with them and end up focussing upon them again (or fighting against them) when we encounter them, all of which makes the affect of them even stronger. It takes a heightened awareness and true inner strength to choose to step back, vibrate higher and see beyond 'what is'. It is important that you allow negative feelings, without allowing them to steal your undivided attention. See through them to their real purpose, which is to remind you to centre yourself and to see everything, including yourself and this current situation, from a higher perspective.

IT'S A NEW DAY

Today make the choice to live each moment fully. Although it might look and feel like yesterday, it's different. It is a brand new day, one that none of us have ever seen before. You have been given another chance to be yourself, to do your best and to follow your dreams, take it. Appreciate it fully. Savour this day, don't rush through it trying to get to tomorrow. Centre yourself here and now, that is where you'll find lasting peace and happiness. Actively find reasons to be happy today, find peace and joy in the smallest of moments. Understand that your life is happening now, and that if you're not choosing peace, happiness and love right now, then you won't see it in the 'then' that you're trying to get to. Today take the time to really 'see' and appreciate the people around you too. Choose to see the good in the world, see all of those people who are making the world a better and brighter place just by being themselves. The truth is that the more that you accentuate the positives the more that they will appear in your life.

IT'S NOT MY FAULT

It is so important that we are accountable and responsible for our own actions, or at times our lack of action. In order for you to be the person that you desire to be and for you to live the life that you desire to live, the actions that you take must support the vision that you believe in. When you blame others, the past or someone else you won't be able to claim back the power to change things. The universe will continue to reflect that perspective back to you until you change how you're seeing things. You'll always be a victim of circumstance, rather than a conscious creator of it. Question your actions and reactions, or your lack of them, and you'll find most of the blocks to that which you desire. Ultimately don't let fear make your decisions for you.

CENTRE YOURSELF THERE

It is important that you allow your actions to be determined, inspired and led by your higher self / the universe / God (or however you choose to identify that supreme and loving energy). Every day make it a priority and your responsibility to connect to that energy within yourself. Step back and centre yourself there, see the world, yourself and others from that perspective. Ask that higher power (which you are a part of, not apart from) to guide your thoughts, actions, and interactions today. Always take a few moments to connect to that energy daily. Align yourself with it fully. Energise yourself from that place of power and peace. When you let go and allow that 'God' like energy to take over, you allow it to support and lead you towards even greater. Things will automatically begin to flow with an undeniable ease when you let go and let yourself be led.

IT ALL UNFOLDS OUTWARDS

Just like a flower grows, life unfolds from within. The flower, like life, opens up and continues to expand outwards and keeps expanding and growing. All growth comes from within. When you centre yourself and align with who you really are on the inside, you allow yourself to be energised from that place and you allow everything that feels like that to flow through you, out and into your environment. You will allow the path that you are seeking to reveal and unveil itself before you. Life unfolds effortlessly from you and for you, if you allow it to.

HOW WOULD MY HIGHER SELF SEE THIS?

When you find yourself in the depths of a struggle, challenge or obstacle, step back and ask yourself, 'How would my higher self see this?' or 'What would the greatest version of myself do in this instance?'. Asking any of those questions will help to take you out of any lower frequency perspective that you're currently 'stuck' on. It will help, even for a few moments, to shift your attention, awareness and current point of focus which is currently holding you back and holding you down. The more narrow that your point of focus is upon a particular problem, and the more that it is fixated upon something in particular that you have deemed as being 'negative', the more pain and discomfort that you will tend to be in. You will unknowingly continue to focus upon and resonate at that specific lower level which will automatically allow in even more thoughts, feelings and events that generally feel like that struggle or obstacle. In addition, you can't see anything clearly when your point of focus is so narrow. A negative and narrow point of focus is always a reminder to broaden your perspective. So in moments like that ask yourself, How would my higher self see this? What would my higher self encourage me to do right now? What would it encourage me to become or encourage me to let go of? Those simple statements have the power to take you right out of a negative thought pattern and help to broaden your awareness just enough to begin to allow in possible solutions or a new positive perspective, point of focus or way of seeing things. When you affirm to yourself and the universe that you're going to respond to life from a higher perspective, instead of 'unconsciously' reacting to it, you allow that to become your new response to life and any obstacles or struggles that you may face. Your reactions will in time start to help you, rather than hold you back.

DON'T LET ANOTHER YEAR PASS YOU BY

We often waste so many of our years waiting around for things to change or for things to happen. Don't let another year go by, start today, save yourself. All of those excuses and reasons that you have for why you can't do or be something are just a reflection of a lower frequency, not a reflection of the truth. Rise above them all. It is time to claim back responsibility for what happens next. Don't let your fears keep you from what you love any longer. Move towards your dreams and your best self with courage and determination. Let your passion and purpose pull you forward. You know better now, you've gained perspective and you're beginning to recognise and remember your power as a creator. It's time to try again.

BELIEVE IT'S POSSIBLE

Did you know that you don't even need to believe that you're capable of doing and becoming the great things that you desire in order for you to 'achieve' them? All that you have to do is allow them in, and you'll do that just as long as you don't have an active and consistent belief in the way that says that you can't. You don't have to 'attract' in your desires and success, you only need to allow them in. You receive your blessings, you don't achieve them. The moment that you have an active and consistent thought in the way that says that you can't have, do or be that which you desire (or that you don't deserve it) you cut yourself off from your blessings and you place a limit upon what is possible for you. When you take your undivided attention of that which is holding back your desires you will automatically start to release the resistance and begin to allow them in. Knowing this, allow those limiting thoughts, don't push against them or try to 'beat' them, as that is giving them your attention and power. Let them be and in time you will begin to let them go, which will allow in your blessings again. Please understand that you don't have to beat your old 'negative' thoughts in order to remove the power from them, all that you need to do is give your attention to new empowering and positive thoughts. When you align with who you really are at the highest level, that too will automatically begin to bring you new empowering thoughts that are a reflection of that higher frequency. You will automatically believe in the 'impossible'. If you happen to encounter any limiting beliefs, allow them, let them be which in time will begin to let them go.

WHY DO YOU WANT IT?

Why do you want to be successful, rich or powerful? To please or impress others? To finally feel worthy and good enough? What is the intention for that which you desire the most? Is there a lack within you that you are trying to fill on the outside? Do you want success so that you will be respected, validated or accepted by others? If that is the reason why you desire something then the intention or the reason for desiring success will be inspired and powered by the frequency of lack and pain, which can only ever bring back results which are on the same frequency as that, therefore more results that will make you feel weak and insecure. Until you allow 'what is' or 'what was' you will continue to create from pain rather than from a place of peace and power. Don't let your desires be solely inspired by your present or past environment, but from your own inner being too. Let them come from a place of love and peace, not need or lack.

DON'T GIVE UP BEFORE THE MIRACLE APPEARS

Every single person that you will ever meet will have their own set of problems and issues. You're not the only one struggling (although it might feel like that at times). No one ever lives a life free of pain or struggles, there will always be 'ups' and 'downs' in life, just don't let your ego tell you that everyone else has it all sorted out except you. Things might not be going the way that you imagined and envisioned, but it won't be like this forever. Changes and miracles can occur at any time, and they will manifest, just as long as you don't give up before they appear.

ALL EMOTIONS ARE POSITIVE

Be comfortable with every emotion, don't make the mistake of labelling some emotions as 'good' and some as 'bad'. Thinking that certain emotions should be avoided is detrimental to your healing. It is essentially that fear of certain emotions that stops you from being able to use them for their intended purpose. Emotions are only 'energy in motion', that is all that they are, energy that is moving. They are not meant to be held onto or meant to be analysed by you, when you do that, that is when issues will arise. They're meant to be noticed, understood, expressed and used to make necessary changes in your life.

HOW DOES DIVINE AND PERFECT TIMING LOOK?

In life we are all going at different paces and running different races. What happens to work for one person won't necessarily work for you. Your life has its own perfect timing, and its own perfect pace. It has its own unique course with each 'detour' bringing you a new lesson and blessing that will allow you to grow and know yourself to a higher degree. Struggles often instil deep within us the key qualities and characteristics that we need to succeed at the level that we desire to succeed at. Don't let detours fool you, your time is coming, you're not lost, this is just the training ground for success and it's all unfolding in divine timing.

WHERE CREATIVITY COMES FROM

Have you opened up that spiritual space to allow the universe to communicate clearly and directly with you? The full power of the universe and your higher self can only flow through you unrestricted when you are centred within yourself, essentially when you have leaned back from your thoughts (and when you're no longer associating yourself fully with them). When you closely associate yourself with your mind or your current circumstances, that energy which brings forth all creativity, clarity, blessings and abundance can only trickle through bit by bit. Allow that energy to flow freely through you. Open up that space and let it in. Allow what is ready to come through you be born into the world. Remember this isn't about trying to make anything happen, this is about allowing things to unfold by themselves when they're ready and able to. So relax, trust and let go.

PERCEPTION OF WHAT IS POSSIBLE
The more that you expand your perception of what is possible for you, the more space and freedom that you give the universe to deliver your desires to you. Always leave room for the universe. Be flexible in your approach to life. When you stay open to all the opportunities and possibilities that come your way, you open up a new path and possible angle that your desires can arrive.
Ultimately it is your perception of your reality including your perception of who you believe yourself to be, and your perception of what you believe is possible for you (including how you see the world or your desires) that is manipulating and controlling your reality. Until you step back into your higher self and see things from that unlimited place and perspective you will continue to live a life within the boundaries of your own fears and limitations. To change your experience in life, all you need to do is change how you're experiencing life and yourself. Expand your perception of what is possible. Be a person of no limits.

HAPPINESS BEGINS WITH YOU
Do you believe that your current unhappiness can be solved by getting something or by being something? Do you believe that something or someone else will make you genuinely happy? Please understand that happiness is only ever an inner state, it is not the result of something else. If you aren't happy now, in this place, chances are that you won't be happy 'then' in any place.

Until you are happy and content with yourself now, things can't change. Until you're happy now, you'll end up looking to your results or your relationships to make or keep you happy. Things should only ever be able to add to your unconditional happiness, not take away from it or be the sole reason for it. If you're allowing some external thing to define or determine your happiness you'll never find lasting or authentic happiness. Be self-full enough to be happy now. It might seem impossible at times to be happy without that which you desire, but that perspective is only ever a reflection and a manifestation of the frequency that you are currently at and currently seeing things from, it's not the truth. When you begin to feel genuine inner joy, things begin to come together.

HANDLING YOUR EMOTIONS

Cultivating the ability to deal with and handle your own thoughts and emotions is the single biggest ability (and habit) that will change your life for the better. Learning to acknowledge your thoughts and feelings (rather than associating yourself with them) will allow you to recognise them for what they are and allow you to direct and refocus your awareness upon greater. When you learn to see your emotions for what they are, as reflections and indicators of the frequency that you're currently on, you will be able to create the future that you desire rather than getting distracted fighting against the present or the past that you don't like.

I HAVE SO MUCH POTENTIAL

The world can't see your potential and purpose if you keep it hidden within you. People can't see your skills, talents and abilities when you are still holding onto them in fear. Although people may not be aware right now of what you have to offer, you can't sit around and wait until they discover you. Create the inner state of success and greatness, become your best self and meet the universe half way. Remember that success is not a result, but a state of being. When you feel successful within, you will begin in time to see it expressed and reflected on the outside. The inner state helps to create the outer circumstance and opportunity which will lead you to results that feel like that inner success. More accurately, success is a state of allowing. Put yourself, your work and your talents on display, no more wasting time and allowing fear to keep you small. Don't let those gifts and talents within you go unused in the present, give them to others. Other people need to hear the messages that you're here to bring. Those gifts have purpose, they're here to help others. Take the time and effort to put something 'out there' that best encapsulates and represents who you are and that which you are capable of doing. You never know who is watching and listening.

AFRAID OF SUCCESS OR LOVE?
Do you desire success or a relationship yet at some level fear that it will change you? That fear based thought and perspective is just a refection of the frequency that you are resonating at in regards to that topic. That thought is not a reflection of the truth, it is just a reflection of a pain, fear or lack based perspective. Those fears are a reflection of how you are used to viewing yourself and that which you desire the most. Maybe you have placed a fearful belief in between you and that which you desire, to help ease the pain of not having it. Maybe you are using your faith in that fearful perspective regarding a relationship or success as an excuse for why you haven't got it yet, or maybe you're pretending and trying to convince yourself that you don't want it just to ease the discomfort of not being it or not seeing it? Those type of beliefs and perspectives aren't helpful, they're not protective. They turn you against that which you desire the most. You can't have a positive experience with that which you desire when you consistently fear it, especially when you are viewing it from that lower perspective. How you feel when you think of your desires is how you'll feel when you see and experience them. When you release the fear and embrace the best possibility of what things can be, you will then begin to see clearly that a relationship or

success won't change you, but that it will only ever make you into an even better person (which is the type of relationship that you'll allow into your reality, rather than a relationship or a result that would confirm to you that it will change you for the worse). When you're already grounded, nothing or no one will have the ability or power to affect or change you for long.

SOUL MATES
You are never alone in this world, only your ego likes to tell you that you are. Your heart and inner being knows better though. You came here into this world with many different 'soul mates'. Don't fall for the lie that you only have one soul mate. Every soul is a part of you, not apart from you. You have many soul mates. A soul mate doesn't even have to be a lover or a partner, it could be someone that you meet once that changes your life for the better and forever. A soul mate could also be your best friend. Before you came into this body you made an agreement with and a promise to your soul mates that you would find each other in this life, that against all the odds and even in the darkest of moments, you would find each other and prove just how strong the power of love is. Always remember that you are never alone in this world, there are soul mates everywhere thinking of you and sending you love. They are there ready to help you. Sooner than you even realise, they'll come into your life and help bring you even higher.

WORTHY OF SUCCESS
Please understand that worthiness is never ever achieved through a result, those type of 'big results' stem from already feeling worthy within. Until you feel happy within, nothing (or no one) will make you feel happy or bring you lasting joy. In addition if you're still waiting to achieve something before you believe in yourself or your abilities, you'll be waiting forever. Always remember that your results are reflections of who you feel and believe you are and what you feel and believe is possible for you. If you want to see success 'then' you have got to be it, feel it and believe you are successful (or worthy of it) now. When you don't

believe in yourself and that which you do, then what you're really saying energetically is that what you do and who you are isn't good enough. At a vibrational level you are saying to the universe, 'Give me confirmation that I'm not good enough in everything that I do, everywhere that I go and in everyone that I meet'. When you change how you see yourself, you will begin to see those changes reflected everywhere that you go. Start cultivating self worth and self value on the inside rather than trying to achieve it on the outside.

HOW TO CENTRE YOURSELF

It is so important that you take some time to centre yourself. Those people who don't actively centre and 'ground' themselves will find that they will take on the emotions of those people around them and that they will be too easily affected by life and other people. This is particularly true for those people who feel everything deeply. When you're not centred you will often pick up on the emotions, needs and feelings of others. You will tend to 'absorb' the emotions of the environment that you find yourself in. Everything and everyone else will end up determining your frequency. To centre yourself bring your focus within, feel the love and peace that is deep within you. Feel the power of the entire universe flowing within you. Imagine that when you are grounding yourself you are opening up a space within you to allow the universe to flow its love, blessings and healing through you unrestricted. Grounding yourself is just like plugging into the power source of the entire universe, it is tuning into the frequency of your highest self. Grounding yourself gives your mind enough room to silence and completely restore itself. Your thoughts will then likely begin to reflect the inner love and peace that you feel within, rather than being a reflection of your current frequency and feelings such as worry or fear. Grounding yourself removes your focus from the outside reflection and brings it within to the inner vibration. It allows you to receive the guidance and clarity that you're seeking. Learn to ground yourself in this moment fully, be fully present in the present moment. Close your eyes and begin to feel the love of the entire universe protecting and healing you right now. Feel your mind being fully restored, and your frequency rising.

WHY ANXIETY IS A WRONG PERCEPTION

If you are facing current feelings of anxiety, fear and inadequacy there is often one underlying cause, that you have attached wrong perceptions and analysis to your past experiences or that current situation that you're facing. All current feelings of fear, despair and pain come from errors in your way of thinking, also from wrong perceptions (and subsequent attached meanings) and also negative associations that you have made in your past, especially from a distorted sense of self. Remember that all 'negative' feelings are here to make you aware, and to get you to see things differently. When you release those wrong perceptions, you can begin to see things clearly again and start to attach new useful and empowering meanings and definitions to everything.

STEP BACK FROM YOUR REACTIONS

When you come across a belief regarding money, success or love (or that which you desire) that feels 'bad' to you or makes you feel uneasy, that is a reminder that something needs to change. Your reactions allow you to see where you are vibrationally in regards to your highest self and that which you desire. Take any negative or 'bad' reactions or feelings as an indication to step back into your higher self and to view that lack or fear based thought or belief from a higher perspective. Observe that limiting belief but don't give into it. Recognise that the real reason why it feels so bad to you when you think of your desires that way is because your highest self is showing you through your thoughts and feelings that you're not vibrating in harmony with the experience that you prefer to have with it. It is giving you a preview through your feelings of how you'll feel when you see your desires, and a glimpse of the experience that you're currently allowing into your reality regarding them. How you see your desires is how they'll appear in your reality. Until you change how you're seeing them, or how you're seeing yourself in relation to them, things won't change. You can't keep giving into those 'negative' thoughts or reactions in regards to your desires, challenge and then change them. Become aware of what those 'negative' reactions are really trying to tell you, which is to start responding in a way that lifts you up and lets in your desires.

IS THE WORLD FALLING APART?

The world isn't falling apart, the old way of seeing and doing things is. This isn't the end of the world, it is just the beginning of a better way. The old way of seeing and doing things is 'dying' in order to allow in a new way of living and being. This is the painful birthing process of bringing in change. Please understand that the darkness only ever comes into the light in order for us to see it and challenge or change it. Don't be afraid of it.

FIGHTING THE PRESENT?

When you make the present moment your enemy, the future often ends up feeling like that too. The energy that you are focussing upon and resonating at in the present moment is what you are (often unknowingly) sending ahead into your future. That is why it is so important that you allow 'what is' instead of focussing upon it or fighting against it (fighting against it is still focussing upon it at some level) all of which would send it into your future. No matter what you're currently facing right now, acknowledge, accept and allow it and allow how you really feel about it, all without making it or the present moment your enemy. Only from that place of non resistance will you then be truly able to release it, and move through it and beyond it. You will then be able to focus upon and envision all that you desire and prefer to be and see, rather than fighting against 'what is' or 'what was'. When you allow and let go of 'what is', you open up a space to allow what is next to flow into your life. Learn to acknowledge and anticipate the miracles that are coming. When you do that you won't have to constantly fight against yourself or fight against 'what is' which would continue to call in even more of what you don't want into your life. Always use the present moment as an opportunity to become more, to change, to start something new and to begin again. Live productively in the present, rather than getting lost in thoughts of yesterday or tomorrow.

FEAR

Fear has a clear purpose. The real purpose of fear isn't to stop us from taking action, nor is it there to tell us that we shouldn't do something, it is not even there to stop us from moving towards our goals, it is simply there to help us and make us aware. When you feel fear, the purpose of that feeling is to make you aware that your current perspective, or more accurately those definitions or beliefs that you're currently focussing upon are not aligned with your highest desires, your highest self and your highest good. In essence that you are not vibrating in harmony with that which you desire at the highest and deepest level. Your higher self is giving you a little indication and reminder (through that fearful feeling) that you might want to update those particular beliefs or change that particular perspective if you want to succeed at the level that you are capable of succeeding at. When we feel fear we should take that as an indication to step back and change our perspective, however what tends to happen when we feel fear is we focus upon that feeling or we fight against it and we allow that momentum to 'carry us away'. We tend to give into those feelings or in an attempt to soothe those feelings we end up either giving up or going back to our 'comfort zone' (which could be more accurately described as our discomfort zone). What also tends to happen is we begin to analyse or inspect that feeling (or we even begin to fear the feeling of fear) which creates even more of it in our conciousness and reality. We end up creating fear that has no purpose, fear that continues to make us feel how we are already feeling now, which is anxious, scared and fearful. 'Real' fear has purpose, it is there to make us aware, it gives us an opportunity to change. However when we begin to fear the feeling of fear we lose any real purpose that it had. When this habit goes unchecked, we start to either define ourselves as being a fearful person or we begin to normalise fear or we even begin to expect to feel anxious and scared throughout our day (and feel fear when we think of our desires) all of which separates us even further from what we desire and from who we really are. It is so important that we learn to let go of all of those definitions, perspectives and misconceptions regarding fear, and that we begin to start again with a new definition of fear, especially a new way of seeing and interpreting it, and a new way of seeing ourselves in relation to it. When you understand what fear really is, everything changes. Fear is in essence an optical illusion that we continue to make real. It's time to see beyond it.

LET GO AND LET 'GOD' TAKE OVER

When you have worked upon the inspiration that the universe has supplied you with, with duty and care, and you have expanded those ideas to the best of your ability, it is time to detach. Hand the work back over to the universe. Let the universe / God do with it as it pleases. Recognise that what has been handed to you by the universe you must hand back. When you know that those ideas aren't yours to begin with, you won't get attached to them or the results that they bring. You can let go fully and let 'God' do the rest. When you know that 'God' is working on it you can rest assured that what manifests is ultimately what is in your highest good.

FEELING MISUNDERSTOOD?

Sometimes in life people will misunderstand who you are and what you do. No matter how clear you make your intentions, some people will just seem to misunderstand you, they will often read too much into what you do, and often see things that just aren't there. They're seeing in you what they fail to see in themselves. Sometimes in life you may encounter those people who have committed themselves to not understand you or understand others, ultimately because they don't understand themselves. Please understand that they can only see you and what you do from their limited perspective. They will often see something very different from their wavelength. Your actions will look very different to them from down there. However as long as your intentions are clear, and your actions come from a place of love, peace and compassion, you will leave enough room for other people to see and understand who you are and that which you do in the best possible light. Those who can 'take' from it will. However don't fall into the trap of feeling like you have to defend or justify your message or constantly explain yourself to others. Explain things only to those people who are willing and able to listen, those people who have committed themselves to not only listening to you, but understanding you and that which you're trying to do (rather than just defending their position and perspective).

TRUST THE PROCESS, INSTEAD OF RUSHING IT

The simple fact is that you won't become your best self overnight, becoming your true and best self is a steady and gradual evolution process. Only the ego believes that it has to happen all at once. You might not be where you desire to be just yet, but you're closer than you were before. Being your best self is a commitment. Make peace with where you are right now. Trust the process instead of rushing it. You're still growing, healing, learning new habits, unlearning older ones, remembering your own power and instilling self worth in yourself maybe for the first time. There is no rush. Healing takes time.

I'LL BE SOMEONE SOMEDAY

Instead of saying, 'I'll be someone someday', start saying and believing 'I am someone now'. If you're not choosing it now and believing in yourself and your success now, you won't see it 'then'. If you say to yourself that you'll be someone someday, 'someday' won't come. What you are really saying vibrationally is that you aren't great or good enough right now, which is what the universe will respond to and reflect back. Know that you'll become your best self soon, but claim it now. No matter what you desire to achieve or be, you've got to start claiming and accepting it today. Be it now, become it this instant.

THE MAP OF YOUR LIFE
Right now you might not know where to go, or what to do, but please understand that the universe and your higher self always knows the way forward. It not only knows what is next for you but it knows what is best for you too. It can see the aerial view of your life and the complete map and overview of the maze of your life, as well as the best way 'out' of that maze too. Any time that you feel lost or unsure of what to do or where to go, reach out to that power, tap into it within yourself. Ask it for guidance, help and support. Ask that higher and inner power to guide you, to protect you and to choose a better way.

FEELING DOWN IS A GOOD SIGN
Feeling 'down' is an indication that something within you is seeking to be released. Any negative emotion that is in your awareness is only ever there because it is seeking to be freed. It is not there to be pushed down, fought against or ignored. Instead of fighting that feeling, seek to understand why it is there. Negative emotions are often an indication that you believe something that either isn't true or isn't in your highest good, about yourself, others or that which you desire. Take some time to meditate. View everything through the lens of love, allow it and be patient. The false belief and resistance will reveal itself in time and let itself out.

LIMIT YOUR SUPPORT
Like everything in life, boundaries are necessary, this too includes limiting the amount of help and support that you're willing and able to give to another. Limits stop you from betraying yourself and from giving away too much. They stop you from losing yourself in the process of helping others. The moment that you go over that limit you start to disrespect yourself. You start to make other people's stability, happiness and peace a priority over your

own. Limit yourself to helping those people who have committed themselves to improving, those people who are doing the necessary inner work, those people who are responsible for their own peace and happiness and those people who are consistently making an effort to grow and heal.

IGNORANCE ISN'T BLISS

Ignorance isn't bliss, ignorance causes us to view everything and everyone through a distorted lens. When we believe that things or people behave in a certain way, then that's how they will appear to us. We'll be seeing our own ignorance and not the actions of another. You'll misjudge their intentions, for your own ignorance. You can only see that which you believe. Your expectation to see a certain result or behaviour will at a vibrational level help to call that type of behaviour or result out and into your environment. You'll be so busy looking for and expecting that one thing that you'll miss everything else, including the truth. Always be willing to be 'wrong', or at least be willing to see things differently.

ACCENTUATE THE POSITIVES

What are you giving your undivided attention to? Are you focussing upon what is working, or what isn't working? Are you focussing upon what you like about yourself, or that which you don't like? Whatever you give your attention to, you are powering and making stronger. Your energy flows into that which you focus upon consistently and that which you rest your awareness upon. Guide your attention upon that which empowers you. Accentuate those thoughts or things which make you feel good, and that which empowers you and lifts you and all others higher. Every single day actively look for and accentuate the positives. Make the positives bigger and brighter, focus upon all that is good in life and all that is right. The more that you accentuate the positives, the more that they will make themselves known in your reality. Try it and see it for yourself. Please note that this doesn't mean that you should ignore any problems that you encounter, it just means that in order for things to change you have got to rise above the issue to see the solution. Only from that higher frequency place are you then able to see and then provide a solution to any problems that you happen to encounter. The only reason why you keep seeing 'problems' now is because you are on the same frequency as them. Learn to reside at the same frequency that the solutions reside at instead.

THINGS WILL STILL GO WRONG

Things will still go wrong when you're 'spiritual' and when you're consciously applying the 'Law of Attraction' principles, however being spiritual will allow you to see beyond it all. Things will no longer have the same power or be able to affect you at a deep level like they once used to. They won't be able to affect you for long. You'll no longer call things a disaster because you will know that how you label something is how it will appear in your reality. You'll be able to allow life to unfold naturally and be able to go with the flow rather than constantly fighting against it. You'll be able to step back and see the divinely inspired plan. You'll no longer hold on in fear, you will be able to let go, trust and go with the flow knowing that you're being led to more.

POSITIVITY IS A MANIFESTATION

Often when we begin to think positively and step into our best self, we will tend to look around for results and proof that our positivity has 'worked' in our reality, however the first change and manifestation of positivity is often overlooked and misunderstood. Feeling good is also a manifestation. It is often one of the earliest manifestations of aligning with your best self. Having slightly better feelings and thoughts regarding everything and yourself is often the first sign and manifestation of allowing in your desires and your best life. That better, more optimistic and hopeful feeling alongside slightly better and more positive thoughts in regards to yourself and that which you desire is a reflection and a manifestation of the new frequency that you're on now, it is proof that things are changing. That is often the first stage of your

161

desires manifesting. In time that positive outlook will tend to become your new and most consistent state of being. You'll find that you will begin to reside at those higher frequencies for even longer periods of time than ever before, which will begin to allow in those positive circumstances, things and people that you're looking for, all of which occurs much quicker and even more effortlessly than ever before. Positivity is one of the greatest manifestations, and it is vital that you acknowledge those happy and empowering thoughts when they occur. Appreciate them when they happen, become aware of your positive thoughts and more optimistic outlook. We often tend to only acknowledge our thoughts and feelings when they're negative, which ultimately powers them and allows in even more 'negative' thoughts or how those 'negative' thoughts feel into our awareness and reality. Acknowledge and appreciate when you're feeling better and thinking more clearly. Help solidify that as your new preferred perspective by appreciating it. Ultimately what you focus upon grows until it begins to show in your current reality. Positivity is the first step towards becoming someone who is able to receive their desires.

EXPLOSIVE OUTBURSTS
Any time that we feel 'negative' emotions a few things tend to happen. We first start to vibrate at that lower frequency and begin to allow in everything that feels like that (such as negative thoughts and feelings). The longer that we hold onto those emotions the more that we will begin to allow in everything that feels like that and all those situations, people and things that will ultimately leave us feeling that way. However more importantly, the longer that we stay on that frequency, the more that we will awaken within us and allow out everything that feels like that to us (especially any feelings that we haven't healed or released from our past). Those feelings will often come rushing to the surface to be set free. That is often one of the main reasons for those explosive outbursts that you see in others. Those explosive outbursts don't come out of nowhere, they are often the result of

consistently resisting how we really feel. Those explosive reactions from others are nearly always triggered by a small resentment or upset in the present moment, one that has caused that person to vibrate at a lower frequency which has subsequently released and awakened those deep and pent up feelings of anger, frustration and pain regarding the past. Any time that your current emotional reaction (such as anger) isn't in correlation or proportion to what has occurred, it is time to become aware. The real reason for your explosive reaction isn't because of this current situation, it is primarily because of what this current situation has reminded you of and awakened within you. It has awakened a feeling or a situation that you haven't fully processed, released, accepted or recovered from. One that you're currently being encouraged to process and let go of now. So remember, any time that a small issue creates a strong emotional reaction within you, it is time to look within. It is time to express those emotions in a healthy and helpful way rather than compressing and suppressing them again. You can't continue to push down or ignore those emotions within you any longer, when you do that you'll end up causing them to build up and pop back up somewhere else. This is an opportunity for you to grow, take it.

THE SIGN THAT YOU WERE LOOKING FOR
This message is meant for you. It is a very real reminder that things are changing even when you can't see the concrete evidence of it. Right now, this very second, something that you have been dreaming of, wishing for and working towards is in the process of manifesting. Real progress is being made. The universe is currently working on your dreams and goals and will continue to do so, just as long as you work on yourself. It is bringing people and ideas together that will take you higher. The universe is asking you to start expecting greatness now. It is time to believe in yourself and take action. Your life is about to change forever and for the better. You have asked for proof, and this is it.

USE IT, OR LOSE IT

It is so important that you act upon and use those incredible ideas that the universe has supplied you with. You received those ideas for a greater reason, the universe knew that you had the ability to do something incredible with that idea. However be warned, if you don't act upon those ideas, the universe will tend to give the same idea to someone else who will use it and make the most out of it. Someone who will bring that idea to its full fruition. So use it, or lose it.

WHEN YOU HEAL, OTHERS HEAL TOO

We often believe that we're the only one going through something, that is until someone else opens up and speaks their truth in an open and honest way. When someone else opens up and speaks about their past, and their struggles, feelings and pain, they unconsciously give us permission to do the same. When we honour how we feel without feelings of guilt and shame, and we embrace vulnerability and we speak from the heart, we not only let the pain out however we also bring in the healing for ourselves and everyone else too. The space in which you let out the pain allows in the healing.

TOO AFRAID TO TAKE ACTION?

Feeling scared isn't an excuse to not take action on your dreams and goals. It is in fact a reminder that you need to. A fearful perspective and those feelings of fear are always an indication to change how you're seeing yourself and how you're seeing this current situation. They aren't reasons to give up. Fear will keep you from your dreams if you let it. Fear isn't keeping you safe, it is actually keeping you from what you love. It is keeping you from growth and from new experiences. Those who achieve greatness do so by moving beyond their first fearful reaction and perspective. They continue to take action in spite of their fears. You can't allow fear and your reactions to carry on creating and sustaining your reality any longer. It's time to consciously respond to life, rather than just reacting to it.

LET LOVE IN
Often when we have been badly hurt in the past, we tend to close our heart off to protect ourselves from feeling any more hurt or pain in the present, which unknowingly blocks us from feeling, receiving and giving love too. When you block one emotion you end up blocking them all. Closing your heart off to fear or pain, separates you from all that you love and from all that you desire too. When you begin to acknowledge and allow how you really feel and you start to practise forgiveness, compassion, empathy, self love, self acceptance and self care, you will begin to open your heart back up to receive your blessings.

TOLERATING ABUSE AND HURT?
People will tend to disrespect you to the level that you disrespect yourself. Relationships are the greatest example of this. Relationships allow us to see ourselves in relation to another. They especially show us how we treat ourselves and what we accept and tolerate. You're not only 'attracting' (or more accurately allowing) into your life people who are on the same frequency as you, however you're being drawn to them too. The only reason why we tolerate abuse in the present is often because someone else treated us that way in our past (which caused it to become normal and almost expected) or we are used to treating ourselves that way now in the present. Once you heal and redefine yourself, everything changes. When you begin to respect, accept and love yourself unconditionally, you won't tolerate someone else treating you badly simply because you no longer treat yourself that way any more. Your relationships also help you to see on the outside what type of love you have been giving to yourself on the inside. We have got to choose love that matches the self worth of the person that we are becoming, and not the person that we were.

YOU ARE ALREADY WORTHY OF IT

You can only ever accept that which you believe you are worthy of receiving. Your ability to receive is key to allowing in all that you desire. Know yourself as being worthy of receiving that which you desire. Don't think of your desires as being something that you have to achieve, instead see them as being something that you have to align with and receive. Please understand that you are already inherently worthy of all that you desire right now this very second, so claim that. You don't need to do or be something else first in order for you to be finally worthy of receiving or 'achieving' something. You were born worthy, you just learned your unworthiness. It's time to let that go, it's not who you are, it's who you were. Release any unworthiness that you have carried with you since your childhood. That 'not good enough' mentality isn't who you are, it is in fact holding back and blocking the person that you are meant to become.

STOP DEVALUING YOURSELF

When you stop hurting and devaluing yourself, everything changes. When you start to show yourself more compassion, moment by moment (and you begin to release all that guilt and shame that you have been carrying with you) you allow yourself to grow and become an even better version of who you really are. That is how all great changes come about, through consistency and through love. The greatest changes rarely happen all at once or overnight. All great things take time and are often a result of practice, commitment, courage and dedication. Decide to love yourself a little bit more a decision at a time. Claim your worth moment by moment and practise being kinder to yourself each and every moment of your day. Remember that you don't have to do or be anything to finally be worthy of love or success, you just have to stop blocking it. Allow yourself to claim your own greatness, and to recognise it within yourself. Know your worth and value in this world, and that the universe brought you here for a greater reason, a reason that you might be unaware of as of yet. When you start to love and value yourself consistently and genuinely, you will begin to allow into your reality everything that feels like that, including a higher purpose. Your natural state is love, trouble only begins when you let something or someone get in the way of you remembering or recognising that.

THEY DISLIKE YOU FOR NO REASON?

You won't get along with everyone in life, and that is perfectly OK. All interactions, whether brief or long lasting, whether positive or 'negative' are all learning tools. When you shine bright, your light will awaken others to the fact that they are not living up to their highest potential, which is often a painful reminder that some people don't want to acknowledge or accept. Those who dislike you (without valid reason) will very often dislike you not because of anything that you have said, done or failed to do, but because you remind them of something that they are not ready to face within themselves. In addition, someone who is not aware of their own pain or purpose, will often project their frustrations and inadequacies onto everyone else. Rise above it all.

YOUR PAST

Please understand that your past isn't who you are, it's only where you have been. It doesn't matter if the past was years ago, or if it was yesterday, it has served its purpose. You have got to give up the habit of defining yourself based on what you encountered in the past, how you were treated or what you did. Redefine yourself now as the person that you're becoming. You're not a product of your past, you are the result of your present choices. Instead of being held back by your past be pulled forward by your future. If at some level you feel like you were better in the past, or that you miss the 'old' you, take inspiration from that. Decide to move towards an even better version of who you were with every single decision and choice that you make. Know that you'll be your best self again, which is just a version of you that is closer in alignment with your highest self and who you really are at the highest level. Please understand that when you're constantly reminiscing about that past 'you' or viewing the difference between you 'then' and you 'now', then you'll end up 'attracting' (or more accurately allowing) into your life everything and everyone that will confirm to you that you're not good enough now, and that you're not the same 'old' you. Believe with every single fibre of your being that the best is yet to come for you, and just watch how the universe responds.

FEELING STRESSED?

When you find yourself lost in feelings of stress, that is always an indication to step back and centre yourself. The only reason why you are currently getting thoughts that feel stressful to you is because you are currently vibrating at a lower frequency and because you are viewing yourself and this situation that you're facing from a place and perspective that is based on fear, pain and powerlessness. You are currently seeing yourself as not being good enough, not being strong enough or not being able to handle 'what is' or what is next, which is always the work of the 'ego'. Stress is always an indication to step back, to rest and to centre yourself. Feelings of stress come from the stress and strain of holding back the fullness of who you really are. When you centre yourself you will begin to see everything much more clearly, and if any 'stressful' situation should happen to occur that required action from you, you would be on the same frequency that the solutions reside at.

FOCUS ON THE NOW, NOT THE HOW

It is so important that you stop trying to guess how and when your desires will show up. Instead of doing that just learn to persevere in the feeling that they have already manifested and that they are here now in your current reality. Focus upon how it feels now to be your best self. Focus right now upon feeling good, upon doing your best, upon allowing yourself to feel good and upon going with the flow. When you let go of the 'how' it might appear and you live into the 'now' that you desire and prefer (which is the best version of now, essentially becoming your best self now) the universe takes care of the rest. Forget the 'how' and focus upon the 'now' that you prefer. When you do that, you will begin to open up a space in your current reality which will begin to allow in that which is best for you. You let the universe choose the 'how' and 'when' things will manifest, which is always the path of least resistance and in perfect and divine timing. Learn to find the feeling of the reality that you prefer (or find the feeling of that which you desire to be or see now) feel it now fully without needing to see the proof of it in your current reality. Faith is needed when it comes to creating miracles.

SOOTHING THE PAIN

You will find that the more that you meditate, the less that you will need to medicate yourself with damaging habits and things such as alcohol and drugs. Only someone who is (at the deepest level) unhappy or in emotional distress, will need to 'self soothe' with those harmful substances or toxic patterns of behaviour. It's too easy to numb the internal pain with external things, because when you are in pain those things are on the same frequency as you. It is so easy to do that from down there. What tends to be difficult is reaching for something that is on a higher frequency, such as healing. Those self soothing tools such as alcohol won't get rid of the pain, they'll only ever mask it and ultimately make it worse. If you find yourself in this situation, it's important that instead of numbing the pain, you begin to acknowledge first that you are in pain and that you're acting from pain, and second that you need to start doing something about it. Until we face our pain we will continue to resist and persist the original hurt and pain that is within us and we will continue to avoid our own healing. When you 'numb out' with substances or unhealthy patterns of behaviour (including things such as purging on food, denial of food, reliance on pornography or impulsive gambling) all that does is cover up that original pain and issue, which tends to create even more of how that feels within you which will be reflected in your reality, your results and your relationships, all of which creates even more secrets and patterns of guilt and shame within you. You'll end up chasing a high, instead of healing and dealing with the low. Most people fear giving up their self soothing 'crutches' (which often by that time have spiralled into a reliance, co-dependence or addiction) because they know that when they give up 'the crutch' they will have to face and feel that which they are afraid of, and that which they have been pushing down and ignoring and fighting against for years. However it is vital that we begin to understand that the only reason why it feels too hard to heal is because of the frequency that you are viewing yourself and viewing healing from, that perspective is not a reflection of the truth. The only reason why you are in so much pain in the first place is because you are refusing to let that pain out. Any emotions and feelings that are in your awareness are there to be acknowledged, healed and released, they're not meant to be pushed down or 'drunk' away. Remember, when you numb the pain, you will also numb feelings such as joy too. Healing begins the moment that you choose to no longer numb the pain, and you begin to work through your emotions. When you do that you will begin to reconnect with your inner being and joy again.

LISTEN TO YOUR OWN ADVICE

Do you find yourself helping everyone else but just can't seem to really help yourself? Often our own way of seeing things (or more accurately our frequency) prevents us from seeing and then acting upon the advice that we desperately need. If you find yourself in this situation, it is best to centre yourself and rise above it all. Maybe even try to offer advice to an imaginary someone else from a higher perspective. Imagine that someone else is going through what you are currently going through. What advice would you give to them? What would you say and how would you say it? Don't filter your answers. Take that advice and 'insight' and implement it in your own life. In addition learn to listen to the advice that you are giving to someone else and apply it in your own life too. Often the advice that we are giving to others, we are actually giving to ourselves first and foremost. So what are you encouraging others to do or be? As that is often exactly what your inner and higher self is saying to you too. In addition, please understand that until you are vibrating at a higher frequency you won't have access to the advice that would be able to help others and be able to change things for the better and for good. The advice and ideas that you are looking for always resides at a higher frequency. So before helping others, step back and vibrate higher. In addition it is so important that you don't allow your vibration to be determined solely by what you are viewing (including the problems of others) if you do you will begin to come into harmony with how that problem feels, rather than coming into harmony with how the solution feels. Until you vibrate higher you will tend to allow their lower vibration to drag you down too.

FEAR IS ALWAYS A REACTION

Fear is always a reaction, never a response. No one consciously chooses to feel scared or anxious, however when you don't take responsibility or accountability for how you respond to life, then fear will react for you. All fear is, is a reminder that you are currently not seeing yourself and that which you are perceiving, the way that your higher self or the universe sees it. Fear is an opportunity to think and look again. Fear is always felt in reaction to something else. That fearful reaction to life or that which you're observing is often just a re-enactment of what you did and how you felt when you last encountered it. It is an automatic reaction. However when you believe that you are your thoughts and feelings you will then tend to listen to and fuel that first reaction, which takes away the opportunity for you to step back and respond to life. You will fail to use those feelings, and lose the purpose that fear had, which is to remind you to think and look again. When you follow fear you are in essence re-acting to the situation, acting again as the person that you were. Things can't change when you do that. However once you begin to consciously respond to life from a higher perspective and with a higher awareness (without letting fear automatically choose for you) your life will begin to change for the better.

HATRED

We often think that when someone hurts us and we hold onto that pain and hatred it will somehow at some level punish them too, when in reality it can only ever affect and harm us. Please let that hatred go, it is never worth it. Let the universe or 'karma' handle it. Give up needing to get revenge, it ultimately harms no one but you. In addition don't need to hear 'sorry' or need to know 'why' they did what they did for you to finally let go, heal and move on. Needing to know 'why' and needing to hear 'sorry' won't give you the peace that you are seeking and the peace that you think that it will. What if they apologised to you and you felt as though it wasn't done in a way that was genuine, what then? Or what if they never apologise and you never get to know 'why' they did what they did? Your inner peace and healing is more important than that. You can't move on when you're still waiting for an apology and when you hate someone, as doing that will cause you to still focus upon them or focus upon how they made you feel. Hate is a barrier that will cover up and separate you from all that you love and all that is meant for you. Once you have done the inner work and healing by processing and acknowledging your own feelings and experience, you will be able to move on.

HOW YOU SHOULD START YOUR DAY

Every single day, decide to start your day with enthusiasm and passion. The intention for the day will directly affect the result. How you start the day will help to determine the energy that will flow throughout your entire day. How you start your day helps to determine not only how your day will go, but what and who you will call onto your path that day. So every single morning make it your responsibility and a priority to connect to the best possibility of that day. Connect to the peace and the presence within you and ask that energy for guidance and support. Open up and let yourself receive the best, knowing that you're worthy of it all. If you begin the day with enthusiasm and excitement, you allow everything that feels like that to appear on your path. Spending 10 minutes every morning getting into that feeling good place will feel like it saved you 10 hours throughout your day. You'll no longer feel like you need to try and force things into being, or feel like you have to fight against yourself or 'what is'. When you actively focus upon feelings of love, joy, passion, excitement and appreciation, things change. Throughout your day, choose to see things and speak about things how you prefer them to be. This doesn't mean ignore 'what is' or pretend that it isn't happening, it simply means allow 'what is' and how things currently look, but see beyond them. Start the practise of seeing and believing in the greatness that is within you and all around you, acknowledge the abundance everywhere that you go. If you happen to lose enthusiasm during the day, allow it, centre yourself and refocus. Start again from that place of power.

IT'S HERE TO HEAL YOU, NOT HURT YOU

Until we learn the lesson that each situation and person is here to teach us (and we also apply that lesson in our own life) it will continue to happen to us again and again (in a different disguise) in order for us to finally 'get it', apply the lesson, heal and move on. Take a look at your own life right now and find those lessons that are still waiting to be learned and applied. Do the work. Circumstances can only change and improve once you change. Remember, everything that happens to you is here to help and heal you, not to hurt you. It's happening for you, not to you. There is a blessing hidden within every lesson.

GOT TO DO SOMETHING

Sometimes saying and doing nothing just isn't good enough. Sometimes we have to stand up and speak out when we observe something that angers or upsets us. Especially when we witness despicable acts of injustice and prejudice. However please don't allow yourself to get caught up in the 'mob mentality' or allow yourself to get caught up in the traditional reaction of focussing upon or fighting against the issue. Instead, start by acknowledging the issue, the 'real issue'. See through the current reflection of it. This doesn't mean that you should forget what is happening right now or pretend that what you witnessed didn't happen, but that you should instead use it as an opportunity to help create and support a solution. If there is something that you can do to help, then shine a light upon that. Lend your voice to those things that are educating and enlightening others, and towards those things that are making a real difference and changing things. Help to support change from feelings of peace and power rather than fighting against 'what is' from feelings such as fear, guilt or shame. Don't fight against the issue, turn up the volume on the solution. Don't promote hate, pain or ignorance, that is the reason for those horrific incidents in the first place. Hate won't solve anything, it often only makes ignorance and pain shout even louder. Step back, take a deep breath and consciously choose to respond from a higher perspective and a place of love and peace.

FEEL GOOD FIRST
Before you do anything, centre yourself in your own peace, joy and power. When you feel good first, before you do or say anything, you allow yourself to receive thoughts, feelings and experiences that feel like that. You allow yourself to receive thoughts about that which you're doing and observing that are on a higher frequency. Ideas that will lead you to a reality that feels good to you. It is so important that before you begin a task, that you centre yourself and align yourself with your higher self, as how you begin something determines what you're able to receive back from it. In addition the intention, or the reason why you do something is key too. That is the energy that flows into and fuels everything that you do.

PERFORM IN THE MOMENT
We often worry that we won't be able to 'perform in the moment', especially when it matters the most. That thought primarily stems from insecurity, doubt in your own abilities and especially a lack based mentality and perspective. Often when you're in that mindset, you're trying to showcase your abilities with the single aim of impressing others. You're seeking approval at some level,

which often stems from a place of uncertainty or lack. Any time that you're trying to 'get' something from that lack based perspective and mentality you will unknowingly cut yourself off from receiving it. Whereas when you're in a 'giving' mentality the information that you need will flow effortlessly to you (as you're open to receiving it). Therefore to perform in the moment and to do your best, focus upon what you're giving, not what you're trying to get back. As long as you've done the 'work' and the preparation, then trust, detach and go with the flow. Give it everything that you've got and then give it over to the universe. When you surrender all stress and worry about how it will go and how others will respond or react to that which you do, you will stop the resistance against your blessings and greatness and that which you desire. You will return to the natural flow of abundance once again. From that higher perspective you will be able to see that thoughts of worry and doubt in your abilities are often just a manifestation and a reflection of a lower frequency and not a reflection of the truth or your abilities. Always remember that your inner being knows exactly what to do and when to do it, and problems only really occur when you think that you know better from your limited perspective.

DETACH

Although we can't help but be affected by what happens in life, it is necessary for us to practise non attachment. Often the more attached that we are to a particular result and the more that our happiness is dependant upon it, the more that we will unknowingly push it away. The more that we want something (or more accurately, the more that we continue to focus upon the not having of it, and the feeling of lack associated with it) the less that it wants us. You can only ever 'attract' and allow in that which you are, and that which you are consistently vibrating at the same frequency as. Decide from now on that your happiness and peace is your own responsibility and that it is dependant upon you alone, and not dependent upon or invested in a result or a reaction of another person. Detach.

WHAT REMAINS UNHEALED WITHIN YOU?

What remains unhealed, unexpressed and unprocessed within you? What aren't you facing or releasing? What have you been ignoring, resisting, pushing away or pretending didn't happen? Until you honour and move through what and how you feel, that pain and those issues will often be placed in front of you again in a different disguise or a brand new struggle in order to encourage you to look within and heal. Everything that you encounter is an opportunity to heal, but when you are so used to seeing things as being problems, and you are so used to denying your own pain and feelings, things can't change. The clarity can't come through. When you begin to see every situation as an opportunity for growth and as an opportunity to practise love, that is the energy that you will put into it and that is what you open yourself up to receive back from it. The lesson and blessing will reveal itself to you rather than even more problems revealing themselves to you. When you acknowledge, accept and allow how you feel and you begin to move through and let go of the pain, the universe will begin to let in your blessings.

NEED TO HEAR "I'M SORRY"?

If you gave up the need to hear, "I'm sorry" in order for you to heal and move on, you would be a completely different person overnight. At times in life we tend to hold onto our own pain and suffering and refuse to move on, thinking and believing that at some level not accepting someone else's apology or even refusing to let go of the pain, will hurt and punish the person that hurt us. We wrongly believe that if we heal, they somehow 'get away' with it, but that couldn't be further from the truth. Until you heal, things can't and won't change. Healing is your responsibility only. If you're still waiting to hear 'sorry' before you heal and move on, contemplate this, what would happen if they apologised but you didn't feel that it was a genuine or heartfelt apology, what then? Instead of needing to know 'why', or needing to get a full explanation, choose to heal and move on. Start to find some sort of forgiveness today. Forgiveness doesn't mean that you are saying that what happened was OK, it is just saying OK it happened and now it's time for me to heal and move on. It is about being responsible for how you feel and for becoming the best version of yourself. Forgive yourself first for continuing to hold yourself in that place of pain and hurt. Forgiveness is for giving, for giving to yourself first in order for you to heal. It's not for them. Continuing to need to hear 'sorry' before you finally find healing would be giving the person or the situation that hurt you the power and permission to hurt you again. You're letting them decide whether or not you heal and find peace and happiness. No more. You're not going to live your life on their terms any more. It is time to reinvest that energy in loving yourself unconditionally, and in building yourself up, rather than trying to tear them down. This is your time now, it is time to heal.

ACCUSTOMED TO HURT

Often when we have been consistently hurt in the past we tend to become accustomed to it in the present. It not only becomes normal and expected, however it often determines how we see ourselves and how we let others treat us from then on out. Often the only reason why we let others treat us badly in the present is because we're either used to being treated like that in the past or we are used to treating ourselves that way in the present. It's a vicious cycle of pain. In addition the more that we expect to be treated badly and the more that we fight against those people and those situations that make us feel that way, the more that it will tend to happen in our own life. We'll end up 'attracting' and allowing into our reality even more things that will make us feel that way. Until we are nicer to ourselves, nothing changes. In addition, until we set boundaries and limits, people will tend to disrespect us at every given opportunity. Don't betray yourself, set boundaries, know and define your own worth. If you find yourself settling for or making excuses for someone who is consistently hurting you, it's time to reassess your life and it's time to love yourself a little bit more.

FORGETTING YOUR POWER?

Any time that you feel 'down' that is just your higher self reminding you that you are most likely forgetting your own power, that you are more than likely forgetting who you really are and how things really are at the highest level. Any time that you observe lack in your own life and you feel awful, the real reason why you feel bad isn't because you are missing something, but because you think that the lack is who you are or how things will always be. Your higher self is making you aware through that bad feeling, that your current perspective is separating you from who you really are and from that which you desire, that's it.

I HATE MY FLAWS

The more that you focus upon something that you don't like within yourself, the more that it will grow and show in your consciousness and reality. You can't change or let go of something that you don't like by fighting against it or by focussing upon it. This doesn't mean that you should ignore it either. Only once you unconditionally and wholeheartedly acknowledge, accept and allow 'what is', will you then be able to change it from a place of unconditional love. You let it go by first letting it be.

HAPPY 'THEN'

Too often we sacrifice our own happiness in the present moment for the promise of being happy 'someday', typically once we have achieved that which we desire. We often think that it's normal to settle for being unhappy now, because the happiness in our near future will somehow make up for it, unaware that when you follow that approach you'll always be chasing happiness. Any time that you visualise happiness happening 'then' instead of now, what you're really saying at an energetic and vibrational level is that you're unhappy now. You can't put off happiness until a later date. If you're not choosing it now, you won't feel it or see it 'then'. In addition if you're not consciously choosing to be genuinely happy right now, then you'll tend to allow 'what is' or 'what was' to affect and determine your inner state of being, which ultimately determines and creates your reality. You'll tend to allow everything and everyone to separate you from your inner happiness. Until you consistently make the choice to connect to your inner joy now, you are unknowingly allowing your current feelings to create the path ahead, which will continue to lead you away from all that you desire. Let joy create your path. Centre yourself and let your highest self (or God / the universe) lead the way.

STOP 'FITTING IN'
You weren't born to 'fit in', the moment that you try to you will begin to lose all sense of who you really are. There is no need to change and shape yourself to fit into a place, position or relationship that you weren't meant to fit into. Too often we change who we are, make ourselves smaller and shrink down our greatness, power and purpose just to please others, or just to fit in or fade into the background. You will never find lasting or authentic peace and happiness doing that. Always remember that you are who you are for a higher purpose. Becoming someone and something that you are not, won't fulfil you or help anyone. Please stop 'fitting in'. You will ultimately know where you belong by how it feels, you will know because the environment that you're in will encourage you to grow and expand into who you really are, instead of causing you to shrink back.

THE ECHOES OF WHAT WAS
At times when we make those 'big' changes in our life, something 'strange' seems to happen. The moment that you give up feeling sorry for yourself, the universe tends to give you even more situations that will make you feel sorry for yourself again. However please understand that it isn't happening to you to punish you, nor is it necessarily there to test you, it is simply the reminisce of your old energy. It is the echoes or the ripples of who you were and what you used to think you deserved, and what you used to expect to happen regarding that particular situation that

you're currently facing. It is the pre-sent energy catching up to the present moment. The universe will often give you one final situation that will make you feel 'down' again, not to hurt you, but in order for you to see if you still want it. It is giving you one last chance to see if you are certain that you want to change your mind (since you have believed in those old lack, limitation and fear based thoughts and perspectives for so long). It needs to make sure that you are sure. So knowing this when you start to focus upon an abundance of money, the universe may provide you with a situation that will make you feel lack again. It will figuratively say, this is what you usually focussed upon regarding this subject (which is often a lack of money) so are you sure that you don't want this situation again? This is often the point where people give up and go back to their old way of thinking (believing that their 'positive' thinking hasn't worked). Sadly all too often we interpret that situation or experience of lack as being proof that our positive thinking hasn't worked, and we go back to our old ways of seeing and doing things, unaware that we were on the verge of a major break through and blessing. Remind yourself of that when the opposite of what you desire starts happening in your life soon after you start thinking positively. Stay strong, remain focussed upon who you are becoming and what you desire. Don't fall into the trap of focussing upon that which you don't want, or pushing against it, giving into it, fighting against it or allowing it to affect your inner state, rise above it all. Remain centred in your own truth knowing that greatness and your highest blessings are on their way to you.

ARE YOU AFRAID TO BE HAPPY?
Have you ever found yourself in a moment of joy and a thought interrupts it saying something like 'What if that happens?'. Those type of thoughts aren't a sign that something bad is going to happen, they are just a reflection of the wavelength that you're used to seeing and interpreting joy from. Understand that your joy won't harm anyone. There is no need to 'police' your joy or any need to stop yourself from being happy just in case something

bad sneaks in and 'blind sides' you. Fearing unexpected events won't stop them from happening, it will only ever stop you from being truly happy now. Surrender control, trust, have faith and embrace joy.

100% YOU

You will only get 'lost' when you're not being yourself fully. You're made the way that you are for a greater reason and purpose. Your personality is there to help support your purpose and your dreams, you don't need to be someone else to succeed in what you're made for and meant for. When you're pretending to be someone else that is when you'll 'attract' into your life (or more accurately allow into your life) those people who will take advantage of you, as well as all of those people and things that aren't meant for you. They'll tend to disrespect you because at the core level you're disrespecting yourself by not being who you are meant to be. Until you be yourself fully, what is meant for you can't get to you.

THEY THINK THAT THEY'RE BETTER THAN ME

Don't confuse someone who is trying to better themselves as someone who thinks that they're better than you. If someone else's power, greatness, talent or beauty intimidates you, that's an indication to look within and see how you're defining and viewing yourself. Those feelings of inadequacy are ultimately coming from a place of lack and the belief that you're not good enough, which is what you'll put out into the universe and what you'll get back. Other people's success, happiness and greatness should inspire you, not make you feel bitter or feel bad about yourself. Understand that if they can succeed against all of the odds and in-spite of all of those setbacks, then you can too. There is no need to compete against anyone for anything. In addition, instead of trying to be better than others, focus instead upon bettering yourself. Focus your energy in a productive way that will support you and support the person that you're becoming. This isn't about trying to better yourself to finally feel good enough or feel worthy of success, it is about bettering yourself by stepping into a more actualised and complete version of your best self. Finally it is so important that you learn to focus your attention, time and energy upon building a healthy belief system that supports you, rather than powering the mentality of trying to beat someone else for something. Let their success inspire and encourage you, not bring you down or lower your frequency.

YOU CAN HANDLE THIS

The universe will only ever give you what you can handle, when you can handle it, so have faith that whatever you're facing or going through right now, you can do it, you will get through this. This situation is here to help you, not to hurt you. This won't break you, it's here as an opportunity to create and reveal who you really are. The universe won't bring you something that you're not vibrationally lined up with, ready for, or on the same frequency as. Therefore this situation has use and purpose, ask yourself, 'What is this here to teach me?', 'How can I use this to better myself and help all others?', 'What am I being encouraged to let go of and become?'. All of those questions will help to keep you on track and will also stop you from falling into a victim mentality which would ultimately hold you back and keep you down.

LOOK AROUND, DO YOU SEE IT?

Be open to the opportunities that are in your current environment. The universe is always placing opportunities right in front of you, however when you are so busy looking at the opportunities that have already passed you by or you're too busy looking for those 'big' opportunities, you'll tend to miss the smaller opportunities that are right in front of you now. New opportunities are constantly revealing themselves to you, however you'll only be able to see and act upon them when you are fully present. Most 'small' opportunities have the potential to bring big results and become something truly amazing, just as long as you stay aware and remain open.

BELIEVE IN YOUR WORK

It doesn't matter how good or how talented you are, if you don't believe in the work that you are putting out and the message that you have within you, then you won't be able to succeed at the level that you are capable of succeeding at. Constantly remind yourself that you're good enough. Accentuate that message until it becomes a belief. Until you believe fully in that which you are doing and the work that you're putting out, it just won't work no matter how hard you struggle and try to make things happen. Your reality will continue to reflect back to you what you feel and believe to be true or be possible for you until you change how you're seeing yourself, the world and that which you are doing.

NEED TO HEAR THANK YOU?

It's so important that you learn to detach from what you give to the world, especially learning to detach from needing to hear 'thank you' from those people that you have helped. Don't need to hear 'thank you' or need to feel that appreciation back from others. At times other people just aren't able to give you that appreciation back. They don't understand what they have been given in the first place. Often in life you won't get back the help, support and love from the same people that you give to, but don't worry, the universe is on it. What you put out and give to another is already coming back to you in another form and disguise, just as long as you let yourself receive it. When you help someone, the universe is sending someone to help you. Continue to pay that love, help and support forward. What you receive is often an exact reflection of what you have been giving. Please understand that when you continue to give with the intention of needing to hear thank you, or desiring to look good to others, or needing to receive praise for your actions, then you run the risk of it coming from the ego and not from your inner self, which helps no one but you. At times helping others can be a thankless job, however don't do it for the praise, do it to make a difference. Those who are able to accept and recognise what you are giving to them will of course be thankful, however don't wait to hear 'thank you' to feel and know that you have done what is right. Give, detach and accept gratitude if it is given, but don't make that the only goal. It's best to only focus upon that which you're giving rather than what you're trying to get back. Finally, please only ever give to another what runs over from your already 'full' cup. You can only offer any real help when your own cup is already full. Don't give what you can't afford to lose.

FREE WILL?

Although 'fate' may play a part in determining who comes into your life, free will always gives you the choice and freedom to choose who can stay. We ultimately have the choice of what to do next and where to go. Think of 'fate' just as you think of the 'Law of Attraction'. Rest assured that fate will always have your back, putting things on your path to steer you from that which isn't meant for you and guiding you towards that which you're seeking at a deeper level, however it won't intervene, it will only ever give you a subtle sign that you're going off track. The choice is always yours. Always remember that you're the creator of your reality, not just a spectator of it.

IT IS WHAT IT IS

How you perceive something is often a direct reflection of the definition that you have attached to it. It is important that you go back and find out how you have defined yourself and that which you desire. You can only ever become that which you believe yourself to be. When you are not confident in your own abilities and you perceive your work as not being good enough, that will be the result which you're open and able to accept and allow into your reality. Everything in your reality will reflect that thought and feeling back to you, not because it is necessarily true, but in order for you to see it and change it if it's not what you desire or prefer to experience. Fighting against those feelings and that result won't change anything, however changing the inner belief will. 'It is what it is', simply because you have created it that way. Bring an awareness to your beliefs and to your perceptions regarding everything that you are viewing. If you believe something is hard or difficult to do then it will be, if you define something as not being for you, then it won't be, if you continue to think that you will fail again then you will, if you think that you will never make more money than you're currently making right now, then you won't. It begins and ends with you. Things will continue to be as they are until you change, and until you commit yourself to those changes. Be careful what you believe about yourself. It is often said that we are made in 'the image of God' (or I would prefer to reword it to say that we are made in the imagination). The image that you hold consistently in your mind, whether helpful or not or whether true or not, about yourself, others, the world and your desires, you will see manifested in your reality. That is until you think and look again.

THE THOUGHT CAN'T SURVIVE
Do you understand that it is impossible for two thoughts to survive at the same time? You can't think two thoughts simultaneously. When you remove your attention from a 'negative' thought it automatically and naturally begins to slow down and fade away, it can't survive without your attention or participation. Your thoughts need your attention and awareness to survive and thrive, you are the energy supply which is energising them. So which thoughts are you giving your attention, awareness and consciousness to? Any thought that you are focussing upon you are powering. Whatever you draw your attention to you are making bigger. Decide to no longer give any of your 'negative' thoughts your attention and power (even subtly by fighting against them, analysing them, pondering them, fearing them, or trying to replace them straight away with positive thoughts). Your thoughts have no real power without you. Remember you aren't your thoughts, you are the awareness and presence that is aware of those thoughts. If you have 'negative' thoughts, that is perfectly OK. They are just a reflection of the frequency that you're currently at, let them be and you will in

time begin to let them go. You let go of the thoughts that you don't want by first letting them be. When you're centred and you're at peace, guide and refocus your awareness upon a thought or feeling that is closer in alignment with who you really are. This isn't about placing a positive thought over a negative one, or thinking a positive thought to cancel out the negative one. It is choosing a positive thought simply because it's closer in alignment with who you really are at the highest level. Guiding your attention is one of your greatest tools, that's where your power is.

MAKE 'A SCENE'
If someone does or says something that makes you feel uncomfortable, don't be afraid to speak up. Too often we fear speaking our truth in case we 'cause a scene', appear 'difficult' or come across as being 'too sensitive', or even in case we evoke a violent or harmful reaction. Please understand that being spiritual doesn't mean that you have to let people treat you badly or that you need to constantly rise above it or see through their ignorant behaviour. Sometimes being your best self and doing the right thing requires speaking up calmly yet unapologetically from a centred place to make people aware of your boundaries and when they are being inappropriate. Don't be afraid to say no or to let people know when enough is enough. Educate and enlighten them if they are willing to listen, if not let go and centre yourself once more.

TOO SENSITIVE?
It is not weak to be sensitive, or to be sensitive to the needs of others, however it is necessary at times for you to become invisible to the harsh words and cruel actions of others. Learn to protect yourself energetically, not from a place of defensiveness but from a place of peace and power. So many people are walking around with 'open sores' and past wounds which are causing them tremendous amounts of pain when any comment is seemingly directed towards them. The number one reason for their defensiveness is because the wound from their past hasn't

fully healed yet and their energy is still being depleted by that open wound. When you heal, defensiveness no longer becomes an issue and you no longer feel like you have to prove or defend yourself or feel like you're constantly under threat. Be sensitive enough so that you can let your pain out yet stop another person's pain from getting in. Become transparent to the harsh words and actions of others. Learn to ground yourself daily so that you won't be so easily affected by the opinions, feedback, energy or harsh comments of others. Walk tall from your own inner core, knowing that no one has the power or ability to truly affect your happiness and peace for long.

DON'T FOCUS ON YOUR THOUGHTS
Are you focussing upon your thoughts, or are you focussing your thoughts? Although it sounds like a subtle difference, the results will be very different. Focussing your thoughts will have a positive impact on your life, focussing upon your thoughts won't. When you begin to consciously focus your thoughts, you will begin to become a conscious creator of your life, rather than just being a helpless spectator of it. When you begin to consciously and purposely focus your attention and awareness upon thoughts that feel like appreciation, love, excitement, joy and peace (instead of focussing upon or fighting against 'negative' ones) you'll begin to call onto your path, into your awareness and into your life everyone and everything that will make you feel like that. You change your life by focussing your thoughts, rather than focussing upon the thoughts that are already in your head.

PRAYING FOR STRENGTH?
Often our conscious mind believes that when we pray asking for strength, the strength that we desire will just magically be instilled within us, which is rarely the case. When you ask for strength what will often occur is you will encounter an experience or situation that will instil within you the strength that you requested. That is likely when things will 'go wrong' and when you'll face troubles or setbacks. However don't worry, you are

more than capable of handling this. Those setbacks aren't sent to hurt you, they're here to help you and here to liberate you, to give you the strength that you are looking and praying for. Every single situation and struggle that you encounter and go through (or more accurately grow through) adds another tool to your 'spiritual tool belt'. It all has purpose. Each experience that you go through leaves you with a valuable lesson, blessing and spiritual tool that you will need later on to be able to handle what is next for you and the life that you desire. Everything that you encounter on the path to success and greatness will give you a chance to use one of those spiritual tools that you already have, or it will give you an opportunity to gain a new one.

WHY IT ANNOYS YOU
Do you find yourself getting easily irritated or annoyed by the smallest of things? If you're very easily irritated by every little thing in life, that is often a sign for you to detach, and that you are currently vibrating at a lower frequency. When you're on that lower frequency that is when you'll have easy assess to thoughts about everything that will irritate you. You'll draw onto your path and into your awareness everything and everyone that will make you feel like that. You'll constantly see things which annoy you in the world or in the behaviour of others. When you are irritated you'll often find it easy to find and see something wrong with everyone (including yourself and your own life). The real reason why you will find it so easy to find fault with everything is simply because you're on the same frequency that those perspectives reside at and originate from. In addition when you feel that way you will tend to (at the core level) unconsciously look for any excuse to get annoyed, essentially to have an opportunity to release all of the frustration and resistance that has built up within you, which you have been suppressing and pushing down. However if you find that you're primarily annoyed by something within yourself, the real reason why you feel that way is because your inner self is trying to get you to change it or primarily change how you are seeing it. Your inner being is showing you what

needs to change in order for you to be genuinely happy and at peace, it's showing you what's holding you back (which is often only a mindset or a perspective) in order for you to see it and incorporate those changes into your life.

REPELLING YOUR GOALS

It's not necessary for you to chase after your goals to be successful, instead embody the feeling of success and allow 'the way' to come to you. Now this doesn't mean that you shouldn't take action, however if you spend your entire life chasing after something (while viewing it from the vibration of lack, and from a space of desperately wanting or needing it) you are unknowingly repelling it. The energies aren't vibrating in harmony with each other. In addition, the actions that you take will be inspired by lack, which will lead you to a future that feels like that lack. Let your actions be inspired from the vibration of abundance, and not from lack. Please understand that your desires reside on the vibration of abundance, not lack. Once you come into harmony with the idea and the awareness of there being an abundance in the universe and an abundance of that which you desire (which you can do by unconditionally 'allowing' and feeling good) everything changes, which is often the moment that you make peace with not having something and when you stop the resistance that was holding it apart from you.

LABELLING EVERYTHING

Far too often in life we get hung up on labelling everyone and everything. The more that we label something as good and something else as bad, or that as only being a certain thing, we will begin to lose touch and sense of what that thing really is. When you define something with a strict definition, you unconsciously bring your experience and bias with that thing to it, you start to experience it through a block of a belief or a definition. To put it simply when you see someone as only being one thing, you can't see what else they have to offer, or see the person that they have become, you'll miss the fullness of who they really are. You'll see them and that which they do through a filter. You won't be able to authentically connect with them when you do that. We unintentionally bring our bias to that which we are observing and we unknowingly draw out certain patterns of behaviour or a particular experience with that person (or in essence that which we think, feel and believe to be true regarding that subject or thing). Instead of needing to define everything, it is important that we learn to just let things 'be' without feeling the need to contemplate or compartmentalise everything. The more that you feel the need to label everything the more unhappiness that you will tend to have. Be open to all things, and allow them to reveal themselves to you in time.

GIVE THEM ROOM

It is so important that we give our loved ones enough room and space to be who they really are, that we don't impose or project onto them, and that we let them show us who they really are when they are ready and able to. It is vital that we give them enough room to find and figure out who they really are. Wouldn't it be incredible to live in a world where we didn't fear that we might be abandoned when we live our truth, were we could show others who we authentically are all without fearing the repercussions. It is our duty to create an environment that encourages and supports our loved ones as they figure out and come to an understanding of who they really are.

GOING AFTER THE SAME TYPE?

If you are used to getting hurt, stop going after your 'usual' type. Your usual type of partner is an indication of what you expect and allow, in regards to love and a relationship. That type of person feels 'right' to you not because they are necessarily right for you, but because they are either on a similar wavelength to your last partner or they are on a similar wavelength to you. In essence your 'type' will be a reflection of how you treat yourself. They will often vibrate in harmony with how you expect to be treated in regards to a relationship and a partner. They will ultimately treat you how you currently treat yourself, that is why you're drawn to them. They feel familiar to you simply because they're on the same wavelength as you and they are on the same frequency as how you're currently feeling. Things won't change until you change. Those type of partners are a reflection of how love looks and feels to you, and what you feel and believe you are worth, and what is possible for you in regards to love and a partner. Once you love yourself fully and you change how you see love, how you see yourself and how you see a partner, you will begin to find a new 'type', which is a partner who will treat you how you treat yourself. Until then, don't fall for that old type, choose again.

MAGICAL TOOL
Without courage, nothing worthwhile can be achieved. If you haven't got the courage to act upon that which you already know (and that which your heart knows to be true) things can't change. Courage will allow you to try again even after you have failed, it will allow you to be yourself in a world that's trying to force you to fit in, it will allow you to admit that you need help when you're struggling, to leave that troubled relationship behind you even though you still love them, to speak up for what is right even when it's not the popular opinion and to put your work 'out there' even when you're afraid. It's the magical tool that you've been looking for.

THINK LESS
Life isn't always about doing more, it's often about thinking less. Before doing more, try thinking less first. This of course doesn't mean that you should stop thinking logically, stop taking action or stop 'pushing' yourself to be better, this just means that it is important that you centre yourself, take a step back, and no longer allow the thoughts that cross your mind to control your life or determine your future. When you think less, you will allow yourself to feel more. You will allow yourself to rise back up to the higher frequency that you naturally reside at, which will begin to allow in everything that resonates at that higher frequency too.

When you do that, you will no longer try to force things into being, you will instead allow your actions to be determined and inspired by that higher frequency. It's important that you step back from your thoughts. It is truly exhausting to constantly over think everything (as that requires you to hold yourself at a lower frequency, which is not where you belong). Incorporate practises such as meditation, mindfulness, exercise and time in nature to clear your mind. When you do, miracles begin to occur.

ARE YOU HELPING TOO MUCH?

It is vital that you leave enough room for others to solve their own problems and issues. If you consistently solve other people's problems for them, you're cheating them out of the lesson and blessing that was intended for them. That 'problem' was there to awaken and remind them of their own power and strength, not to remind you of yours. Be there to support and guide, but not to force or impose.

BE YOUR AUTHENTIC SELF

Express yourself, be the best version of yourself. It is so important that you live authentically and be who you really are. When you harbour shame and guilt in regards to who you are, how you look or what you do, you will continue to hold back your blessings. You can't let in all that you desire when you are vibrating at that lower frequency. Please understand that you are made the way that you are for a greater reason and purpose. Don't worry about what other people might be thinking about you or that which you do, or worry about what they are actually thinking about you, it has no real affect on you unless you allow it to. Those who attack other people who are different are often uncomfortable within themselves, they ultimately don't like themselves at some level. Their small mindedness is what is the issue and problem, not you embracing and showing the world who you really are. They are intimidated by those people who are themselves, and by those people who have the courage to be themselves unapologetically. It just reminds them that they are not living authentically and not living on purpose, and that they are too afraid to even try. Be yourself. You are going to have to walk your own path sometime in life in order for you to do what you are here to do. You can't reach your purpose when you're not being yourself and when you're too afraid to put yourself 'out there'. Be who you are and be proud of it, don't let the world change you, you're needed as you are. Do you realise that you were created by the entire universe for a greater purpose? A reason greater than you could ever begin to imagine or even comprehend. Let that feeling guide you, it will never steer you in the wrong direction. Don't be afraid to stand out and be original.

WITHOUT THIS, NOTHING CHANGES

If you allow your current emotions to determine your behaviour, outlook or next course of action, you will never be able to become your best self or live your best life. You will continue to react to what you encounter and observe, which will inevitably create even more of what you don't want in your reality. Self awareness and presence is necessary in order for any meaningful changes to occur in your life. Seeing life from a higher perspective and awareness will allow you to see clearly what you need to let go of in order for you to grow and become your best self. When you find yourself lost in a painful or 'negative' emotion, or lost in a downward spiral of 'negative' thoughts, bring in some awareness. Centre yourself in the present moment and see through what is occurring. That brief moment of stepping back will help to allow in clarity and will give you the space to think and look again.

THEY CAN'T SEE YOUR DREAM

Learn to block out the noise, negativity and doubt of others, stay focussed upon your own positive mindset. Don't need others to see, believe or understand what you see. They can't see your dream, they weren't supposed to. They don't know what you know, they can only ever see your dream from their limited wavelength, it looks very different to them. Don't need other people to believe in you or that which you do for you to believe in yourself. Encourage and empower yourself. Focus upon what you're here to do, rather than trying to prove yourself or defend your dream to others.

FEAR STOPS ME
Hiding away in fear won't keep you safe, all it does is hold you hostage, keep you in pain and keep you from your purpose. The intention and reason for the action always determines the result, so what you do in fear (and from the feeling of fear) can only ever bring back a result that feels like that fear. Never let fear make your decisions or choices for you. Don't react to life in fear, respond from love. Closing your heart off in fear will only ever block all that you desire and love from getting to you. Recognise that fear is only ever an indication to start seeing yourself and your desires the way that you prefer to see them, it's a reminder to respond with love.

IT'S SO IMPORTANT THAT YOU SPEAK UP
It is vital that you use your voice, you've got to speak up. When you speak your truth you will begin to vibrate at the level of everything that is right for you, which not only lets go of any resistance that is blocking your highest blessings and greatness, but it allows in everything that is on that higher vibration too, which is everything that is right and true for you. When you continue to live a lie and you hold back your deepest truth, it calls onto your path people, things and situations that aren't in your highest good. This is why it is so important that you be yourself authentically and you live your truth. In addition when you speak your truth you release any guilt or shame associated with concealing who you really are or hiding away from what was. You bring in your healing. When you are proud of who you are and you love yourself unconditionally, miracles will begin to occur. You will begin to allow in everything that is meant for you. It is the only way to live on purpose and to live authentically.

ANOTHER PERSPECTIVE

Learn to step back from your problems and see them from another perspective. You can't see things clearly when you're so close up to them. That is often why you can solve other people's problems but you can't solve your own. You're too close to the situation or vibration, you're on the same frequency that created it. No matter what solution you're seeking, the answer will sneak in when you're not focussing upon the problem, it will appear when you're feeling good, when you're not looking for or needing the answer and when you're on a higher frequency.

MOVE TOWARDS LOVE, NOT AWAY FROM FEAR

Make yourself a promise to consistently move in the direction of the person that you're becoming, to move towards what you love and not away from what you fear. Every single day of your life, with every decision that you make, choose love and peace. Do what you would do if you weren't afraid of failing, and if you knew that you couldn't fail. It takes practise, but once you master it, life begins to flow with an undeniable ease.

GIVE AND TAKE

There is a natural flow to life that goes unseen by many. Simply put, there is always an equal exchange of give and take. However this natural give and take can't occur in our life until we start giving. You must first give in order to start the flow of receiving back in all areas of your life. When you give, you open up that space to receive back. This isn't about giving just to get something back, it means giving without attachment or conditions. If it's not unconditional then it has no real value. If we give with conditions, we receive with the same conditions. When you give freely from an open heart, 'karma' becomes a blessing. Those who give freely do so from the belief that they have something to give, which the universe responds to and reflects back. When you feel like you have something of value to give, the universe will tend to give you even more of that thing back. Once you receive, it is so important that you give again in order to keep the flow going, so that there isn't stagnation. You will find that those people who hold on tightly to the 'little' that they have (and those people who tend to believe that they have nothing or that they haven't got much to give) will find that the universe will end up taking from them that which they have, due to their faith in lack and scarcity. They have unconsciously blocked their blessings and cut themselves off from receiving more. They're vibrating on the frequency of needing - or lack, when 'receiving' is on the frequency of having - essentially on the frequency of abundance. Only when you're focussed upon giving are you then able to open up and receive back that which you desire. It's often said that no one has ever become poor from giving, which is one of the truest statements ever spoken.

DO YOUR DESIRES FEEL BIG?

Your desires won't manifest a moment before you're vibrationally lined up with them. If your desires still feel 'big' to you, or they don't feel like the next logical step for you, then you're not up to speed with them yet, essentially you're not vibrationally aligned with them. The unfolding process should feel easy and natural to you, and feel like it is destined for you. It mustn't feel like something that you have to struggle and strain to achieve. Divine and perfect timing is the time that it takes for you to get on the same frequency or mental and emotional state as your desires. You don't have to 'achieve' success, you only have to align your thoughts and feelings with the idea of how it feels to receive that success and be a successful person.

I'LL BE HAPPY WHEN...

Any time that you think, feel or believe that you need something or someone to be happy or be enough, that's an indication that you're 'disconnected' from the essence of who you really are. What that says vibrationally is that you're unhappy and not complete now, which is what the universe responds to and reflects back. Remember that we are always complete 'as is' and as or where we are. Our results are a reflection and a manifestation of our inner happiness, and not the source of it.

Happiness isn't something that you get, it's who you are, and it's only available now.

BREAK THOSE BELIEFS

Beliefs take years to form but seconds to break. This too applies to all of those old fear and lack based beliefs that have ruled your life until now. Now that you are beginning to see yourself and all those things differently, you have changed the power of those old beliefs forever. They won't be able to affect or control you to the same level and degree that they once could. You can now see them for what they are, you have started to remove the power and fear from them. You have brought in a new awarenesses and a higher consciousness, which in time will create new empowering and expansive beliefs which will take you even higher and even further than ever before.

SYNCHRONICITY

Synchronicity is what occurs when you are in sync with the vibration of who you really are and that which you are seeking at the highest level. They occur when you're at peace, when you're grounded, and when you are going with the flow. Synchronicity and serendipity often occurs in your life every single day (even when you don't realise or recognise it). It can reveal itself to you in forms such as repeating patterns of numbers or aligned time (or reflection time) such as 11:11 or those chance encounters with someone who can assist you in fulfilling your goals and dreams. It is much more than luck, chance or mere coincidence. Please understand that where you are right now has purpose too. This is a part of the natural order and sequence in which you receive your desires and you become your best self. Ultimately the universe will continue to place you in that place, at that time, for a much greater reason and purpose than your conscious mind can comprehend. It is no accident or coincidence that you are where you are right now, it is all necessary in order to help you to know yourself to an even higher degree.

WHY THINGS AREN'T CHANGING

Have you been allowing 'what is' to determine how you feel or what you believe? If you have, then you'll continue to be limited to 'what was' or 'what is'. Instead of allowing whatever crosses your path or comes into your awareness to steal your attention, choose what you give your attention and presence to deliberately and wisely. Decide from now on to only focus, direct and guide your attention and awareness upon that which you desire to see or feel more of.

'BAD' HABITS

We all have 'bad' habits and flaws for a greater reason, they keep us human. Our 'flaws' and quirks allow us to accept other people for theirs. If we didn't have flaws we would spend our entire lives condemning others for theirs. If we were all perfect we couldn't connect with and relate to each other. We connect with others through our mistakes and 'flaws' so don't hide them away from the world, let others see them. No one can relate to and learn from perfection. We are all perfectly made, and made the way that we are for a greater reason. However if your 'bad' habits or unhealthy behaviour is causing you or others harm, it's time to take back responsibility for becoming a better you.

GREATEST LESSON IN 'LOVE'

One of the greatest lessons that you'll ever learn is that you can't love or be loved by someone who doesn't fully love themselves, and more importantly you can't save someone who won't save themselves. In life we often try and save others at the expense of neglecting and harming ourselves, or we end up loving someone else at the cost of us not loving ourselves fully. At times it's necessary to walk away from those situations and people for your own sanity and well being. Remember, that you can only give someone something that they're ready and able to receive. You can't help someone until they decide to help themselves, and more importantly you can't do anyone else's healing for them. Choose you.

LOOK AFTER YOURSELF

Learn to care for yourself as you would care for a small fragile and vulnerable child. We all have a small vulnerable child that is hidden within us that still seeks and needs love, support, acceptance, validation, encouragement and comfort. Be willing to be that loving parental presence for yourself. Instead of neglecting or rejecting yourself, love and accept yourself fully and unconditionally and continue to do it until you believe it. Start by talking to yourself in a kind, sympathetic and loving voice rather than a harsh or critical tone of voice. Listen to how you're feeling, find comfort within yourself, be gentle with yourself, nurture that inner child and very soon they'll become an empowered adult.

EMBRACE SETBACKS

A setback always comes right before a major break through. A setback is setting you up for a leap forward. You aren't being punished or tested by the universe you're simply being reminded of your inner strength. A setback gives you the opportunity to take a step back and refine your approach. This isn't the time to give up, this is the time to step back, look at things from a higher perspective and frequency and try again. So pick yourself up, breathe deeply, look again and know that you can do this.

STILL SUBTLY HURTING YOURSELF?

(Trigger warning: This post briefly mentions self harm)
When you don't know your worth and value you'll tend to hurt yourself in subtle little ways, you'll often hold yourself back and continue to ignore your purpose and desires. You'll also tend to allow others to hurt you, disrespect you and take advantage of you. Every time that you don't believe in yourself you are subtly sabotaging and harming yourself. Self harm is not only the things that you do to hurt your physical body, but the things that you say to yourself too, as well as how you treat yourself, how you see yourself and how you think about your mistakes. It's time to build yourself back up and heal.

THE POWER IN A DECISION

The moment that you make a 'final' decision, the universe will start to rearrange itself in accordance to the choice that you have made. There is an unseen power in making a decision. When you decide that you're going to do something or be something (not from a place of pushing against what is, but from an approach such as 'I am going to do this' or 'I know that I can do this') things start changing. Making a decision from a place of 'I'm not sure' isn't going to change anything. It is your certainty and faith in yourself, your abilities and that end result that gets things moving. Get clear on what you want and what you're going to do and start making those 'big' decisions. Until you decide, nothing changes.

CAN'T RUSH DIVINE TIMING

You can't rush divine timing, all great things take time. When you try and force something into being, especially before it is ready, it often ends up not being worth it, simply because your desires didn't have enough time to fully develop. When you force something, it never ends up being what you deserve or what you are looking for. Your desires only ever feel like they are taking a long time to manifest when you think that it has to happen fast or happen your way, and especially when you're still waiting for them to manifest for you to be happy. The ego always thinks that it is taking too long. Please understand that the universe is not working on your time scale. We all have our own perfect timing. Divine timing looks different to everyone. The universe will bring the opportunities and events into your reality in divine order, not a moment too late or a second too early. Be OK with this process. Until you accept and allow perfect timing to do its job, you'll tend to constantly focus upon the lack in your life and your current environment, and consistently ask yourself 'Why aren't my desires here?' and 'Where are they?', unaware that doing that will continue to block the blessings and miracles that were just about to unfold. You'll end up holding them back even longer. Focussing upon lack won't bring you abundance, happiness or peace. Allow 'what is' and how it looks. Remember that it is here for a reason. Instead of wishing it away, make the most out of it.

SNAP

Have you ever played the card game 'snap'? Imagine that life is just like that card game. If you haven't heard of that card game, I'll summarise it for you. The aim of that game is for each person to put out a card until there is a match, which when you see it, you put your hand down on top of the cards and shout 'snap' and you win the game. Think of life being just like that game, however every single card that you put out the universe shouts 'snap' to, it's always a match, however you always win. So what cards have you been putting out lately? The victim card? The 'poor me' card? Or are you putting out the self empowered card? The cards that you choose to put out and put down the universe will continue to match you with. There will always be a match until you change which cards you're putting out. When you change the cards that you're dealing, life will begin to respond. However it takes some time, so be patient. In time, once you have lifted yourself up, the cards will begin to match that improvement. Soon the cards that you put out and what you get back will be in alignment, and you'll be able to shout 'snap' and win the game.

I WON'T DO WHAT THEY DID

When we experience something painful and traumatic in our past environment, we often promise ourselves that, 'I'm not going to do what they did'. However when you do that, you unknowingly make that thought and painful experience your point of focus. That is where your energy and attention is focussed, and that will be the frequency that you will reside at in regards to that thing or experience. That is where your intention is formed, which will determine the energy that will flow into it, which ultimately determines the experience that you will have with it. So when you say 'I'm not going to do what they did', that means at some level you are still focussing upon it or resisting what was or how it feels, which will continue to create even more of that (or how that feels) in your future. In addition, your resistance against the past or how it made you feel, ultimately causes it to persist in your reality. It is important that you start afresh, simply focussing upon what you do want without viewing it in relation to the past or through a filter or definition. This isn't about ignoring, denying or pushing against the past, it is simply about affirming the future. When you accept the past, you won't feel the need to 'beat' it. You will be able to overcome it and move beyond it to that which you desire and prefer to experience. When you acknowledge 'what was' and how you feel about it, you will begin to open up a space which will allow you to learn from that painful past without making the pain the focus. You will be able to grow from and move beyond what they did or what they failed to do, and you'll be able to do it all from a place of peace rather than pain. You will be able to end the cycle of hurt and have the power to start a new cycle of healing, peace and power.

COURAGE

Courage is making a decision to no longer allow your first reaction of fear or pain to stop you from saying, doing and becoming that which is in alignment with your best self and your best life. Courage (and bravery) are in essence, fear management. Courage is no longer allowing fear to control you or your destiny. Everyone experiences fear at some point and to some level, however courage is choosing how you interpret and use those feelings of fear. Courage is answering your heart's call. It is following your heart in spite of your fears. Courage is the bridge between the life that you have and the life that you said you wanted, which is the life that is waiting for you. Courage is consistently choosing to bravely follow your heart in spite of appearances, it is embracing the vulnerability of being authentic and being yourself and doing what is right even when it is not the popular opinion. It is embracing change instead of running away or hiding from it. Courage is choosing discomfort in the moment while cultivating the strength, confidence and determination to live your truth and speak your truth no matter what or who you face. Courage will allow you to stand up and speak out when it matters the most. Courage is the act of casting aside fear and fully embracing love.

PROBLEMS
Problems aren't here to define you, they are here to simply help you to define yourself, to make you into the person that you need to be in order for you to do the work that you're here to do. Problems don't happen because you weren't thinking positively enough or because you have done something wrong, they have purpose. Problems are opportunities for you to know yourself better, to know your strength, to better yourself, to redefine yourself, to try again and to lead and inspire you to even greater. Everything that occurs in your life is leading you towards something greater. Problems are therefore chances for you to practise those lessons that you already know (but haven't yet applied in your own life) as well as being opportunities for you to be your best self and to do your best. Each problem is an opportunity for you to learn a new lesson that will help you to succeed at the highest level. Don't get lost in the problem, or how that problem feels or looks, rise above it all. Rise up to the frequency that the solutions reside at by centring yourself. From there everything will become that much more clearer to you.

THE NEED TO APPEAR PERFECT
Perfection isn't something that you can achieve, it isn't a result. Trying to be perfect and appear like you have it all together is the biggest weakness, not the greatest strength (don't confuse perfection with doing your best or expecting the best from yourself). Seeking perfection is the ego, it stems from the feeling of not being enough, and from the feeling that you have to prove yourself, it originates from fear and pain. Be yourself, be the best version of yourself, that is enough. Please understand that seeking validation or praise for your 'perfection', is often fear (and a lack of self acceptance, self worth and self belief) in disguise. Until you see the perfection that already exists within you, you

will spend your entire life chasing it and trying to emulate it on the outside.

YOUR POSITIVE THINKING NOT WORKING?
Just because you can't see the reality or results that you desire doesn't mean that they aren't on their way to you. Your thinking positively has worked and is continuing to work, it just takes time for it to come into focus and for it to appear in your environment. Until then detach, let go and allow. Let go of the hidden resistance. Don't allow yourself to get distracted or caught up fighting against how things currently look to you from the frequency that you're currently residing at. Look beyond 'what is', see through it, rise up. When you see through it, you will see it through. Have faith that miracles are about to unfold in every single area of your life. You have no idea the size of the blessing that the universe is holding on reserve just for you.

THEIR WAY WON'T WORK FOR YOU
We all have our own journeys to success and 'enlightenment'. Don't make the mistake of trying to recreate other people's miracles in your own life. We often think that it's what they did physically that caused those incredible results and success, when in reality it was what was going on energetically and internally that caused it. When you find yourself trying to recreate someone else's path to success, recognise it as an indication to step back and let go. Relax, trust, centre yourself and let your own path reveal itself in time.

THE WINDOW TO THE WORLD
Your beliefs become the window in which you see the world from. It becomes the lens in which you see and filter all things and all people through. It's important to find out whether or not your own lens is clouded or distorted, as what you believe and expect to see you will make real (which will become your reality). Ultimately you can only ever see that which you're looking for. The lens in which you see things from and through will continue

to provide you with proof of that which you already believe to be true. You won't see things as they really are, but as you believe them to be. Until you change the lens in which you're seeing all things from, including how you're seeing yourself and your desires, things can't change. When you change the perspective that you're seeing everything from, everything changes.

HELP RATHER THAN JUST SUPPORTING YOUR FRIENDS

Real friends support and encourage each other to grow, they seek open and honest communication with each other and they make each other aware by telling the 'truth' even when it is not the popular opinion. They seek to deliver the truth from a place of love (not to instil shame, guilt or pain) but with the intention of enlightening and lifting them up. Being a friend doesn't mean that you have to support everything that someone does, but that you support their overall growth and well being. Support their ventures, yet don't be afraid to make them aware when what they're doing isn't in alignment with or a reflection of who they really are. If they can't receive your advice, let them be, they might have to learn it their own way and in their own time which is perfectly OK too. Be there to assist and support them, if and when they're ready to grow.

THE INTENTION OF THE QUESTION

How you ask a question has a direct affect on the result that you will receive back. Before every question that you ask, find out what is the intention of that question, and find out which vibrational place it is being asked from. For example, two people can ask the exact same question, such as 'How can I do this?'. The first person could ask the question from the feeling place of openness, they could say it asking for guidance from a place of little to no resistance, and from a place of peace and power. That person is open and able to receive a solution and answer that will help them. However the other person who asks the same question yet who asks it from a place of fear, panic, frustration and desperation, will get a very different response back. Although they've asked the exact same question, the answer that they'll receive will be very different. It's important therefore to understand that it's not the questions that we ask or the words that we use that are important, but the vibrational place that we are asking them from that truly matters. Although they asked the exact same question they had two very different energies and intentions behind their questions, which can only ever bring back two very different results. It is always the intention, feeling and energy behind the question that matters and not the actual words that you speak. It is 'how' and 'why' you do what you do that creates the results. It is not what you say, but how and why you say it that truly matters. The power of the entire universe flows through your thoughts, feelings, intentions and decisions. Always find out which frequency you're asking your questions from.

WHY 'I AM' MATTERS
Ultimately we are what we imagine and believe ourselves to be. That is why 'I am' statements are so powerful. You are what you say you are. You will become the person who you feel and believe yourself to be right now. You are 'attracting' (or more accurately allowing) into your life and consciousness that which is on the same frequency as you, which is often based on who you feel and believe yourself to be right now (or who you already are or were in the past). If you believe that you are a successful person, or a person of success, you will help to allow into your conciousness and reality, successful ideas or those results that feel like that success. However when you feel that you are poor or that you're someone that has to struggle to get what they desire, then that is what you'll get back, all those ideas and situations that will confirm that poverty and struggle to you. Everything is 'attracted' to you based on the person that you think, feel and believe that you are now. That is why self belief, self confidence and self acceptance are so important to your overall success. Whoever you think, feel and believe yourself to be today, is who you will become tomorrow. See yourself as the person that you're becoming before you 'become it'. Speak from there, feel from

206

that place, think from that space. Incorporate a belief system that supports the person that you're becoming, rather than a belief system that just repeats the perspective and thoughts of who you were (which would resist and deflect the results that you ultimately desire). You have got to give up seeing yourself and others as they were. Remember that you are not a victim of the past, you are the creator of your own reality and future, and you create that future now. Be who you prefer to be, rather than being the person that your past made you into. Be a winner, think, feel and act from that place now. Say it with faith and power. Always remember that you are creating your reality moment by moment based on who you feel you are, when you change today, everything changes.

OTHER PEOPLE'S OPINIONS OF ME
Everyone will have an opinion about you, but don't let that stop you from living. Their opinion of you is based on their own frequency and rarely has anything to do with you or that which you do. They can only see you from their limited perspective, which is just a reflection of themselves and their own frequency. When someone has a negative opinion about you (that isn't based on facts) they're really only ever showing you who they are and what they think, feel and believe (often about themselves). They're not telling you who you are, they're just showing you who they are. What they reject in you is often what they're silently rejecting in themselves (or what others have rejected in them). They're projecting pain and self hate, and are operating from the level of fear. Rise above it all.

CAN'T FACE IT?
That which you are afraid of facing is never as bad as it first seems. It only looks and feels that way because of the perspective that you're looking at it and yourself from. From there you can only ever see more perspectives that are similar to how you're already seeing things. You can't see things clearly from that lower frequency. Only when you're at peace can you begin to see things

as they really are and allow things to reveal themselves to you, rather than allowing your expectations and lower perspective to draw a particular 'negative' behaviour out from them. When you move through that which is holding you back, you free yourself, and you release that which was stopping you from recognising and accessing the peace that was within you all along. You release the resistance against that which was holding back your blessings and joy.

THE UNIVERSE'S JOB

It isn't your job to create the way that your desires will manifest, that's the universe's job. Let the universe handle the precise details of when, where and how it will all manifest. Get out of the way. All you need to do is 'allow' it in, you don't have to 'attract' it in. It isn't your job to create the result, opportunity and success that you desire, your only job is to imagine, believe and feel the reality of that which you desire which will begin to allow it in, and you do that best by being on the same frequency that it resides at. Please release all the blame, guilt and shame that you have been carrying with you because your desires haven't shown up yet. Release all the stress and struggle to create the results that you desire. When you think that you have got to struggle to succeed then you will, when you think that you're going to have to fight against life and struggle to find the opportunities for success then that is exactly what will happen, when you think of life as being hard then it will be. Don't make life any harder than it needs to be. What you think, feel and believe to be true, will be reflected back to you, in order for you to see it and change it if it is not what you desire or prefer to experience. Release all that strain and pressure to make anything happen. Surrender all control and let the universe do its job. Relax and get into a place of allowing. When you step back and 'allow' you will begin to allow in that which is trying to get to you. 'Allowing' is just complete acceptance, it is surrendering and faith in action. So relax, allow, trust and have faith that the universe is bringing you where you need to be and when you need to be there, and that it won't happen a second too late or a moment too early, all in divine timing.

YOUR DESIRES ARE HERE
The universe is responding to your desire for more every single second of the day. It is waiting patiently for you to get into alignment with how those desires feel, for you to vibrate at the frequency that they reside at, in essence waiting for you to become the person who is able to open up and receive them. When you are consistently only focussing upon getting something, and you are vibrating at the level of how it feels to not have it, or at the frequency of how it feels to be a person who hasn't got their desires, you're unable to receive your highest blessings which reside at the frequency of abundance. Open up that space and let them in. Every single day the universe is giving you what you desire in subtle little ways. It often gives you what you desire in a disguise, especially when you have so many blocks in the way, so that you won't cheat yourself out of it. It will often place opportunities that will eventually lead to your desires fulfilment in your current environment, to primarily see if fear will stop you again. Don't worry if you have allowed your fears to stop you from acting upon those impulses (to go somewhere or to do something). The universe will continue to bring your desires back around in another disguise so that you can try again. You can't miss what is meant for you.

IT'S THE THOUGHT THAT COUNTS
We often hear the phrase that it's the thought that counts, and although the thought truly does count, it is the feeling and the faith that is placed within that thought that gives the thought its power supply. Without the feeling, the thought is less 'powerful'. Thoughts and feelings work side by side they're reflections of each other. Often when we focus upon a feeling we vibrate at that frequency which naturally and automatically begins to 'attract' and allow in even more thoughts that feel like that into our consciousness and our awareness. In addition when you focus

upon a particular thought you will begin to reveal the frequency or perspective that you're seeing things from, you will also begin to feel and generate an emotion within you, which is 'energy in motion', which will begin to automatically and naturally 'attract' and allow in even more thoughts that feel like that, all of which ultimately acts like a self perpetuating cycle. The cycle which goes as follows, your thoughts affect (and can determine) your feelings, which are also a reflection and a manifestation of your feelings or frequency, and your feelings 'attract' and allow in similar feeling thoughts and perspectives which will in turn determine your feelings, all of which affects your overall state of being and what you're 'attracting' or more accurately allowing into your reality. However please don't worry about 'negative' thoughts, as thoughts without your attention, have no real creative power. Your thoughts need your attention and awareness to stick around. So although it is the thought that counts, it is the feeling that really matters, and when you gently and consistently focus your attention and awareness upon thoughts and feelings that are closer in alignment with who you really are (which are thoughts and feelings which empower you, such as joy, love and peace) the self perpetrating cycle begins to help bring you even higher and higher.

HIGHER SELF LEAD THE WAY
Your higher self knows exactly what you desire to have, to be, to do, to see, to become, and to achieve and receive. So let it direct your path. There is no point in trying to struggle and force things into being. There is no need to stress or worry about what you should do next or where you should go, just let your inner spirit and higher self lead the way. Let things unfold naturally for you, trust and listen to the guidance that your higher self is bringing you. Hand over any stresses or struggles to the universe or your higher self. Release the need to try and make things happen, there is no need to try and do the universe's work, let it create the way and arrange how your desires look and when they'll arrive (just as long as you keep meeting the universe half way). Release

the attachment to the strain and struggle of success. Step back, let go and allow. Let your higher self rearrange the path and your desires, let it sort them out and bring everything together. Learn to have a 'care less' attitude. Trust that your higher self is on it. When you ease up, relax and care less about 'how' and 'when' your desires have to manifest, you will begin to allow them in. You will begin to release the resistance and go with the flow. Follow the care less approach, it's careless to do anything else.

DEALING WITH LONELINESS

Being alone and being lonely are two very different things. Being alone and having your own alone time is critical to your overall well being and growth, it is necessary for your own stability and inner peace. However being lonely and feelings of loneliness can be very damaging and isolating. Loneliness can cause you to 'fall off track'. It can cause you to go back to your old ways of seeing and doing things. Loneliness can cause you to make irrational decisions, such as choosing a relationship not out of love, but out of pain or fear (in essence doing it to 'numb' the inner pain). That intention or reason for choosing a relationship isn't to grow or because it would ultimately empower or uplift them, but because they can't face being alone or having to face their own feelings. Only someone who doesn't know themselves fully will feel that they aren't 'enough' being alone. Any time that you feel alone, connect to the energy that is within you.

DISCOMFORT ZONE

Get out of that comfort zone, or more accurately 'discomfort zone'. That discomfort zone has nothing new to teach you, it is made up of old beliefs, perspectives, feelings and experiences of who you were. That comfort zone feels so comfortable to you simply because it is resonating at the same frequency that you have been vibrating at in regards to yourself and that which you're facing. We often think that it is keeping us safe when in reality it is holding us hostage. It only feels safe in comparison to the unfamiliar vibration of that which you are about to face. That 'discomfort zone' is not a castle, it is a prison. It is called the discomfort zone, because only someone who is in discomfort needs a 'comfort zone' to feel safe and at peace. Real and lasting feelings of peace can only be found within yourself and within the present moment. In order for you to get something different you are going to have to do something different. You are never going to find lasting or authentic happiness in your 'comfort zone'.

BREAK DOWN YOUR GOALS

Break your goals down into small bite-size pieces. When you first begin working towards any 'big' goal it can often leave you feeling overwhelmed. From that perspective you will often want to walk away or give up. However when you break down your goals and dreams, they will seem that much more manageable to you. The energy that you will then approach them with will be one that assists you and empowers you, rather than one that holds you back. If you approached your goals from the energy of, 'This is too big' or 'I can't do this' or 'I'm not sure I'm ready', that energy is what flows into that which you're doing and stops you from receiving the ideas and perspectives that would help bring it to its highest potential. You would be unconsciously limiting what it can become before you even begin. In addition that 'negative' and fear based approach will stop you from receiving the results that you're seeking. It's important that you learn to step into the 'feeling state' of the end result. When you break down your goals and take action on those smaller bite-sized pieces in faith (knowing your greatness and knowing that you're being led to even better and that the universe is right there with you every single step of the way) things will begin to flow with ease. Step into the end state by contemplating what you would do, how you would feel and how you would act if you knew that you already had that which you desire now? Think, act and feel from that place. When you remove your attention from those lack based thoughts or perspectives for just long enough, you will stop persisting the reality of its absence and begin to allow it in.

LOVE WHAT YOU DESIRE

What do you want most of all? What do you desire with your entire being? That which you desire is calling you to love it unconditionally, and to move from desiring it to feeling unconditional love for it. What you desire is always an indication to start loving it. Desire is a creative force, however instead of wanting something, show it love. When you allow yourself to feel love for what you desire, it begins to reflect that love back to you. Love yourself, love your desires, show everything unconditional love. Love and appreciate what you have (please note that this isn't about loving situations that you don't want, just accept and allow those). In addition you can't receive love from that which you desire when you hate those who have it. The frequencies aren't in harmony with each other. You can't hate something for them, but love it for you. In addition, you can't fear something and love it at the same time, the most consistent feeling always wins. Remember that the universe is responding to and reflecting back that which you feel and believe most to be true regarding yourself and all things. You help to create the life that you desire by focussing your feelings of love. When you observe that which you desire from a place of love, joy and appreciation, and you contemplate it from a loving gratitude and appreciation, it helps to draw it even closer to you and into your current reality. The moment that you desire something with your entire being, switch to feeling and believing that you have it, feel that desire turn into love for it now. Love it with your whole heart, unconditionally, whether you have it or not. Sadly most people never even allow themselves to want or desire something. They cast those feelings off, feeling and believing that it's impossible or that it is not meant for them simply because it never happened before (unaware that it is their faith in that lack based perspective that is stopping them from having that which they desire). Always remember that your desires will appear in your consciousness and reality the way that you have been viewing them most often and how you have been feeling about them now. Have you been viewing that which you desire from a place of abundance and from feelings of love or from feelings of (and faith in) lack? Let yourself love it, as that is showing the universe your preference regarding that situation or thing. Your love for it calls it even closer to you. The love that you place in it will be reflected back from it. Finally focus upon showing yourself unconditional love, until you do, that which you love can't get to you since the frequencies aren't in alignment with each other. When you love yourself and your desires unconditionally, miracles occur.

USE YOUR VOICE

Bring the darkness within you out and into the light. Speak your truth, speak out even if your voice trembles and your legs shake. What you witnessed, experienced and endured had purpose, it all was necessary in order for you to help spark the need for things to change. Stand on the shoulders of those brave souls who came before you and speak out. Release any shame or guilt within you and use that energy to help change things for the better. Before you came into this life you understood that you would have to walk through the darkness so that no one else would have to face it again. Looking back you will see clearly that what you previously believed was sent to destroy you, was really sent to liberate you and all others. Use your voice and speak your truth. You are needed.

A BROKEN RELATIONSHIP VS AN UNHEALTHY ONE

It is important that we recognise the difference between a broken relationship and an unhealthy or toxic one. A relationship broken by poor communication or unconscious behaviour can of course be fixed and will often improve with effort, open and honest communication and commitment from both individuals. A broken relationship can inspire and encourage healing and can drastically improve when each individual faces their own issues, feelings and pain instead of running away or blaming each other (and especially once both partners have worked on themselves first and have committed themselves to doing the necessary healing and inner work). That type of relationship can help us to grow, however an unhealthy relationship won't. Things never really change or improve in that type of relationship, promises are meaningless and empty, and 'love' is only ever fleeting and temporary. Trying to fix an unhealthy relationship is always dangerous. Sadly too many people convince themselves that a toxic relationship is just a broken one, and that it's worth saving, or worth saving over themselves. They often commit themselves to keeping that unhealthy and harmful relationship alive (often from fear, believing that it is the source of their worth, validation and happiness, and the only 'love' that they'll ever receive) when they should instead be focussing that time, effort and energy upon fixing and loving themselves fully and unconditionally.

ABANDON YOUR PLANS

Goals help to give us something concrete to aim at and focus upon. They give us something to believe in and something to move and work towards. They allow us to believe in ourselves, which helps to inspire us to take action and call into our reality everything that feels like that. However please understand that the universe always has a bigger plan for your life. Leave enough room for that divine plan to unfold. Your plans should always be abandoned (or at the very least be modified) for greater when it comes along. When you think that your plans and goals are better than the universe's plans, and when you need things to go your way only, you cut yourself off from letting in even better. Leave enough room for serendipity to occur. Go with the flow. See and follow the 'bread crumbs' of the universe. Ask the universe for more, and to always lead you towards even greater. Say 'if not this, then something better'. Always remain open and able to receive even greater. However please understand that planning for success is so important. Planning allows you to get into the 'end state' and embody how that success feels now, which will begin to allow in ideas, people and things that will take you to success. Getting into that end state ultimately calls you forward and towards a result and reality that feels like that.

TICK OR TOCK?

If you have a ticking clock near you (that makes a ticking sound) take a listen to it now, what sound does it make? A 'tick' and then a 'tock' sound? Or maybe you hear a tick, tick, or a tock, tock sound? Things change and sound different according to what we expect to hear. Listen to that clock again and expect to hear 'tick, tock' and more than likely you will, and then take another listen expecting to hear 'tick, tick', and in time you will. This is a prime example of how our attention and expectation changes what and how we experience something, which is the exact same way that we affect our own reality. Start expecting the best, anticipate it, know that you will see it. Direct your attention and awareness upon greater, and just watch what happens in time.

SHOWER AND STREAM OF BLESSINGS

Imagine that right now there is an abundant and never ending stream of blessings being showered down upon you. When you are in a state of complete allowing, the energy and love of the entire universe can flow through you unrestricted, however when you begin to consistently focus upon something that brings you down (or more accurately takes you out of that stream) the blessings can't flow through you like they once could. They can now only trickle in. However the moment that you step back into the stream (by taking your attention and awareness of that which caused you to step out of the stream, and you begin to refocus upon genuine feelings of joy, peace, gratitude and love) you will begin to open up and allow in the stream again. You will begin to go with the flow once more.

EVOLVE INTO GREATNESS

Life is a never ending process of change and evolution, every single day you are learning and growing into an even more actualised and complete picture of your highest self. However in order to do that, it is necessary to let go of what you are conscious of being in order to allow yourself to focus upon what

216

you desire to become. You've got to let go of the old story in order to write a new one. Begin by letting go of who you think you need to be, who you were and what you believed was possible for you. See beyond your past and your current environment. When you let go of 'what is' you allow yourself to be 'born again' as the person that you desire to be, which is the person that you're destined to become. Continue to remake and redefine yourself in the vision and name of greatness.

I SHOULD BE 'X' BY NOW
Are you still subtly comparing yourself to others? Maybe you're stuck in the mindset of comparing your results to someone else's results, e.g. that someone else achieved 'X' by your age? That sort of thinking keeps you stuck in a cycle of guilt and shame, and continues to separate you from your blessings. It will keep you small. Understand that everyone has their own journey which always unfolds in divine timing, and not in our timing, fundamentally there is purpose to the wait. It is time to think and look again from a higher perspective. Remember, there is no time limit attached to your true purpose.

STEP BY STEP
Just as a journey of a thousand miles begins by taking one step forward, the changes that you desire to see in your life will begin to come into your reality by taking that first step in the right direction. Every moment that you make the conscious choice, effort and decision to keep on moving in the direction of who you're becoming, things begin to change. It doesn't matter how long you have been going in the 'wrong' direction for, the moment that you get back on course things start to change. Have the inner strength to consciously and consistently choose to step in the 'right' direction even when things don't look like they're changing much, even when your fears are giving you a thousand reasons not to act, and even when it feels like those changes that you desire are still a million miles away. Every single step in the right direction adds up. Day by day you will get closer to your

blessings and your best self. However if you allow yourself to get caught up looking at what you did wrong, where you are currently 'stuck' or where you still need to go, you will not only give your attention to not being there (which will perpetuate it) however you will also tend to want to turn around and give up. You can't see where you are going when you are constantly looking behind you. Try and focus instead upon your next step, rather than the whole journey, you will find that much easier to do. All of the greatest changes are applied step by step, moment by moment, thought by thought, and not all in one go, so go easy on yourself.

FLIP THE SCRIPT

Many of us are still unknowingly playing the victim in subtle little ways, either by believing that we are a victim of the past, of the present, or a victim of circumstance. When you define yourself as being a victim at any level (or you hold onto that mentality) it often becomes your reality. Just like a character in a movie, if you see yourself as being a victim that will become the storyline and script that your life will follow. The universe is always taking its cue from you. The script is being written by your most consistent thoughts, feelings, intentions, beliefs and your current and most consistent sense of self. 'Flip the script', see yourself as a winner and watch what happens.

WHAT IS MEDITATION?

Meditation isn't about going within to escape life, it is about going within to connect to the true essence of life and who you really are. It is not about avoiding your feelings, but allowing them and letting them be, which begins to let them go. You don't need to silence the mind, but allow it to silence itself. Meditation is about grounding yourself in the present moment and allowing what is ready to reveal itself to you to come to the surface and let itself out when it's ready to. All we need to do is hold that space for it to happen, and we can do that by being aware of what comes into our awareness and viewing it from a place and space of unconditional love and allowing. Meditation is not about making anything happen but allowing it to naturally happen by itself. Meditation allows you to acknowledge and process your feelings with clarity and from a higher perspective and a place of non resistance. It allows you to have a clearer understanding of why those thoughts and feelings are there and what they are blocking, resisting or persisting within you. When you meditate into the peace that is within you, you allow yourself to go beyond your current reactions and reality. You begin to remove any resistance that is holding back your peace and preventing you from consistently feeling your inner power, which is who you really are. You don't need to do anything to feel your inner peace. This is not about doing more, it is often about thinking less. All you need to do is take your attention and awareness of anything that is holding you back from feeling and recognising your inner peace and power in the moment. When you meditate you begin to understand that you aren't your thoughts and feelings, that you are the presence that is aware of them. In addition, meditation allows what is best for you and for all others to unfold from within, it allows insight to come forth and assist you (which is hence why it is called insight, it comes from looking within). Meditation also allows you to respond to life. It puts the power back into your hands to choose again from a place of peace, power and purpose.

"HURT PEOPLE"

It is often said that "hurt people, hurt people", however that isn't necessarily the full truth. Just because someone has been hurt badly in the past doesn't mean that they can't love others deeply and fully in the present, they are in fact the people who often love others deeply. However until they are conscious of their own pain (and they begin to acknowledge, accept and allow it and release it) they will tend to either let it hold them back or cause them to tear others down. Having an awareness of what we're doing and why we're doing it helps to bring us higher. Unconscious and unhealed pain gives birth to the term, 'hurt people, hurt people'. We should instead say, "hurt people have been hurt by people". Once you begin to love and accept yourself fully and treat yourself better, you can then begin to treat others that way too.

ATTITUDE DETERMINES ALTITUDE

A simple fact in life is that your attitude helps to determine your altitude, and your outlook also helps to determine your income. Your attitude or your mood is critical to your overall success. When you have a positive attitude you will begin to allow in thoughts, feelings, opportunities and things that reside on that higher frequency. When you are 'higher up', problems will look much smaller to you from there. You can begin to see the full picture from that higher frequency, as you're not so close up to the issue any more or how it makes you feel, you will have gained perspective and distance from it. The ability to determine your own attitude regardless of 'what is', will be one of the strongest skills that you could ever develop. It will cause you to be a conscious creator of life rather than a helpless spectator of it.

CAN'T REMEMBER THE LOVE?

Often after times of major loss, such as the death of a loved one, we tend to believe that we will never be happy again or ever feel love, peace or joy again. I promise you that you will feel all of those things again, however it often takes time to reach that stage. Until then, feel the loss, embrace it. The grief that you feel is often just a sign of how deeply you have loved someone. In time the good memories will come back and the painful memories will slowly begin to fade away. The pain will fade and what you'll be left with is the love that you both shared and the brightest and most colourful memories that you both made together. It is often said that grief is only love with nowhere to go, so instead of holding onto that love, send and direct it to them. They will most definitely feel it. Grief is a reminder to look again, primarily to remember that love lasts forever. Understand that the love that you feel for your departed loved one strengthens the communication and spiritual bond between you both. Most people will never experience the love that you both shared. It is truly a blessing to have had such a bond in the first place. You will smile and laugh again in time, and you will feel and find peace again, and when you do, they'll be right there with you in spirit. There is no need to feel guilty about 'moving on', in essence you're not moving on, you're moving forward with them in another form. No matter what you do or where you go, they will be right there beside you encouraging you and lighting up the path ahead. They want you to be happy, because when you feel good you will automatically begin to vibrate at the frequency which they reside at, which will allow you to open up and communicate directly with them.

FOR-GIVING

Forgiveness is for-giving, for giving to yourself and to others in order for you to heal and move on. You don't forgive by fighting against or focussing upon the problem, situation or event (or by focussing upon how that feels) but by embracing the solution. Forgiving someone or something doesn't mean that you're saying that it's OK that it happened, however it is saying, OK it happened and I refuse to allow that to hurt me any longer, or separate me from love, who I really am and the life that I desire. Forgiveness frees you, it is claiming back your power, and making your happiness and peace a priority again.

RUNNING AWAY FROM YOUR FEELINGS?

It is important that we face our feelings instead of continuing to run away from them. Running away from uncertainty, uncomfortable feelings or situations which frighten you, won't keep you safe. What you're really doing is running away from your growth. Feeling uncomfortable is often the first stage of growth. What you're avoiding and running away from will ultimately continue to come back around in another disguise until you finally 'get it' and you apply that lesson in your own life. Hold yourself accountable for facing your fears, for choosing what happens next and for facing the lesson and uncovering the blessing that is hidden within it.

YOU WON'T ACHIEVE EVERY RESULT

You are not meant to achieve every goal, some goals are only meant to get you moving. They're only something to aim for, something that keeps you moving so that you can reach the point where 'fate' and the universe can intervene and lead you to even better. That is why flexibility is key. Stay open and aware for those opportunities and people that come onto your path and into your life. Be open and flexible in your plans and approach to your goals and desires with the faith that the universe will at times intervene and lead you to even greater. Knowing this, if things don't happen the way that you have planned, or they don't go the way that you had expected or preferred them to go, you will be able to allow it and let it go knowing at the deepest level that it's only happening because you are meant for more, and that even better and greater is currently on its way to you.

ACTION IS FAITH IN MOTION

What you continue to act upon will bring back even more of the same, just like an object in motion stays in motion. Ask yourself what beliefs and actions did you focus upon and add momentum to today? Action is in essence, faith in motion. What we tend to take action towards is what we are most sure of. When you take action towards anything you are combining and solidifying your current feelings, faith and beliefs, which is a powerful force. What you act upon you are showing the universe, at an energetic level that 'this is what I believe most to be true and what I want more of'. Your action towards anything shows your commitment towards and preference for what you desire. Only take action towards that which you prefer. Instead of choosing the less painful option, start moving towards and taking action upon your goals. When you do, the universe will begin to meet you half way. In time you will begin to allow your actions to be inspired by what you are focussing upon and moving towards, which will be your highest success and best life.

CONTROLLING YOUR THOUGHTS?

Inner peace is not achieved by controlling your thoughts, but by controlling which thoughts you give your attention and awareness to. There is no need to monitor each thought, and ask yourself, "Am I feeling nervous?" or "Is that a negative thought?". Doing that calls those type of thoughts and feelings into your awareness. Your expectation of there being a 'negative' thought or feeling in your awareness causes them to appear, you are calling them in. Give up constantly monitoring your thoughts and instead allow whatever thoughts are passing through your mind to move on. Don't give into them or hold onto them. Acknowledge them and then let them go. Remove your attention and awareness from them. There is no need to fear, push away, work out or analyse any 'negative' thoughts or feelings either, let them be, centre yourself and choose peace again.

NEVER RESPOND IN ANGER

Never react in a moment of anger, as that will only ever create a result that feels like that anger. The intention for doing something, and the energy that you bring to it always directly affects and determines the outcome. Anger solves nothing and destroys everything. The moment that you raise your voice, you will always lower your argument, your point and your vibration and cut yourself off from receiving all that you desire, including peaceful solutions. Step back, centre yourself and respond from a place of love, compassion and empathy.

FEAR FAILURE?

One of the biggest obstacles that prevents us from taking action towards our dreams is the fear of failure. Ultimately it is not that we fear failing, it is just that we fear failing publicly. We are often afraid of looking stupid, afraid of looking not good enough or afraid of appearing not strong enough. However please understand that those type of thoughts are always thoughts of the ego and manifestations of a lower frequency and perspective. Someone who knows their true inner power and worth, and centres their being there, won't allow the thought of one 'small' or 'big' failure stop them from trying. They ultimately know that failure is guidance from the universe, and that it is often the method in which the universe redirects us towards an even better way. Only someone who operates from the level of the ego seeks to win all of the time and fears embarrassing themselves or looking like they aren't in control of their own life. Risk the humiliation, it is always worth it. Often when you risk nothing, you risk losing everything that you have dreamed of and worked towards.

STOP EXPLAINING YOURSELF

Please give up trying to explain yourself to everyone. Not everyone is going to (or even wants to) understand, like, or 'get' you. Everyone that you encounter isn't going to understand what you do or what you like, and that is perfectly OK. You don't need to be understood by anyone but yourself. Only an ego seeks and needs to be understood, respected or admired. Not everyone needs to understand or respect your decisions or your choices. Don't fall into the trap of believing that you have to justify or constantly explain and defend yourself either, especially justifying any decision that serves your greater good. You don't owe anyone an explanation, if they ask for one, just summarise it in a simple sentence such as, "It no longer serves me" or "I'm choosing me". There should be no guilt in choosing to empower yourself, or making decisions that support the person that you are becoming.

JUST DO YOUR BEST

All you can do is your best. Some days doing your best is getting out of bed, other days it could be running a marathon. Doing your best isn't always going to look the same, and it isn't always about giving things your all, sometimes it is just giving what you can and doing what you're able to do right now. That is all that is needed, just do your best. Give up measuring your success or failure in results too, measure your success by whether or not you're currently doing your best and giving things your best effort, and whether or not you're currently doing that which you know that you are capable of doing right now. Your best is always better than nothing at all.

IS THERE AN EQUAL ENERGY EXCHANGE?

Are all of your relationships and interactions an equal one? Of course there will be times when the exchange isn't exactly equal, however overall is there an equal exchange in all of your relationships? Is the amount of support and love that you are giving to someone / something, and the amount of support and love that you're getting back or willing to accept, equal? It is often said that there are two types of people. Those people who draw energy from the room (and the people that are around them) and those people who give that energy back to others. It is important that there is a delicate balance between both of those sides in your own life and in all of your interactions. Don't allow your precious energy to be taken advantage of. People can unconsciously feel your energy. It is important that you protect it from time to time, yet still leave enough room and space for you to receive love and support back too. You don't need to protect yourself from the world, just protect your energy by grounding and centring yourself properly. You deserve to be honoured and respected in all of your relationships. Don't let others leech of your good nature. Find balance or you will end up doing for them that which they fail to do for themselves. Try and aim for an equal energy exchange in all of your relationships and friendships, or you'll end up feeling drained and depleted of energy.

PUT YOURSELF OUT THERE

Serendipity and 'fate' can only occur once you put yourself out there. That job, opportunity, relationship or life that you have been seeking can't find you when you're hiding away from the world. Hiding away in fear won't make anything happen, it won't change things. Trust your greatness, have faith in your abilities, know your worth. Trust that the path will unfold, however that can only happen once you take action and you meet the universe half way. Take that first step and allow 'the way' to appear.

BE IT NOW
It's never too late to become the person that you have always dreamed of becoming. Decide to become that person today, choose it, claim it as who you are right now. Step into that vision with faith. You are more than worthy and capable of living the life that you desire. Recognise and claim that. There are truly no limits to what you can become and what you can achieve (or more accurately receive). The only thing that is holding you back is your current mindset and outlook. Think and look again. Ultimately you can't allow in that which you feel you are not. Until you 'be it' now, you'll never see it 'then'. Your reality is a reflection and an extension of who you already feel and believe you are. It starts and ends with you.

I WANT TO BE LIKED BY EVERYONE
You will never find lasting and authentic self worth, peace or happiness trying to please others or trying to get them to like you or that which you do. One thing that will keep you small and timid is trying to be liked or respected by everyone. That will cause you to water down your personality just to please others, to get their approval or to make them feel safe and secure in your presence. You'll live a life dependant on the approval and validation of other people who probably don't even like themselves. Life just doesn't work that way, not everyone is going to like or understand you or that which you do, sometimes being yourself will upset a few people and that's perfectly OK. But when you validate and like yourself it won't matter.

WHAT DID YOU EXPECT?
What you expect directly affects the result, which is often why you will hear people asking you, 'What did you expect to happen?'. What you expect, you birth into your reality. So what do you expect to happen next? Do you expect to win or lose? How do you

expect your life to turn out? How do you expect others to treat you? What you expect you let into your reality. Only once you get clear on your expectations can you begin to change your life. Your expectations are often a reflection of what you're able to accept and receive. This isn't about expecting anything to feel better, or needing something to finally accept yourself, it is about knowing and claiming your value and worth and having healthy expectations that reflect that. Until you expect more, you'll continue to accept less than you're worth. When you stop accepting less than you're worth, you can start expecting and accepting more.

MAKING BIG CHOICES?
When you are faced with the big choices and questions in life such as what next and where now? Centre yourself, go within and let the answer and guidance reveal itself to you. The answer isn't out 'there', it is within you. Hand over your questions, fears and uncertainties to that presence within you, then detach and allow. That presence not only knows what's next for you, but what is best for you even when you don't. So relax. Know that the universe is 'on it', that it's already done. The answer will appear in your environment in divine timing, which is often when and how you least expect, just as long as you leave enough room to let it in. Make it your duty to stay open and aware.

IT IS NOT FOR YOU
Do you ever find yourself wanting something with every fibre of your being, only to later look back and realise that if you had gotten it you wouldn't have received that which you have right now? That if things had happened the way that you wanted them to go, things wouldn't be as good as they are right now. At times not getting what you want is the biggest blessing and stroke of 'luck', however we can often only see that looking back. Sometimes our desires weren't meant for us, they were only a reflection of the vibration that we were at, and not what was ultimately best for us, let your goals change and evolve as you

grow and as you know yourself to a higher degree. They were likely only desires from your ego, rather than your higher self. Sometimes in life you won't get what you want, because at the core level the universe is protecting you. The real reason why you didn't get what you wanted isn't because you weren't good enough, or because you didn't think 'positively' enough or because you didn't do enough, but because you deserve so much more. Therefore knowing this, if you don't get what you want (be it a relationship with that particular person or that particular job) that only ever means that you deserve better and even more. The universe won't let you do yourself out of even greater. Always be open to more.

FAILURE

How you define failure is key to your overall success. Failure is a symptom of success. Don't take failure personally, it's there to allow you to grow and to better yourself. Give up the idea that you're failing because you're not good enough. Failure isn't a reason to give up, it's just a reminder to try again. It's a sign that you're closer to success than ever before. If you're not failing, then you're not trying anything new. As long as you're still learning from failure that is a sign to keep going.

ANGRY PEOPLE

'Angry people' unconsciously call into their life things, events, and people that will awaken that suppressed, compressed and unexpressed anger within them. They're unconsciously seeking something to be angry at, that will allow them to release all of that anger, frustration and pain that is deep within them that is seeking to be released. At the core level they're vibrating at the frequency of anger, so everything that they see will make them feel that way (as they're viewing life from that lower frequency). An angry person will always have something to be angry at (their expectation helps to call it in too) that is until they express or release that anger in a safe manner. When you're angry you are deflecting the manifestation of every desire and you are pushing away and holding back all of those opportunities that the universe created just for you. If your heart is closed off to love, gratitude and joy you'll never be able to receive your blessings and desires.

I NEED TO SAVE THE WORLD

If you think that the world needs saving and that it is a bad place, then that's how it will appear to you. That will be the filter in which you see the world and other people from. You will seem to continuously 'attract' into your life those events and people that will confirm to you that which you already feel and believe to be true on the inside (that the world is falling apart, that everyone needs your help and it is your job to save others or save the world). You won't be able to be truly and authentically happy when you make it your job and duty to save everyone. You will always see another person or another cause that needs your help. The problems won't seem to end. Every area of your life will end up feeling like that. You will find that everyone that comes into your life and environment will primarily want one thing from you, for you to help or 'save' them. You will 'attract' (or more accurately allow) into your life those people who will rely upon you for everything, or those people that you constantly feel that you need to save, all of which will continue to cut you off from the joy, peace and blessings that you desire and deserve. It will stop you from fulfilling your highest purpose. When you change your definitions, and change how you are seeing the world, others and yourself, and you especially change how you see your role in the world, things will start to change for the better.

PREMONITION

Do you know which frequency you are currently residing at? Those people who consistently reside at high frequencies of joy, love and peace are open to receive information and guidance from the universe and their higher self. Those who are centred on that higher frequency are often the same people who tend to 'feel' that something isn't right. They can at some level feel that something is going to happen before it even happens. Their frequency allowed their inner being (or higher self) to communicate directly with them in the least restricted way. They are able to receive a snippet or an indication of what is about to occur and how to handle it, which others often call intuition or premonition. However don't get intuition confused with your fearful thoughts. Your inner being will always deliver you information when you are at peace, not when you're afraid. Intuition doesn't come from thinking, it comes from allowing. It comes through when you are not thinking. Fearful thoughts and 'what ifs' aren't the truth, they're just manifestations of the frequency that you're currently vibrating at. Intuition comes from within, not from looking on the outside and guessing what is going to happen. Intuition always leaves you with a sense of peace and knowing, fear won't.

STOP WAITING FOR MOTIVATION
Are you waiting to feel motivated before you take action? If you are, you'll be waiting forever. Motivation is overrated. Focus, discipline and dedication are more important than motivation. When you have a goal to focus upon, that energy will pull you forward and open up doors. A goal that you feel empowered by and passionate about will give you drive and direction that motivation can't and won't. At times you'll feel motivated and other times you won't, but focus and dedication will get you moving and allow in the motivation to keep going once you're already 'out there'.

YOU LEARNED CONDITIONAL LOVE
As children we often believe that our parents and those who raised us know everything and that they know better. They are often the authority figure in our life, and at a young age, our only source of information. Unfortunately when they don't know how to love themselves, they often place conditional love upon us. We learn from them how to conditionally love ourselves, including everything and everyone. We learn to see everything through a filter of lack or fear, everything becomes conditional. The belief

that you have to strife and struggle to get anything in life starts to take centre stage. Love will always seem to be limited or lacking in some capacity in your life. When we operate from that level we think, feel and believe that love, peace or happiness is something that we have to get or something that we need to achieve, and therefore something that we can lose. We see love and happiness as being on the outside of ourselves, rather than being within ourselves, which often causes us to either try and impress or please others to get it, or trying to control others and our environment to get that love, validation and worth that we never got growing up, which we still feel we lack within. From that limited perspective, once we get love or happiness, we either end up desperately trying to hold onto it, or we don't know how to handle it, which can cause us to control others and also betray ourselves to try and maintain it. When you let that limited perspective 'be' and you forgive the past and you begin to vibrate higher, you will begin to understand that you don't have to do or be anything to feel the love that is within yourself. You will begin to recognise that all you had to do was remove the conditions that you placed upon yourself in regards to happiness, peace and love. Recognise that any time that you see joy or love as being conditional, that it is the work of the ego, and an indication to step back, centre yourself and think and look again, and most of all to practise self love, self acceptance and self worth.

PAIN IS AN ANCHOR

If a thought doesn't lift you up, empower you and make you feel good when you think of it, let it be, and you'll begin to let it go. Don't analyse, hold onto, fight against, try and fix, or attempt to analyse any of those thoughts. Let them go, only focus upon a thought if you want more of how that thought feels. Imagine that those 'negative' thoughts and feelings, such as anger, are just like an anchor. The longer that you hold onto those thoughts and feelings, the faster and deeper that you will sink down, and the lower that your frequency will become. However the moment that you let that thought go, by removing your attention and awareness from it, you will automatically begin to rise back up to the highest frequencies that your being naturally resides at, you will return to the natural flow of life.

ANOTHER DAY, ANOTHER TRAGEDY

In moments of unimaginable terror and pain your love is needed the most. Love is the most powerful and creative force in the entire universe, one that we all must use to heal and bring peace to those people who need it the most. We can't lose ourselves in the chaos, terror, pain and anger. We have a responsibility not to retaliate with hate, but to respond with love. A heart full of hate and anger has no room for love or healing. That hate and anger truly only affects us, it doesn't affect those who commit those heinous acts of terror. That is exactly what they aim to do, to separate us and take away our peace and love. When fear and evil arises in the world, we must unite, come together, and find and focus upon love.

A BETTER WAY OF SEEING THINGS

It is always healthy and wise to step back from your current way of thinking, seeing and doing things. Standing back allows insight and clarity to show you a better way of operating. In order to do that you need to ask yourself, 'Is the way that I'm currently seeing and doing things a healthy, empowering and stable way of seeing and doing things?'. Ask yourself, 'Could there be another way, an even better way of seeing and doing this? Or an even better way to think about this?'. It is so important that you word the question in a positive context and manner, such as, 'Is there a better way?', rather than, 'What am I doing wrong?', as that would cause the universe to highlight the problems rather than the solutions.

THINK BEFORE ACTING

Are you consciously responding to life, or are you just reacting to 'what is' or what was? When you react to life, what you're unconsciously doing is re-enacting what was and how you felt before, which will often continue to allow in even more of what you don't want. It is necessary to respond to life if things are to be any different. In order for any real change to occur it's necessary to step back and respond to life, and to see beyond 'what is' to the possibilities of what things can become. A great principle to follow is that with new enlightened beliefs, act before you think (so that your lower perspective won't supply you with thoughts that will encourage you to stop, which are just a reflection of how you are used to seeing things, and not reflections of the truth) and with old beliefs think before you act (so that you don't continue to unconsciously react and perpetuate that which you don't want, which would allow you to step back and see things from a higher frequency and perspective, and then allow you to consciously respond to life). Doing that will give you enough time to reflect on whether or not what you're choosing is ultimately helping or hindering you. It will give you the opportunity to respond to life rather than just reacting to it.

ADD TO THEIR PEACE AND HAPPINESS
Today before taking action, making any decisions or saying and doing anything, ask yourself, will this add to the happiness and peace of myself and all others, or will it take away from it? That simple question will keep you grounded, allowing you to do what your higher self would do. By asking yourself, 'Will this truly benefit and help others as well as myself?', you will not only allow in further clarity, however you will also allow in a better course of action.

YOUR TALENT WILL TRIUMPH
Trust that your talent will triumph, that you're destined to win, that people will find your talent, that the way will reveal itself to you and that it's inevitable. Know that with every fibre of your being, understanding that at a vibrational level it has already happened. Silently know that you're a superstar and that you're someone special. Trust and know that no matter what you do or where you go, that the universe favours you. Take action from

that faith. Let any lack based definitions fade away, trust the universe, and let it do its job.

SECRETS?
Secrets don't make you sick, they keep you sick. Secrets close you off from others and from that which is meant for you. Secrets don't keep you or others safe, they keep you in pain. It's so important that we learn to embrace vulnerability and be open with those people who have earned the right to hear our story and our truth. When you hold back and hide your secrets in fear, you not only hold onto that guilt and shame but you allow it to 'fester' and appear elsewhere in your life. It affects everything. Only once you release your secrets can you allow in healing and authentic connection with yourself and others.

STILL COMPARING YOURSELF?
If you are going to have lasting peace and happiness you are going to have to give up comparing yourself to others. Comparing yourself to others is a symptom of believing and feeling that you are not good enough. When you make comparisons you will often unknowingly compare your 'weaknesses' to other people's 'strengths'. You can't see their struggles from that perspective. We all have our own unique strengths and weaknesses, and none of those make us any less or any better than anyone else. No one person is better than any other, only an ego believes that they are. Please give up checking to see if you are better than others or if they are better than you. It isn't helpful. Comparing yourself to others comes from the deep rooted belief that you are not enough, or somehow not good enough, or that you are powerless, unlovable or unworthy. It is important that you detach and focus upon your own journey, rather than looking around at what everyone else has and what you don't have. In addition, give up comparing what they have done and what you haven't done. In life some people will have 'short-cuts' to success and other people will have 'detours', however we all get 'there' eventually ('there' may not even be a physical place, but a place and a state of being

within ourselves). Only ever compare yourself to one thing, and that is whether or not you are currently in alignment with your best and higher self, or the greatest version of yourself.

REPLAYING MISTAKES
Are you still punishing yourself over the same mistakes? Especially over those things that you did when you didn't know any better? Please understand that you couldn't see what you see now, you weren't on the frequency that you are on now, so forgive yourself. There is no benefit in replaying the same story and finding fault, let it be and let it go. Release the guilt and shame associated with the mistakes that you have made in the past. Until you do, that guilt and shame will reappear everywhere else in your life. Mistakes are only 'missed takes', so dust yourself off and try again.

HOW TO CHANGE THE WORLD
The only way that we can 'change the world' is by changing how we see ourselves and how we see others. All lasting change on the outside must first and always begin within. Only once we start to practise more compassion and love with ourselves, can we then begin to be more compassionate and loving with others. That is how you change the world. You change the world by being nicer to yourself first. When we change the lens in which we see ourselves, others and the world from, things start changing for the better and for good.

ANGER ISN'T POWER
Those who are in pain will often use anger and violence as a form of power and control, and as a method to be heard, understood or respected. It is the only way that they can get their voice or 'point' across. From that lower perspective, anger and violence (including shouting, bullying and threatening others) feels like power. Only someone in fear thinks that they need to shout to be finally heard or understood, or needs someone 'below' or 'beneath' them to feel their own power. Those type of people are

not expressing anger to heal, but to regain control, or prove their power. Anger that is expressed in an open way is healthy, it assists in the healing process, however anger expressed without purpose or direction is damaging. Anger is only ever a pit-stop on the way to healing, it is not the final destination. Real power is being authentic, being vulnerable, opening up and expressing how you really feel.

THE SELF HATE CYCLE
Self hate is often caused by a 'feedback loop'. When you find and focus upon a thought or thing about yourself that you don't like, you'll inevitably begin to feel bad. The more that you focus upon feeling down or bad the more that you'll begin to vibrate at that lower frequency, which will cause you to have easy access to other perspectives that also feel like that. All of which will cause you to either feel even worse or cause you to fight against that negative thing or feeling, which will of course power it even more. That's when self loathing begins to feel normal because it's the frequency that you're vibrating at consistently regarding yourself and how you see yourself. The cycle ends when you begin to step back and find self love.

THINK, JUST DON'T OVER THINK
Most problems can be solved by taking the time to think properly and to think things through, however most problems are caused by having too much time to think. It is all about balance. Thinking about things helps, but over thinking doesn't. Take the time to think things through from a logical stand point and a higher perspective. Just don't spend too much time over thinking as that introduces doubt and fear, which will cause you to vibrate at a lower frequency allowing in even more ideas that feel like that, which will take you off course and away from that which is meant for you. Think, just don't over think. Over thinking won't help you to see things clearly, it will in fact cause you to see things in a distorted manner. However over thinking helps you to see clearly which perspective you're seeing things from and what frequency

you're currently on. How your thoughts feel is an indication of the frequency that you're currently vibrating at, or what frequency you're vibrating at in regards to that situation, person or thing. It's all an indication to vibrate higher.

FEELING STUCK?

The universe never gives you an experience that you can't learn from or a situation that you can't get out of. No matter what situation you are currently facing or feel like you're stuck in, there is always a way out of it. There is never a lasting excuse or a valid reason for giving up on yourself, there is always another way, it's just that chances are you can't see it from your current perspective or frequency. Take that as an indication to step back, rather than a reason to give up. Everything changes when you change your current way of seeing things. Never give up hope. You'll get through this.

THE NEED TO PLEASE

Are you a people pleaser? Are you someone who is afraid to say no, or feels like they can't say no? Someone who wants to keep everyone else happy? Someone who seeks to always keep their friends, family or partner happy? When you try to please everyone, what you are ultimately saying to the universe is that your well being and happiness doesn't matter, so that is the type of people that you will 'attract' and allow into your life. People who will use you. What you're saying vibrationally is that your happiness isn't important. You'll always end up feeling that way until something changes. The main reason for needing to please others is often our attempt to get the love and validation that we never got in our early years. We secretly want others to like us or appreciate what we do, or desire them to need us at some level, so that we can like and appreciate ourselves and that which we do, it allows us to be 'seen'. When you solely define yourself in relation to what others say or think about you, you won't want to give them a reason or a chance to dislike you, so you'll continue to do what they ask of you even when you desire to say 'no'. It is so important that you learn to say 'no' and you start to please yourself first, not in a selfish way, but in a self-full way. Give yourself the validation, love and praise that you never got growing up, so that you won't end up seeking it in others and in your results. Know that you're enough with or without the validation and opinions of other people. Until you do, you will continue to look for it in the opinions of others and ultimately be affected by what they say and do, or that which they fail to say and do.

HATE MONEY?

Often when we don't get what we desire, especially money, we tend to either resent it or silently resent those people who have it, or at some level we condemn it, finding reasons to not want it any more, all the while secretly desiring it. In reality we don't really hate it, we just hate that we don't have it yet. When you hate what you want the most you'll end up pushing it further away from you and you'll continue to separate yourself from it even more than ever before. Until your thoughts, feelings and beliefs regarding yourself, your desires, the world and others are in harmony and alignment with each other, you won't be able to allow in the experience that you're seeking regarding money.

YOU DIDN'T KNOW ANY BETTER

You can't continue to hold yourself back and punish yourself over something that you did when you were in pain, and for that which you did or failed to do (or even continued to do) when you didn't know any better. Punishing yourself now over something that you did 'then' isn't helpful, even if 'then' was yesterday. When you were in pain, the momentum was too strong for you to see clearly and think logically. The perspective, awareness and wisdom that you have access to now was on a different wavelength to you back then. You know better now and you can see the situation clearly, you are a different person, so forgive yourself. Accept what was, learn from it and grow because of it, and most important of all find inner peace.

START APPROVING BEFORE IMPROVING

You can't progress, better yourself or become your best self without self love or self acceptance. They are the corner stones of all self improvement. All lasting self improvement stems from self acceptance. You have got to approve of yourself before any and every attempt to try and improve yourself or improve your circumstances. Until you do, things won't change. Start now by loving yourself a little more each day. You've practised your unworthiness, now it's time to start the practise of claiming, affirming and confirming your inherent worthiness. It doesn't matter what happened before or 'what was'. You are good enough and you are worthy of love now.

JUST LET GO

Life unfolds effortlessly if we allow it to, we just have to get 'out of the way'. Let the universe do its work and stop holding onto things that weren't meant for you. Instead of holding on in fear, let go in the faith that you are being led to something better and something greater. What is not meant for you is trying its best to get away from you, and that which is meant for you is trying its best to get to you. The space in which you let something go is often the space in which you let something new in.

WHAT IF I FAIL AGAIN?

Just because you failed before doesn't mean that you will fail again. When you think, feel and believe that you're going to fail again, you'll not only stop trying, but you'll stop imagining, expecting, anticipating, feeling and believing in your own success too, and stop believing in yourself and your greatness and purpose. From that lower frequency you'll start to have thoughts that will convince you that your desires aren't for you, in time you'll start accepting and tolerating less than you deserve. Please understand that since the last time you failed, things have changed, you have grown, things are different now. It's time to try again. It's important to remember that all failure is temporary. What happened before isn't an indication of what will happen again or what can happen now. If you think, feel and believe that the way that it was in the past is the way that it will always be in the future, then you'll end up holding yourself and your blessings back. It is only once you stop seeing things as they are or the way that they have always been, can you see the possibilities of what they can become. It's time to try again.

USE YOUR TALENTS

You have a responsibility to grow and develop your talents, and to bring them to their peak. We are never given a gift or a talent that we're not meant to use to help the greater good in some capacity. Someone somewhere needs what you were sent here to do. When you are stuck in the mindset that you're not good enough then you'll never have the opportunity to become the person that you were destined to become, and the world will have to go without your message, talent and purpose.

REALITY IS A REFLECTION

The universe is always drawing to you people, opportunities and events that are vibrating at the same frequency as you. Your reality, results and relationships are a direct reflection of the frequency that you have been frequently resonating at. Until you change within, things can't and won't change on the outside. The moment that you begin to consistently and genuinely embody the thoughts, feelings and qualities of your highest self, everything changes. Redefine and remake yourself in the vision of greatness and watch what happens.

CHANCE MEETINGS

When you step into and stay in the feeling place and frequency of all that you desire, the universe begins to respond. You will begin to allow in events and situations that will feel like that inner peace and happiness and those people who will make you feel that way too. It will be those 'chance' encounters, when and how you least expect that will be the turning point and beginning place of allowing in all that you desire. You'll constantly seem to be in the right place at the right time. Other people will look on and call it coincidence, chance or luck, but you will know better. You will know that the universe is naturally responding to your new thoughts, feelings and beliefs (or your vibration) and that it is orchestrating a plan to fulfil your highest dreams and desires. Have faith and stay in that feeling place of your highest self and your highest desires. Very soon things will begin change.

IT ISN'T A COMPETITION

There is no need to compare yourself to others or compete against anyone for anything, the moment that you do, you will always lose in some aspect. They'll always look better, prettier or more talented from your limited perspective. The belief that you have to compete with someone else for your desires is fundamentally blocking your blessings and keeping you 'small'. There is no need to fight over a small part when there is truly an unlimited abundance available to you. They can't take your blessings and you can't take theirs, we all have our own unlimited stream available to us. Open up and let yours in.

EXPECT AND ACCEPT THE BEST

No matter what you're doing, expect and accept the best. Expect to have the best thoughts, feelings and experiences regarding that which you're doing. Expect to think positively and in a way that is encouraging and empowering. Anticipate all of the positive thoughts that you'll have regarding everything and how great all of that will make you feel. When you do that, you will help to make room for greatness to flow into your life. You will allow your current point of focus to allow in even more things that feel like that to you, all of which will help to set you up for success. Accept those blessings, knowing that you are truly and inherently worthy of them all, and that it is what is meant for you. In addition, expect to be the best version of yourself, and to have the clarity of mind to know what to say and when to say it too. Anticipate the ease in which you will have positive thoughts and positive expectations regarding all things, and especially anticipate how all of that makes you feel now. Go throughout your day simply expecting and anticipating the best, yet detached and at peace simply knowing that the universe is 'on it'. That intention has the power to work wonders on your entire life. If we can unconsciously train ourselves to expect the worst, then we can consciously train ourselves to expect and accept the best. So remember, no matter what you do or where you go, expect the best. When you consistently affirm that you deserve the best, you will naturally begin to accept the best too, which will in turn cause you to start expecting the best, all of which helps to allow it into your life. It becomes a cycle that takes you higher and higher.

SELF DOUBT

Self doubt is one of the most common killers of our happiness, peace and dreams. All self doubt really is, is an indication that you're not seeing yourself or this current situation clearly, or seeing the fullness of who you really are. In essence, when you closely associate yourself with your mind, you will tend to believe everything that it says. Your current thoughts (which include thoughts of self doubt) are showing you what your current frequency and perspective is limiting you to, it is showing you what you believe you are currently capable of achieving and becoming, not what you are really capable of achieving and becoming. Self doubt isn't the truth, it is just a manifestation of a lower frequency and a reminder to vibrate higher.

MANAGING THEIR ANGER OR PAIN?

Trying to keep other people happy all of the time is damaging and dangerous, not only for your happiness, but their healing too. First of all it isn't your job or duty to make or keep others happy, no matter how good your intentions are. Trying to please them or make them happy, won't heal them or really help change anything. What you are really doing is unconsciously assisting them in resisting their healing. It isn't your job to maintain someone else's level of peace either, that isn't your purpose or responsibility. You are not here to be anger management for someone else. Let them feel anger, let them speak up, it's necessary in order for them to heal. Let them express what's going on in a healthy way, rather than trying to compress or suppress their current outburst, their chronic unhappiness or every trace of pain. Only then can you assist them in being genuinely happy and at peace.

THE BRIDGE TO YOUR DESIRES

You might not be exactly where you desire to be right now, and that is perfectly OK. However please understand that all things are unfolding in perfect timing and in divine order. The changes that you are seeking are currently in the process of unfolding, even when you can't see them. Divine timing is often the time that it takes for everything to come into harmony with each other. You wouldn't want one thing to unfold before the other things are ready. Every circumstance and experience in your life happens in divine order. Think of the process of your desires unfolding as being similar to the process of building a bridge, a bridge which is taking you from 'here' to 'there'. The bridge to your desires is under construction, with each and every new experience adding a new brick to the bridge which is taking you higher and further than ever before. In time you'll reach the other side and look back and see just how far you've come without even realising it.

HOW TO FIND YOUR PURPOSE

There is no one specific way to find your purpose, it can be from trying out new things, often it comes from combining your passions or that which you're passionate about and other times it can come from taking the time to become aware of what you have of value within yourself that can help others as well as yourself. Take some time to become aware of the message that you have within you. What do you know that could help others? What have you been through that others need help, support or guidance with? Create a purpose from your passions, but also your pain and your past. Stop waiting for a purpose to come along for you to feel fulfilled, create a purpose now, when you do that you allow room for your 'real' purpose to find you. If you don't know what you are passionate about, start by trying new things, and make sure that you give them enough time and space to develop into more. Passion often comes after we try new things, not before we try them. Stop waiting for passion to appear before you begin. Often when you do that which you're passionate about, it ultimately leads you to your highest purpose or that which you feel called to do. Your passion might not necessarily be your purpose but it's there to help guide you towards it. Maybe combine your passions into a unique service or product, make that business or product that you have been looking for, and start now. Fundamentally your only purpose is to be your best self. Every other purpose will manifest from that. If you feel lost when it comes to your purpose, ask the universe or your higher self for help and guidance. When you ask the universe to use you for a higher purpose, it will. In addition, when you know that you are made for a higher and greater purpose, the universe will begin to bring you proof of that.

YOU CAN'T TAKE THEIR BLESSINGS
Other people's success, happiness, love, health, beauty, freedom, money and talent isn't taking away from yours. We all have our own unlimited supply of abundance available to us. You have your own stream of abundance and blessings which only you can tap into, and other people have theirs, which you can't tap into or access. Please understand that there is no limit to the blessings and abundance in the universe, the biggest place of lack and limitation is often in our own minds and imagination. The belief that others success is somehow taking away from yours, is holding you back and holding back your desires and results. Believing that someone else's happiness, abundance or wealth is somehow stopping you from tapping into and accessing the abundance that is available to you, is blocking your blessings. We all have an endless supply of miracles and abundance that is available to us, and all we need to do is let them in, and we can do that by focussing upon how they feel or by coming into vibrational alignment with them (by stepping into your higher self and seeing

things from a higher perspective). When you detach and open yourself up to the possibility and reality of abundance, you let abundance flow first into your mind, feelings and then reality.

IMPOSSIBLE

To achieve greatness it's not even necessary to believe that you can have, be or do all that you desire, all that is necessary is that you don't have a lack, limitation or fear based belief in the way that says that you can't or that it is wrong to have, do or be something. Having the belief or hope that anything is possible for you, leaves enough room for your entire life to be transformed. Give the universe enough room to work miracles on your life. Greatness is often only achieved by those people who believe the 'impossible' can somehow happen for them and to them. The only real limit is our own imagination.

HAPPINESS FIRST

Genuinely embrace joy now, allow yourself to be happy. Every single day consciously make the decision to be happy. I know that all of those struggles and heartaches that you've been through makes it seem like happiness isn't a choice and that you'll never be happy, however please understand that happiness really is a choice, and you can (and you will) be authentically and genuinely happy again, but only once you choose to. You've got to rise above the perspective that you're currently seeing yourself, the past and happiness from, and begin to see that happiness really is a choice and an option for you. I know that it might sound flippant to say that happiness is a choice, especially if you're dealing with a chronic illness and when your current reality is draining you, however you can still choose joy. Happiness is still an option. You still have a choice regardless of 'what is', 'what was', how you're used to seeing things and how you are used to feeling regarding it all, you can choose again and decide how you're going to feel about it all from now on. Once you allow how you really feel, and you begin to make peace with it all, you can begin to choose again. Only once you make peace with how you feel (and with 'what was' or 'what is') can you then begin to connect to your inner being, which is where that genuine and lasting joy and peace can be found. In time you'll begin to see that all you had to do was remove any resistance to your happiness, by removing your attention from any thought, feeling or perspective that was separating you from feeling and reaching it. Joy and peace is who you really are, it is how you're supposed to feel. You don't have to fake joy, you only have to uncover it within yourself. Ultimately until you choose to be happy now, you will unknowingly allow yourself to be affected by everything and anything that comes onto your path and into your awareness. You've got to be unconditional in your joy, not just faking it to make something happen, but choosing joy because you recognise that it is who you really are at the core level. Focus upon being authentically happy above and before everything and anything else. When you decide to focus upon feeling good now, you'll find that everything that you are seeking will naturally come looking for you.

YOUNG AT HEART

In life it's important that you remain humble, that you stay like a child, always open and curious about all things. It's important to be like a child, yet not childish. When you stay humble the ego can't survive or thrive. Having that young at heart, fun, adventurous, open and innocent, yet wise approach, is so powerful. When you release your expectations regarding all things, and you approach everything with that innocent optimism, you allow the best result to unfold. This is especially important when you are being creative. Continue to believe that anything is possible for you, 'get out of the way' and know that the best result will always manifest. Release all pressure and strain, and let things be what they need to be. Staying young at heart stops any cynical or fear based thoughts or beliefs from your past being able to block your current results or blessings. The more that you think that something won't work (simply because it hasn't worked before) the more that you will end up blocking it from happening. You have got to see that which you do and who you are from a higher perspective. You have got to have faith in more. Be like a child, believe in the impossible, knowing that you'll be fine regardless of what happens. In addition when you continuously bring a cynical approach to things, it will immediately shut down and limit the possibilities of what things can become. Always give things enough room to reveal themselves to you. When we grow up we tend to approach things from a place of, 'It won't work' or 'This can't work', simply because it never worked before. Our knowledge and experience tends to hold us back and limit our current success. We begin to approach everything from that place. The intention for all things becomes 'negative' or pessimistic. It's time to bring that childlike innocence and optimism back to everything that you do. All great findings will come from that innocent, non attached optimism, inquisitiveness and openness.

YOU WEREN'T TO BLAME
Are you still punishing yourself over a situation that you probably had no real control or power over? Or punishing yourself over a situation that you didn't know how to handle. Please understand that you did what you could with the limited amount of knowledge and experience that you had at that point. Only now, that you know better and you are removed from that situation, are you able to see what you could have or should have done better or differently. The clarity of the solutions that you can see now weren't available to you 'then'. They weren't on the same frequency as you, they were out of reach. This knowledge and insight that you have now wasn't vibrationally available to you then, you weren't in the same vicinity as it, you only had easy access to ideas and thoughts that were on the same lower frequency as you. You've probably been punishing yourself over something that you had no real experience or ability to handle. Let that guilt and shame go now. It's good to look back and learn from our mistakes and learn from those situations in our past and grow from them, however don't over analyse things and punish yourself for what you did or what you failed to do. Trust that you did what you could with the knowledge that you had or knew how

to apply at that point in your life. Learn from other people's mistakes too, you can't make them all on your own. Look consciously once at the mistakes from your past, take the lessons and blessings that they were there to bring you and move on stronger and wiser for them.

ASK YOUR ANCESTORS

In moments of fear, stress and the unknown, ask your departed ancestors for guidance and support, they have your back. You are a part of them, never apart from them. No matter what difficult situation that you are currently facing, ask them to guide you along the path ahead, they can see the short-cuts, obstacles and the pitfalls. Ask them to comfort and support you, ask them for wisdom and clarity. They will rise up to meet and support you every single time that you ask them to. Relax knowing that regardless of what you face or how things might look, that your ancestors have your back, and that they are silently encouraging you every single step of the way.

"THANK GOD"

We often hear the phrase, 'Thank God I did that', or 'Thank God I didn't go there'. However do you really listen to what that sentence says? Do you actually thank God / the universe? (or however you choose to define that supreme and loving energy). That simple sentence is always an indication to actually thank God, to thank the universe for its guidance, protection and blessings that it has bestowed upon you. When you are genuinely grateful, the blessings get greater, and when you purposefully thank God for something, you allow in even more things to be thankful of and thankful for.

ANGER IS A GOOD SIGN

When you find yourself feeling down, upset or angry, that is a good sign. It is an indication that something within you is seeking to be released. Any negative emotion that is in your awareness is seeking to be freed. It's not raising its 'head' to be pushed down or ignored, it's there to be seen, felt and released. This doesn't mean that you should act out in anger though. You should instead take that as an opportunity to understand why it's there. Negative emotions are an indication that you are believing something that either isn't true or isn't in your highest good about yourself, others, your desires or the world. Take some time to meditate. View yourself and that 'negative' feeling through the eyes of unconditional love. Allow it, see through it and be patient. The anger or pain will reveal itself and let itself out in time.

WHERE IS LIFE LEADING YOU?

Imagine this for a moment, that there is a never ending path that is unfolding directly in front of you. But where is that path taking you? Is the path taking you towards your goals and blessings, or towards more of the same? You'll know by how you consistently feel. What it leads you towards is dependant upon you, and your current frequency. When you feel good, a path that feels like that (which will naturally lead you towards everything that is on the same frequency as that) will unfold before you. The path changes in accordance to what you continue to give your attention to now. Your focus creates the path. When you centre yourself and you align with your best self, the path that unfolds will guide you towards greatness.

DISTANCE AFFECTS DESIRES

Do your desires feel close to you or do they feel far away? Distance really does affect how your desires look and appear in your reality. To show this, imagine an airplane that is flying at top speed. If you were up close to it while it was going at that speed, you would be able to see and understand just how fast it is going. However when you're on the ground looking up at it flying high in the sky, it often looks like it is going at a much slower pace from down there. Which is the same way that distance affects how your desires look to you. Your perspective changes everything. When you feel that your desires are close to you (and that they're in your close environment) they will manifest into your reality much faster. However when you feel as though you're separated from them (or that they're separated from you) they will appear and manifest at a much slower pace.

HAVE A REASON, NOT ANOTHER EXCUSE

Often the only thing that is holding us back is ourselves and our current perspective. It is so important that we don't allow our first reaction to determine our next course of action (which would determine our results). We have got to respond to life rather than allowing our first fear, pain or lack based reaction of, "I'm not good enough", "I can't do this", "They won't like me", or, "I don't have this or that", stop you from taking action and stop you from believing in yourself. Once you condition yourself to have a reason to succeed rather than having an excuse or a reason why you can't, success will be yours.

LAW OF ATTRACTION MISCONCEPTION

The biggest misconception about the 'Law of Attraction' is that your desires will come to you, when in reality you can also go to them. Your feelings of worthiness, success and joy will naturally begin to draw to you all that resonates at that same level, however your desires are also always pulling you towards them too, which is often that intuitive feeling drawing you to people, events and places that will begin to allow them in. Follow the call.

ARE YOU OK?

There is no shame in telling the truth and being honest with yourself and admitting that you're not OK. It's perfectly OK to not be OK, and to be unsure of what to do next. It's the belief that it's not right or OK to feel those emotions (or in other words it is your resistance against how you really feel and your refusal to acknowledge and feel it) that causes the most pain. Open up and be vulnerable with others, let that trapped emotion out. There is no weakness in admitting to yourself and to others that you haven't got it all together. Doing that is one of the greatest strengths. Every time that you do it, the ego weakens and loosens its grip upon you. There is no need to pretend that you're OK when you're not. A problem shared is more than a problem halved. When you're feeling down, don't give up, just give up fighting against yourself and fighting against how you really feel.

MIS-TAKES

Instead of judging or criticising another person's mistakes, see them as missed-takes, let them try again. It is often because of those mistakes that they have an opportunity to learn, grow and become their best self. They aren't mistakes if they allow us to grow. Find compassion and empathy instead of finding fault or blame. Judging another ultimately only affects you.

THE YELLOW BRICK ROAD

When you're centred upon feelings of a higher frequency such as joy, peace and love, you will allow the path ahead of you to be created from those positive emotions and feelings. Those high frequency feelings will automatically begin to lift you up to a higher frequency and will place you onto a path that feels like that, which will in turn lead you towards everything that is on the same frequency as it. Instead of letting fear create the path ahead, let joy create the path. There is no need to fear, just relax and trust. Meditate and allow your inner peace and joy to lead and create the way forward. When you do you'll always find yourself on the 'right' path. Let those higher frequency feelings create your 'yellow brick road' that will lead you towards your blessings and your best life. The path ahead is always rearranging itself to match and come into harmony with what you are consistently focussing upon and how you are feeling right now. It is always changing in accordance to your most consistent frequency. It doesn't matter what you felt before, if you change how you feel now and what you focus upon now, everything changes. The path ahead isn't set in stone, when you change it changes. It doesn't matter what happened before or how things were yesterday (or even just a few moments ago) when you change today, everything changes. The moment that you change, the universe begins to rearrange itself to come into alignment and harmony with your new outlook and frequency. When you relax, feel good and feel the peace that is within you, the path ahead will piece by piece come together for you.

WHO DO YOU BELIEVE YOU ARE NOT?

It is rarely who you believe yourself to be that is holding you back, it is who you believe you are not that is the issue. So who do you believe you are not? Do you still see yourself as being someone who isn't capable? As someone who is never quite good enough? When you continue to focus upon 'what' and 'who' you believe you are not, you'll continue to allow in even more of that into your life. Instead start focussing upon who you can be (and who you will be). Let that be your focus, invest your faith there. Bring that to life within yourself.

DON'T IGNORE YOUR FEELINGS

When you continue to ignore how you're really feeling you will fail to recognise the purpose of your feelings. They're ultimately there for you to feel them and then release them, and for you to honour those feelings that you never allowed yourself to feel in the past. Remember that your feelings are an indication of your frequency, they're letting you know whether or not you're currently in alignment with your highest self. One thing that is for certain is that when you acknowledge, allow and accept your feelings you will begin the process of letting them go. You'll free them and simultaneously free yourself.

THE POWER IS WITHIN YOU

Take a moment to connect to the power that is deep within you, become one with it. When you recognise and acknowledge that universal power within you, you'll intuitively see yourself and others through the eyes of greatness. You'll feel at one with all things. You'll never feel lost when you ground yourself in that peace and love. Let it take your fears and worries, hand over your goals too. Connect to that energy, breathe in that unconditional love and centre yourself there. Let that be the source of your peace. Energise yourself from that place. See yourself and all others from that place of love.

I SHOULDN'T BE ANGRY

Being spiritual doesn't mean that you don't feel 'negative' emotions any more, or that you won't get upset by anything, and it especially doesn't mean that you should ignore how you are currently feeling or those things that irritate or anger you either. Being spiritual gives you an understanding of why you are feeling that way, and why things are the way that they are. It allows you to use your emotions rather than being used by them. Being spiritual allows you to no longer allow your happiness or peace to be conditional or be affected by things for long. It brings you clarity and allows you to see negative situations or problems from a higher perspective without being 'negative', and it helps you to detach and recognise the real reason for the issue, and it undoubtedly allows you to connect to the solution. Being spiritual enables you to use your 'negative' emotions for their intended purpose, and it allows you to maintain and access your own source of peace, power and joy within yourself. It is often the belief that you can't be angry or that you shouldn't be, that causes resistance and even more pain in your life.

ACCEPT HOW YOU FEEL

Whatever emotion that you are feeling right now, stop for a moment and take full responsibility for it. It doesn't matter what someone else has said or done, or what has occurred and whether or not it was even your fault. You have got to accept and claim responsibility for what this situation has awakened within you. Only you can be responsible for how you feel and for improving things. How you react to what you encounter allows you to see and feel clearly what needs to be healed in order for you to become your best self. Anything that needs healing will come rushing to the surface to be acknowledged, felt, understood, healed and released. Anyone or anything that stops us from acknowledging and allowing how we really feel is ultimately not in our highest good. Only once you allow how you really feel can you stop the resistance against your natural state, which is peace, love and joy.

WANT TO RUN AWAY?

Everything is scary when you are doing things for the very first time (primarily because the frequency and perspective is currently unknown to you, you can't see things clearly until you come into harmony with that situation and frequency). Until we are comfortable with where we are and until we get our 'bearings', our initial perspective will often be a fearful one, which will supply us with fearful thoughts such as 'run away' or 'give up'. Those thoughts will try to convince you to go back to your comfort zone (or a frequency that feels comfortable to you). Don't give into them, see them for what they are which is a reflection of the frequency that you're at and not a reflection of the truth. Use that as an indication not to give up but to centre yourself and to step forward into your highest self and to take action. That uncomfortable feeling won't last, stick it out, it is always worth it in the end.

TRUST

When you can't trust others without a valid reason for doing so, it is often a result of your own fear, pain or guilt. You're likely seeing them through the lens of your past (especially when you've been hurt badly before or you still haven't recovered from it). When you fear that a partner will hurt you (and you expect them to) that is all that you will look for and see, you'll immediately become defensive and try to prevent something from happening. It will also cause you to see everything from a lower frequency and perspective too. It is what you will expect to happen which will help to allow it into your reality. You'll continue to 'attract' and allow into your life people who will hurt you and leave you feeling that way. They'll reflect back and confirm to you that which you already feel and believe to be true regarding yourself and love.

That will be the behaviour that the universe will highlight in all of your relationships. In addition you will be so busy looking for reasons why you can't trust them that you will miss everything else or discard it because it is not in alignment with your current perspective, thoughts or beliefs. You have got to see your partner through the lens of the present, rather than seeing them through the eyes of your past experiences with love. The real reason why you can't trust someone is ultimately because you can't trust yourself. When you learn to genuinely trust yourself, you will begin to trust others. You've got to focus upon loving, accepting and trusting yourself first, before seeking a relationship.

PROCRASTINATION

Procrastination is so stressful and painful in the long run, it is often said that nothing is more tiring than the endless hanging on of an uncompleted task. Please understand that things are never as hard and as difficult to do as your procrastination likes to tell you that it is. Once you start to take action, your perspective will change and momentum will begin to pick up and build in the direction that you prefer. Soon you will start to get even more thoughts that will support that new perspective and new way of seeing the task that you're doing. Once you begin to take action, you will often wonder what took you so long to act in the first place. You will begin to see things clearly again. Things often only feel like an impossible task when you are resisting doing them. Once you start the task and you have been doing it for a while (and once momentum has begun to build in that direction) the vibration or perspective will begin to support you, rather than hold you back. Completing the task is always much more rewarding than giving into procrastination. There is also another subtle type of procrastination too, which is doing the work that doesn't need to be done right now just to convince yourself or others that you're working hard. Doing that won't help you in the long run. When you continue to put off the work that you have defined as being 'hard' or 'difficult', it will continue to look and feel that way to you until you rise above it. What you are really only ever doing is putting off your success. Until you rise above it and see the next course of action clearly, your lower frequency will continue to hold you back. (Please note, don't confuse procrastination with time of rest and recuperation, rest heals and refuels you, procrastination doesn't, it is resistant by nature).

LEAVE ROOM

Of course it's necessary to have a clear idea of what you desire to be and what you desire to see, however always leave enough room for the universe to bring you even greater. Always leave the door open. The universe can dream an even bigger dream for your life than you could ever begin to imagine for yourself. Allow that higher vision to unfold. Hand your desires and goals over to the universe, let go, detach and allow even better to grow and show in your reality. Don't look for it, let it appear when it's ready. Until then, act upon your inspiration and follow the signs, knowing that you're being led to something incredible.

ARE YOU PLASTERING POSITIVE THOUGHTS OVER NEGATIVE THOUGHTS?

Give up the belief that you have to beat 'negative' thoughts or that you have to replace a negative thought immediately with a positive one. You don't 'get' peace by beating negative thoughts, you 'get' peace by choosing and claiming it within yourself. There is no need to fight one thought with another thought, all that you need to do is lean back from your thoughts by removing your attention from them (as it is your attention which is powering them). When you allow your thoughts and you stop engaging with them (by giving up fighting against them or pushing them away) you will learn to let them be and they will begin to let go of you. By replacing a negative thought with a positive one immediately, you are trying to think your way out of 'negativity', which is impossible to do. You feel your way to peace. Those 'negative' thoughts will go away by themselves when you don't fight against them or fear them. When you begin to detach and vibrate higher you will immediately begin to allow in better feeling thoughts.

BE YOUR BEST SELF

If you can't imagine how it would feel to be your best self or your highest self, emulate someone that you admire. Emulate how they act, and the way that they carry themselves and present themselves to the world. Step into that vision and take inspired action from that state. Don't become them, but simply embody how they see themselves, others, the world and that which they're doing. Imagine that you are just as confident, powerful, happy and at peace as they are. Be yourself but see everything and approach situations with inspiration from someone that you admire. Step into your best self taking inspiration from how it feels to be that person you admire, step into the new and improved version of yourself. Walk in that state of being, think from that space, see from those eyes. Do all of this not from the space or place of the ego, but from knowing your true power. This isn't about necessarily 'faking it until you make it' (as you're not pretending) as you are choosing to really become your best self. Doing that will allow you to come into harmony with how your higher self feels and how it sees things, which will begin to allow in everything that resonates at that level.

YOU ARE YOUR HABITS

You are what you think, feel and do consistently, not what you do sometimes. Therefore don't worry about those passing 'negative' thoughts that cross your mind, they have no real power. We are that which we do most often, not that which we do sometimes. Knowing this it is therefore important to remind yourself to purposely think positively and to see things from the perspective of your highest self more consistently. A few positive thoughts 'here and there' isn't going to change things. You are a product of your habits, that which you do most often and the decisions that you continue to make or fail to make. Being your best self is a habit that you need to begin today. The quality of your life is an exact reflection of the quality of your most consistent thoughts, feelings and actions, or those thoughts that you give your attention and awareness to most often. So ask yourself, what is the most consistent and common feeling that you are emitting out to the universe daily? As that is what you're currently allowing into your reality.

WAITING FOR FEAR TO DISAPPEAR?

Are you still waiting for fear to disappear before you take action? If you are, then you will be waiting forever. Fear is never a reason not to take action, it is only a reminder that before you do, you need to update your sense of self, your definitions and your beliefs to match your ambition and desire, especially for you to start seeing things how your higher self sees them. If you feel fear in regards to your goals, take action anyway. Being scared isn't an excuse to not go after your dreams. Those who succeed often feel scared, yet they still act anyway. Don't let fear make your decisions for you and allow it to keep you from what you love. Move towards that which you love not away from that which you fear, that subtle difference is life changing. Act from a space of expecting the best. If you act from a place of 'I'm not sure' or a place of fear, then you won't be able to receive the result that you prefer. Act from peace and power. When you step into your best self you'll automatically expect and accept the best, which will help to call it into your reality.

BELIEVE IN YOURSELF

You have a responsibility to believe in yourself fully. Until you do, no one else can. Please understand that each of us are born with at least one unique gift within us. We're not given a gift that we're not meant to use and share to some degree. The power that created the entire universe gave you that unique talent and skill set for a very specific reason, the universe doesn't make mistakes, there is a purpose to everything that it does. It gave you that talent because it knew that you alone could be trusted with it and be responsible enough to use that gift wisely. It knew that you could bring it to its highest and fullest potential. If the power that created the whole universe believes in you, then you should start believing in yourself and your gift too. You have no right not to believe in yourself.

NO LESS THAN $1,000,000
Often when we are so transfixed upon getting a certain amount of money we unknowingly limit ourselves to that amount. Of course a goal of a certain amount is helpful, however when we say that it has to be that amount only, we often unintentionally block all of the other smaller amounts that would have totalled that amount from coming into our reality. We also tend to block all of the other available ways that it could have arrived. Be open to all amounts in all ways and let the path of least resistance bring them to you in the easiest manner.

SEE YOUR EMOTIONS CLEARLY
It's so important that we learn to bring an awareness and clarity to all of our emotions and feelings. Too often we misinterpret our own emotions which are fundamentally holding us back and causing us unnecessary pain. It is time for us to reinterpret our emotions and to see them for what they are. All it takes is a small change of perspective to see things clearly and to release all of that unnecessary suffering and pain. In essence start to see all 'negative' emotions (such as anger and frustration) as primarily being an indication that you're not seeing things in a way that empowers or helps you. See any lasting, genuine and consistent emotions that feel good to you (such as appreciation or joy) as an indication that you are in alignment with who you really are and with how your higher self sees things. That is it.

GIVE NO EXPLANATIONS
You don't have to explain or justify your emotions, your responses or your reasons for doing or not doing something to anyone, especially to those people that continuously hurt you. Refuse to give into their need to know why their words, actions or lack of actions have hurt you. Stop giving into their request for you to explain exactly what they did wrong. That is for them to figure out,

that is about their growth, not yours. It is not your job to sit down and continuously explain to someone what they did wrong, that is their duty, it is necessary for their growth not yours. Yes of course doing it once (at the most a few times) can assist your growth but no more than that. Your growth is primarily about no longer accepting their pain or abuse and having the clarity to finally recognise and understand that those people who act that way are already in pain. Rather than lowering your vibration by getting into an argument with them and blaming them again, rise above it all. Send them love and healing, detach and move on. Know that ultimately until they heal, they will continue to hurt others and fail to see the real reason why they act the way that they do.

REMAIN TENDER AND SOFT
We can't let the harsh actions of others or the harshness of the world turn us cold. Hold onto your gentle, soft and innocent nature. I know that you have been hurt badly in the past, so you are used to having to protect yourself from others and the world, however you don't need to protect yourself so much any more, you're safe now. Let that guard come down. Soften your approach and outlook to life. Release all forcefulness. Centre yourself in peace, not pain or the past. When you approach life from a defensive, cynical or fearful place you will unconsciously call into your life everything that feels like that to you. Until you have processed your feelings and begun the healing process, you will continue to block your blessings and joy.

NEVER GIVE UP IN ANGER
Never give up on something in a moment of fear or anger, you can't see things clearly when you're operating from that negative feeling or lower frequency and perspective. When you feel better you'll be able to think clearly and see things from a higher frequency again (which is where all the answers that you are seeking reside). In addition, only ever make decisions, start a new project or bring up an issue once you're on a higher frequency, as

the intention (and the initial vibration) always determines the result.

SERENDIPITY

Serendipity and coincidence is often the universe's way of bringing even greater to you. Watch out for serendipity and be aware of those things that are happening to you right now. Be aware of any 'bread crumbs' in your current environment. That is often the universe's way of encouraging you to follow it. For example those 'bread crumbs' could be that new opportunity that just happened to present itself to you. In addition just feeling and believing in success is enough for serendipity and 'chance' to intervene and create an event which would lead you to your blessings and guide you towards your best life, which is often the path of least resistance too. Those coincidences and serendipitous moments are often the universe's way of guiding you towards even greater than you could have ever imagined for yourself. It is the 'short cut' to your blessings. However don't go looking for or trying to force 'serendipity'. Those moments will only reveal themselves to you when you are in alignment with who you really are.

LOOK ONCE

After we do something embarrassing or 'wrong', we tend to hold onto that situation and replay it numerous times. We analyse what we did wrong from every possible angle, from everyone else's eyes, asking ourselves why we did it, all of which often makes us feel even worse. It is important to understand that we can't see the solutions when we are looking at those situations from that place of guilt or shame. We can only get back thoughts and perspectives regarding that situation and ourselves that will feel like that guilt and shame. When those 'embarrassing' situations happen it is best to step back and allow how we really feel, and then look at it again from a higher perspective and frequency. From there you will be able to see what you did wrong, why you did it and most important of all how to improve it or how to grow from it. Only then can you take back responsibility for changing things. Doing that will empower you and allow you to better yourself because of it. Feelings such as guilt, shame and embarrassment will only ever compound how you are already feeling even more and create lasting issues within you. It is important to let go of the shame. You didn't know what you know now. Don't 'die' by the same mistake a thousand times. You won't learn anything new by constantly replaying and over analysing the same situation, you will only end up making it worse, you will end up keeping yourself on that lower frequency. When you do something wrong, look at it once from a higher perspective and frequency (and only do this once you are at peace). Learn from it and move on better and wiser for it. Find the lesson and blessing in it. In time you can even begin to be thankful for what it taught you, and for the opportunity of growth that it provided you with. Forget the mistake and remember the lesson. Replaying that situation over and over again won't bring you peace or change the past, it will only ever affect your present and your future.

JUST ACT
Give up the need to know everything before you take action. Way too many times we talk ourselves out of taking action because of an excuse. There is no need to be afraid of failure or be afraid of making mistakes. If you fall down, just take note of where you fell, what caused you to trip and fall, and what you learned as you lifted yourself back up. That is where the growth is, not in hiding or running away. Choose to grow as you go. In addition forget what you're going to do, and just start doing it. You introduce doubt into your vibration when you take too long to act upon your inspired ideas, and you allow that limited perspective to supply you with even more reasons why not to take action, all of which activates procrastination and makes it that much more difficult to act. In addition, don't let your ego tell people, 'I'm going to do this / that', and instead just take action, let your results speak for themselves. Once you have aligned with your best self, act on those inspired ideas.

GROW, RATHER THAN SHRINKING BACK

This is a reminder that you need to put yourself 'out there' into the world and stop hiding away in fear. When you begin to try new things, you will often feel uncomfortable and at times afraid, and you will feel the desire to run back to your comfort zone and the 'safety' of your old ways. However please understand that the thought that is telling you to run away or that you can't handle something is just a manifestation of frequency that you're currently vibrating at and a reflection of how you are used to seeing things, it's not the truth. That uncomfortable feeling is a sign of growth and an indication that you are evolving. It is just the growing pains of becoming more. So no more running away, that is too easy to do, actively put yourself in situations where you're 'forced' to grow, rather than situations that make you shrink back. No longer run away from that which you fear, consciously and consistently move towards that which you love, and that which encourages you to grow.

YOU ARE ALREADY SO BLESSED

You are blessed beyond all description, although I know it might not feel like that at times. Someone somewhere right now is praying for what you already have. Look around you, you already have so much, you have so much to be thankful for and appreciative of. When you're stuck in a mentality of lack, the universe will continue to take from you that which you already have. Never take anything for granted, take the time to consciously count your blessings. There is always something to be grateful for and appreciative of.

CLAIM IT

How you see yourself is so important. We are often conditioned to see ourselves through the lens of the past rather than the lens of what we can become. Imagine if we started to see ourselves from the perspective of greatness and our highest potential instead. Please understand that you have so much to give, you haven't even begun to exhaust the reserves of greatness, talents, skills and abilities that are lying dormant within you, all of which are just waiting for you to acknowledge and claim them. Be still, get in touch within and bring that greatness out and into the world.

THE 'ONE MORE' COMMITMENT

There is one sentence that will dramatically improve your life if you commit yourself to it, it is, before you give up, try 'one more' (this is in regards to that which is a reflection of your best self and your best life). This is what that statement really means. When you're working on your goals, such as writing a book, every time that you sit down to write, write one more paragraph or one more page. Every time that you do 'one more' you grow. 'One more' is when it really counts, that's when progress is made. Up until that point, that is what you have been unknowingly limiting yourself to, but when you do 'one more' you expand your limitations and open yourself up to more. Now this isn't about pushing yourself to the point of exhaustion, it is about training yourself to keep going and to keep growing.

DEALING WITH LOSS

Feelings of loss and grief can be some of the most powerful and all consuming emotions, especially when we don't face them. We must go through our feelings and emotions including grief, in order for us to get to the 'other end' of them. When we lose someone or something close to us, especially in tragic events, we are often left with many unanswered questions and uncomfortable feelings. The overwhelming feelings of denial, grief, hopelessness, confusion and anger (to name a few) become the new norm. It's so important that during this time you allow yourself to face and then process how you are really feeling. True healing can't be rushed, and it can't begin until you're honest. Process and then allow how you are really feeling moment by moment, take it all step by step. Your feelings will often change from moment to moment and that's perfectly normal. You are allowed to feel angry and be left feeling confused about what to do next and where to go, give yourself permission to feel everything fully and deeply. Problems only occur when you resist, ignore, deny or try to cover up how you're really feeling. Emotions are 'energy in motion', let those feelings within you move through you. In time, once you have gone through and 'processed' your emotions you'll be able to centre yourself and find peace again. You will in time begin to remember and feel love and joy again rather than feeling the current pain and loss. Those feelings of love and joy will allow us to naturally connect to the frequency that our loved ones now exist on. They want us to laugh and to have fun. Above all else, know that time truly is a healer.

WHAT MAKES YOU COME ALIVE?

Do that which makes you come alive, that which you are passionate about, that which empowers you and that which excites you. When you do, you will connect to and communicate with God (also known as your inner spirit, the universe etc). To some it could be singing, dancing, painting or writing, to others it might be reading spiritual or religious texts. Whatever it is that makes you come alive, embrace it. Dive into that feeling, expand it, savour it. When you do what you love and that which excites you, that feeling will fuel you and flow into everything that you do and everywhere that you go.

STOP TALKING YOURSELF OUT OF TAKING ACTION

If you are going to succeed at the level that you're capable of then you are going to have to move beyond your own fears and lower perspectives. Stop letting fear talk you out of taking action upon your goals and your inspired ideas. Please understand that your fearful thoughts (and those reasons that you have for why you can't succeed) are only ever reflections of who you were and how you are used to seeing things. They are a manifestation of the vibration that you are at, they're not the truth. They are not reasons to not act upon your dreams, they are in fact reminders that you have to, and that before you do take action you need to change your perspective if you want things to be any different. You're being reminded that it's time to start seeing yourself in your fullness. Those thoughts that say that you can't succeed are just how you are used to seeing your ideas, and how you usually act when you get them and how you are used to seeing yourself. It is time to change your perspective and time to start seeing things clearly again from a higher frequency. It is time to take action, no more talking yourself out of your blessings.

THE PETS IN YOUR LIFE

The pets in your life are some of the most wisest and purest souls. They are first and foremost teachers. A pet teaches you true unconditional love. Their love is pure and knows no limits. By loving them they allow us to love ourselves. The love that we give to them heals us too. Pets give us worth and value beyond words. The love that we feel for them lifts us up too. Each of our pets are unique, yet they all bring us love. We are all better people for having known them and having loved them. We don't 'pick' them, they pick us. They come into our life to teach us valuable lessons, especially how to live in the present moment, how to love and how to let go. When it comes time for them to go, they will leave us knowing how it felt to be loved. That spiritual bond and union between you both can never be broken. Love knows no end. When you find yourself thinking of your pet that has 'passed on' from time to time, know that they're thinking of you at that exact moment too, so send them love, they'll feel it. They will be with you, walking by your side for the rest of your life, as an angel and as a reminder of unconditional love.

MOVING ON AFTER LOSS

It can often be a difficult process to begin to 'move on' after someone we love dies. First of all, it is important to understand that those people who leave this physical body never really 'pass away'. Energy doesn't die, it only ever transcends, transforms and transmutes. Those people who you have 'lost' are very much still a part of your life, they're still around you, beside you, sending you love, and guiding and protecting you throughout everything that you are dealing with and going through. You are not moving on without them, you are simply moving forward with them in another form. The spiritual bond that you both shared can never be broken, it was often formed before you even came into this physical body and it will continue to carry on and get even stronger as you 'move' on. Just because you can't physically see them, doesn't mean that they're not there. It is so important that you understand that those people who leave this 'concrete reality' reside at a higher frequency now, at the frequency of love and joy, and that is the frequency that they want us to be on too. They want us to feel love and joy again. A heart that is filled with sorrow and pain can't connect to the vibration of love and happiness, which is where they are. When you begin to return to that place of peace within you, and you begin to feel love and joy again, you will begin to open up that space and allow your loved ones to connect to and communicate directly with you.

YOUR RESULTS

Your current results are not a reflection of who you are now, but who you were. They often aren't up to speed with the greatness that you have recently claimed, and that which you now know yourself to be. However as long as you define yourself, your worth or your greatness in comparison to the lack of results that you currently have or had, then you will never progress. You will spend your time observing 'what is' or 'what was' which will persist it, or you will get caught up fighting against it which will continue to block the possibilities of what things can become. Your overall results are a reflection of who you feel and believe yourself to be, however they're not determined by or limited to 'what is' or what already was. When your current reality isn't up to speed with the person that you are now (which is often the case) then you will need to look beyond it if you are to know and claim your power and highest blessings. There is often a buffer time until your blessings arrive, and this is just that.

THINGS AREN'T CHANGING

Are you allowing 'what is' to determine how you feel, what you think, how you behave and what you believe? If you are, you'll always be limited to 'what was' and 'what is'. Rather than allowing whatever crosses your path or comes into your awareness to steal your attention, choose what you give your undivided presence and awareness to deliberately. Only focus, direct and guide your attention and awareness upon that which you desire to grow and show in your reality.

FACING OBSTACLES?

When you have a dream that is bigger than the life that you currently have right now, then you will always face 'obstacles' and 'setbacks'. The universe will deliberately place challenges in front of you in order for you to grow. It is all necessary, every single setback and struggle is making you into the person that can handle the life that you desire. This is the training ground for greatness and success.

POSITIVE PROPELLER

Positivity is aligning with who you really are, it is your true power and nature. Every single positive thought and feeling is propelling you in the direction of who you really are and that which you desire. Positivity is power. When you focus upon positivity, imagine it like raising up your sail and allowing the power and energy of the entire universe to take you where you need to be, when you need to be there. Allow the universe to guide, protect and lead you, trust the direction that it is taking you. Point your boat in the 'right' direction and go with the flow.

REPEATING AFFIRMATIONS?

You don't need to say or repeat affirmations to affirm or confirm your own value and worth. Affirmations can be used as a tool to help support you in becoming your best self and most definitely can help you to see things as your higher self would see them, however it is important that you understand that it is not

necessary to do 'more' or think more to be your best self, it is
often about thinking less. Affirmations shouldn't feel like 'hard'
work or feel like they're pushing against 'what is' (or pushing it
away) and they most definitely aren't about ignoring how you
really feel. In essence all you need to do is stop giving your
undivided attention and awareness to those thoughts, feelings
and experiences that are resisting and blocking your worthiness.
Especially those thoughts, perspectives and experiences that you
have replayed, repeated and practised into becoming affirmations
that affirm your unworthiness. If you can learn your unworthiness,
then you can learn your value and worth. Remember happiness is
your natural state of being, you don't have to work hard or do
anything to 'attract' or allow in that which you desire, you only
need to vibrate in harmony with how it feels which will begin to
allow it in.

SELFISHNESS VS SELF-FULLNESS
It is so important that you learn to be self-full. Don't confuse
being selfish with being self-full. Being self-full is key to being your
best self. Those people who continuously put others first, before
themselves, tend to be those people who continue to struggle and
go without. It is not your job to put other people's peace and
happiness above your own. If you're not helping others from a
place of peace, power and self fullness, then it's not worth it. It's
not helping anyone. You have got to give to yourself first. Have
you ever noticed that those people who put themselves and their
happiness first and above everyone else continue to win and
succeed, and those people who give everything to everyone,
continue to fail? Things go 'right' for those 'selfish' people not
because they're technically 'good' people (some of them have a
lack empathy for others) however they succeed because they
understand that self-fullness is the key to success. That is why
everything works out for them. Now this isn't a reason to be
selfish, it's only a reminder to be self-full. Don't misinterpret their
selfishness as a reason not to be self-full, or as a reason not to
help others. Their intention to put themselves first may be a

selfish one, but when they keep making their happiness a priority they will continue to find happiness and success, while you continue to give and struggle in vain, you'll end up giving it all away and be left with nothing. When you give all that you have, and you're constantly left feeling unhappy or 'empty', the universe will continue to respond to that feeling and continue to reflect that back to you in your results and experiences. You'll allow into your life everyone and everything that will make you feel that way too. That is why self-fullness is key to your success. When you feel self-full the universe will continue to give you even more things that will confirm that to you. Redefine self-fullness as being the vehicle that will allow you to give more and be more. Self-fullness is recognising the power in being happy and in being at peace first. It is understanding that what you are looking for can only be found in being happy first. Until you make yourself, your happiness and your peace a priority things won't change.

IT'S THEIR FAULT

When we are so fixated upon blaming other people or the past for where we are right now or for our current unhappiness and lack of success, we will not only persist that which we don't want, but we will also continue to hold ourselves apart from that which we desire most of all, including the happiness, peace and love that is within us. The universe will continue to supply us with experiences that will not only confirm to us that others are to blame for our current unhappiness or the situation that we're dealing with, however it will continue to supply us with even more things that will separate us from feeling the love, peace and happiness that is within us. The more that we 'marinate' in those feelings of pain and blame, the further that we will drift away from our purpose, peace and happiness. We will continue to be unhappy, feel powerless, feel like we have no real purpose, and feel like we have no real control over our life, that is until we change within. When we take an honest assessment of our life, our actions or our lack of actions, we can begin to see that the only thing that is truly holding us back is ourselves and our current mindset. You can't allow in your future blessings when you are continuing to give your undivided attention and awareness to your past troubles or current struggles. Although it may be someone else's fault why you are in pain, it is your responsibility and duty to heal and grow from it, and to move beyond those feelings to peace again. Please choose your happiness and peace now, instead of fighting against the past and that which you don't want. Be accountable. It's never too late.

FAKING JOY?

Are you thinking positively just to try and trick the universe into giving you all that you desire? Or maybe you're pretending to feel good just to try and make something happen? Please understand that it doesn't work that way, the intention always determines the result. So if you're only feeling good to try and get something back, the intention (or the reason for feeling good) comes from a place of lack and frustration, which is what the universe will respond to and reflect back. Only once you genuinely begin to allow yourself to feel good now, can things really change for the better and for good. You don't have to pretend to be happy, joy is who you are, it's how you will feel when you remove your attention from anything that is in the way of you feeling and reaching it within yourself.

SPEAKING ALOUD

It's so important that you speak your desires and goals aloud. The spoken word has more power than we can even begin to understand. It is not enough to just write down your goals and to think positively. Your spoken words must match your intentions and thoughts too. Life tends to move in the direction of your words, and that which you say you are, and that which you speak about most often with passion and certainty. Vocalise your intentions and desires, breathe life into them. Speak things into existence today, see things from the best possible outcome. Look beyond 'what is', don't let your external dialogue be a running commentary on what already is (or what was) or that which you don't like. Start speaking things into being, say that, 'This is going to be amazing' or 'This is going to be incredible'. This isn't about forcing positivity or trying to make anything happen, it is about relaxing and recognising that at the highest level it already has happened. Positivity is a natural affect of feeling good and vibrating in harmony with who you really are. Those who talk the most about what they want or what they don't want tend to create even more of those experiences in their own reality. Which is why it is often said that poor self talk leads to a poor life. Your words really do have a magical affect on your reality. When you speak your words aloud you're literally 'spelling' them and also casting a 'spell' on your reality. It is a creative act. Manifesting that which you desire requires more than just thinking positively and internally focussing upon that which you want. You have got to combine thinking, feeling, writing, and speaking. That union is vital.

THE 'DOWNFALL' OF THINKING POSITIVELY
When you begin to vibrate at a higher frequency, such as the frequencies of love, truth, happiness and worthiness, everything that isn't on that frequency and level begins to fall away. This is often when relationships fail or when you lose your job. Those people who aren't on your frequency and those things which are 'negative' or not good for you will no longer be in your environment (or situations may occur that will remove you from that environment). When you embrace your true self, you will begin to rise up, and those people who are on a lower vibration will begin to remove themselves from your life. You may start to lose friends around this time too, however be OK with it. When you change, everything changes. 'Negative' people who were once around you and who were in essence reflections of how you had been treating yourself or how you had been feeling (or more accurately the frequency that you were vibrating at) will no longer be around you. You're on a different frequency than them now, but don't let your ego 'hijack' that idea and make you feel like you're better than everyone else. You're just becoming a better

version of yourself, you're not trying to be better than anyone else. When you improve and become the best version of yourself, the universe will make room for new people and new experiences in your life. You deserve to be around those people that will love and support you unconditionally, you deserve the best. When things start to fall away don't fall into the trap of trying to hold onto that job or that relationship which ultimately isn't meant for you, or what is best for you. There is no need to worry when the less that you have been settling for begins to fall apart. It is only falling apart to allow even better to come together for you. The universe is making room for what you desire and deserve. Therefore when a 'disaster' occurs, don't panic and label it as such, instead see through it to the possibilities of what is coming together.

THE SKY ISN'T THE LIMIT

The sky isn't the limit. The only limit there is, is in your own imagination. There is no need to place limitations on what is possible for you. The moment that you do, you will begin to limit yourself and your dreams. Let there be no ceiling to your dreams, be limitless in your thinking and your imagination. Give up determining what is possible for you based on 'what was' or what you received or achieved before. Always leave enough room for more than you previously thought was possible. Surrender what you thought was possible for you and embrace the 'impossible'.

IS THAT A COPING MECHANISM?

How many of your current actions are actually reactions in the form of a coping mechanism? (which are essentially actions that you take or don't take in an attempt to protect yourself from perceived harm or pain). Maybe the real reason why you're pushing people away is to finally feel in control or to prevent yourself from being hurt or let down? Maybe the real reason why you're limiting yourself is because you don't feel like you're good enough or worthy of success due to your past? So many of our current actions are actually reactions from pain and fear, and are re-enactments of what was and how we felt. In order for things to change we are going to have to anchor ourselves in the present, as well as becoming aware of our reactions, and above all else being accountable for what happens next.

YOU MUST DO THIS BEFORE ANYTHING ELSE
The number one priority of your adult life should be to heal and recover fully from whatever you experienced or failed to experience as a child and an adolescent. When you're in pain (due to situations and experiences in your past) that is when you are more likely to make irrational and illogical decisions which don't support the person that you're becoming. When you're in pain you can't think clearly, you can't see things or people as they really are. You won't be able to see yourself clearly either. That is when you are most likely to get into the wrong group or an unhealthy or toxic relationship. Until you heal you'll unknowingly take that pain everywhere that you go. Make healing your number one priority above all else. Be responsible. It is time to heal.

WORRYING ABOUT EVERYONE
It is not your job to worry about every single person in your life, or your job to worry what might happen or what trouble that they might get into if you are not there to consistently coach and support them. Release that need to control everyone and everything. That won't keep them safe. It is not your job to look after everyone, if you do that, you will only ever do it at the expense of your own happiness and peace. You didn't come into this world to walk everyone through life, you came here to create your own path and life. Let others learn by themselves, give them enough space to make their own mistakes and to learn their own lessons. Trust that their own higher self and inner being will look after them, and that it will guide and protect them too. Don't teach your loved ones and children to rely solely upon you, but to rely upon themselves and their own higher self. Like a bird raises its young, give them enough room to spread their wings, and

when the time comes, give them a gentle nudge out of the nest so that they can learn how to fly. Give them the tools to live their best life with and without you. You won't be able to create your own path and reach your highest potential when you are trying to create everyone else's path for them. Let their own higher self, intuition and feelings speak to them, let those things assist them in creating their own path, it can do a better job than anyone else ever could. You don't know exactly what they need (and when or why they need it) but their own inner self knows. Learn to detach and surrender control.

FEELING UNCOMFORTABLE?
If you are uncomfortable in your current environment, take a moment to step back and ask yourself, what is seeking to be released within me? What am I trying to avoid or push back down? Ask yourself, what am I being encouraged to let go of? Meditate upon that idea. Hold that space for healing. That which is seeking to be released within you will come rushing to the surface by itself. It will 'open up the door' and let itself out in time. Any time that you try something new or you are placed in a new environment, that which is no longer needed within you (such as any old habits or 'negative' ways of thinking, seeing and doing things) will come to the surface to be healed and released. Anything that needs to be healed will make itself known to you. That is why as soon as you try something new you'll often get thoughts like, 'I can't do this', or those feelings that convince you to run away. You will receive those thoughts and feelings not because you can't handle it, but because your higher self is showing you all of the old ways of seeing and doing things that need to be released or changed in order for you to achieve and receive the result that you're looking for, and the result that you are capable of achieving, or more accurately, receiving. However what we tend to do when we get those thoughts or we feel that way, is we 'follow' those thoughts (or we fight against them) or we listen to and give into those feelings. We tend to shrink back and give up, instead of centring

ourselves and stepping forward with passion, purpose and courage.

BODY IMAGE
Your current outlook and thoughts are a direct reflection of the frequency that you are at. Those with poor body image, a lack of confidence or self esteem issues are often viewing life or themselves from a lower vibration. The real reason why they feel bad isn't because of how they look now, but because of how they're still viewing themselves. When you feel bad that is an indication that you're not seeing yourself as your higher self sees you, that's why it feels so bad to you. Therefore understand that negative thoughts aren't there to get you to change how you look, but to instead change how you're seeing yourself, and to change the frequency that you're seeing yourself and your 'faults' from (and the body 'ideal' that you're chasing after). Essentially, to start loving and accepting yourself more. If you need to improve, your higher self will tell you, not your ego.

DISTRACTION OR DETOUR?
In life it's necessary to understand the difference between a detour and a distraction on the road to success. At times things may take you off your path, and what first looks like a distraction may in fact be a detour to success. It's necessary to look at all things and opportunities from a higher perspective to know the difference between them both. Please understand this subtle difference. Distractions bring you down and restrict you, they may make you feel temporarily happier but they ultimately won't fulfil you. Detours will enlighten and empower you, however they often won't feel great to begin with. Detours will bring you another way to your success, a better and easier way, they will give you valuable lessons which will take you further and lift you higher, they will push you to better yourself, and they will give you the tools that are necessary to try again. Detours are guiding you towards something better and towards greatness, distractions are keeping you from greatness. When you centre

yourself in your own peace and power, you'll intuitively know, feel and see the difference between them both.

IT WAS ALWAYS YOUR CHOICE

You always had the power to create the life that you desired, however when you believed that you couldn't, the universe responded to that belief and brought you even more proof that you were a powerless spectator of life, rather than a conscious creator of it. Every situation and person continued to confirm to you that things were beyond your power and control, and that you were a victim of circumstance rather than a conscious creator of it. Until you know and claim your inner creative power you will often be left feeling powerless. Don't think of what happened to you as your fault, instead think of what happens next as your choice.

HOW DOES IT MAKE YOU FEEL?

How you feel about something is always in alignment with the experience that you will have with it. How you consistently view something, be it a relationship, money or a job, is in alignment with the experience that you are currently allowing and inviting into your reality regarding it. If you feel down, nervous or frustrated when you think of money, that means that at some level your beliefs, thoughts and point of focus is holding back the experience that you desire to have with it. That at some level you are 'unconsciously' holding back the abundance and blessings that are reserved for you and are trying to get to you. Those lower frequency thoughts are always an indication that it is time to align your desire for something with your beliefs about it and your beliefs about yourself. So in summary how you feel when you think of that which you desire is a perfect indication of what you are offering vibrationally and the experience that you will receive back and have with it. Until you think of what you desire from a place of joy and abundance (or more accurately until you stop thinking of it from a place of lack, fear or limitation) and you start to see yourself and all things as your higher self sees them, your desires can't show up in your reality, or appear the way that you desire and prefer them to look.

SELF WORTH VERSUS NET WORTH
Self worth, self love and self care are critical components in order for you to live a happy, peaceful, stable and successful life. Self love and self worth must always come above and before any attempt to increase your net worth. Prioritise developing yourself fully on an emotional, mental and spiritual level, before you try and develop a career or a relationship.

BIG CHANGES ARE ON THEIR WAY
You may have noticed lately that things are beginning to change. Although the changes may be subtle, they're very real. 'Big' and positive changes are on their way. Your new way of seeing and doing things has altered your path. You're beginning to 'go with the flow'. Your higher self is calling you towards your highest purpose, you're being led in an even better direction. You have opened up just enough space to allow in miracles and blessings into your life. What was once out of reach, is now within your grasp. In the upcoming weeks you will start to get even more proof that things are changing for the better. It's time, you're ready for what's next.

YOU ONLY FAIL IF YOU GIVE UP
Failure isn't a reason to give up, it is inspiration to try again. Failure is forever when you give up and you don't use the lesson that it was here to teach you. Stop counting your failures or focussing upon how they make you feel (as focussing your attention upon that calls in even more of how that feels into your reality). When you stop identifying yourself with your results, especially with your failures, you can begin to see and then use the purpose that failure had for you. Failure is always an opportunity to grow, to evolve and to become your best self. Failure always leaves you with a reusable and valuable lesson every single time that you encounter it. However unless you learn

from your failures, you'll never be able to earn from them. Failure isn't a sign that something isn't meant for you either. You have got to stop taking failures and setbacks so personally. Give up giving up on yourself and your dreams simply because you have failed. Only ever give up on something from a place of peace and clarity, and not from a place of anger, defeat or frustration as you can't see clearly from there. Choose again and choose more.

100% OF YOUR ATTENTION

Are you giving your goals your undivided focus and attention? Are you focussing all of your efforts and attention in one place at one time? Or maybe you have unknowingly worked upon your goals giving them 10% here and there? Or maybe you're even giving 10% to 10 different things at one time. In order to succeed at the level that you're capable of succeeding at it is necessary to give that which you're doing your best effort. It takes focus, commitment and determination. You have got to give 100% to your goals, consistently, not just 100% from time to time. Discipline is required in doing anything that is worthwhile. Be like a 'disciple' to your own dreams and goals, to your own highest self and to your highest purpose. Without discipline you'll end up going from project to project, achieving nothing worthwhile and achieving a fraction of what you're truly capable of 'achieving'. In addition, stop trying to do everything all at once and all by yourself, it is great that you have so many goals, however it is important that you take things one goal at a time. Only then can you give them your all. In addition there is no need to struggle doing everything all by yourself, let other people help you. Work on your projects as part of a team. Greatness and the highest levels of success are only possible with team work. Always remember that focus is necessary in order to succeed at the highest level. Focus your attention and awareness upon embodying your best self right here and right now, and not just here and there from time to time. Focus your thoughts, feelings and actions upon the highest perspective and best possible outcome. No more multitasking 100 different tasks all at once.

Once you have achieved that particular goal that you're focussing upon and you have taken that project to its highest level and potential, you can then begin to detach, and broaden your focus and go onto the next exciting idea or project.

WANT TO CHANGE THE WORLD?
It is important that you don't have a goal to change the world or to go down in history. That is often only ever a goal of the ego. Those type of results that change the world are what naturally occurs when people courageously and consistently follow their purpose, and when they do that which they're sent here to do. Going down in history wasn't their main goal, aspiration or aim. Those people that will change the world for the better do so by following their passion and purpose. In addition, let go of the idea that the world needs 'saving'. Although your desire to change the world comes from a good place, it too can be an extension of your ego's desire to be admired, respected and remembered. In addition when you feel like the world needs saving, you will often only ever see a damaged world and you will continue to call into your life those people that need saving. You will continue to hold yourself apart from experiencing and living in a world full of joy, love and passion. You will hold yourself apart from the joy that is meant for you and the blessings that are trying to get to you.

YOUR BLESSINGS CAN'T FIND YOU
You are powerful beyond all measure, however do you truly believe that? The only reason why you won't be able to believe in yourself and your abilities fully now is when you have a belief, thought, feeling, experience or memory in the way that stops you from accessing the faith, power, purpose and self belief within you. You've got to remove your attention, faith and focus from who you were and from 'what was', in order to allow in who you're meant to become and what is meant for you. There is no need to hide away and protect yourself from the world any more. When you continue to hide from hurt you will inevitably hide from your blessings too.

CHILDHOOD BELIEFS

It is important that you leave those childhood and 'high school' beliefs behind you. Until you do, that hurt child that formed those beliefs that you're still currently operating from, will continue to respond first. You will continue to see life, yourself, others and that which you desire from that limited and pain based perspective. You need adult beliefs now, beliefs that are more in alignment with who you are becoming. Just like you wouldn't ask a child for their opinion on what to do next or allow a child to make the major decisions in your life, why would you let your inner childhood beliefs rule your life now? Any beliefs that are based on fear and pain can't tell you about your worthiness, value and abilities. Create new empowering beliefs by stepping into your higher self moment by moment, and by choosing to respond to life rather than just reacting to it.

PRACTISE WHAT YOU PREACH

It's so easy to stay positive when things are going well, it's often only once things go wrong that it becomes more difficult to do, however that's where progress is made. That is when you are able to truly 'practise what you preach', and when you can put into practise all of those things that you have learned. That is when those lessons prove their real worth and show you their value. Everything that you have ever gone through has enabled you to handle what is next, so trust that you can handle this.

BELIEVE

If you desire things to be any different you're going to have to believe in yourself and your purpose. Until you believe in your gift, your message, your blessings and your greatness, things won't change. Your reality is ultimately a reflection of what you believe is possible for you, and what you believe you're currently limited to. Until you believe in yourself, your belief in lack and limitation will continue to create your reality and your results. Self belief changes everything. Believe in the possibility of things getting better. Train yourself to believe in yourself and your blessings, instead of believing in your limitations and failures.

WE'RE ALL THE SAME
Every single person that you will ever encounter will have their own set of struggles, insecurities, problems and pain. Regardless of how 'perfect' their life might look on the outside, they, like us, are still growing, still learning and still making mistakes, that's just a part of life. Make peace with that process. We are all 'a work in progress', there is no such thing as 'perfection'. Please remember that there is no need to compare your current progress to someone else's final results.

READ THIS ON YOUR 'DARKEST' DAYS
Right now, I am going through a powerful transition, from 'what was' to what will be. From this painful situation will come peace, purpose and healing for me and for all others. This is not the breaking of me, but the making of me. I will emerge better, stronger and wiser from this. I will use this situation as a reminder and an opportunity to find lasting peace within myself. This is just the step back that will allow me to make a massive leap forward. There is more in store for me, my story doesn't end here. Deep down I know that I am not the only one going through this or the only one feeling this way, I am not alone. Only my current perspective likes to tell me that I am. My current thoughts aren't a reflection of the truth, they are only a reflection of the frequency that I'm currently at. I will see clearer soon. I know that the universe has my back, as do my ancestors and spiritual guides. In my most painful moments, when I can't see the light or find my way, I know that they will be with me, holding my hand and walking me through the darkness. I am loved, I am needed and I will get through this. Soon, once the pain subsides and lessens, I will be left with a powerful lesson and blessing that will change my life for the better.

A MORNING 'PRAYER'

Dear Universe / God / Higher Self,

Thank you for this brand new day. I open up to receive your love, peace, purpose, protection and healing. Prepare me for this day. Restore and renew my body, spirit and mind. Lift up my frequency. Allow me to see things how you see them. Encourage me to respond from love today. Reveal your presence everywhere that I go, and in everyone and everything that I see. I ask you to bless each and every one of my interactions and experiences today. Energise, heal, empower and inspire everyone that I come into contact with. Guide and transform my thoughts, feelings, words and actions today. Speak to me clearly and directly, allow me to know your voice. Turn up the volume on my intuition and inner wisdom. Lead me to where I need to be, when I need to be there. Light up my 'yellow brick road'. Reveal your truth, unveil your way. Allow me to focus upon that which continues to lift me and all others higher. Rest my attention and awareness upon all that is good. Continue to allow me to recognise and claim my true worth, value, purpose and power, and to accept and love myself even more than ever before. Allow me to rise above and move through 'what is' to what will be. Allow me to forgive even more than ever before. Allow what is in my highest good to come together, and let everything else fall away. Continue to empower, encourage and inspire me. Turn my lessons into blessings, pain into healing and purpose, and fears into peace and clarity. Allow me to learn through love and joy. Continue to awaken and reveal my inner creativity, confidence and courage. May appreciation continue to be on my mind and on my lips today. As I now begin this brand new day, I release and relax into your love and light. I surrender in faith and go with the flow. For now, I thank you, and I love you.

'Amen'

The Backstory...

How and why did
'A Message Of Love' start?

For those of you who are interested in the origins of this book and the 'A Message Of Love' online account, I decided to add this section in at the end of the book.

'A Message of Love' has been years in the making, with more failures than I can count and even more setbacks than I care to remember. From the online account, to the audio book (which a few of you may remember) to this very book that you're currently reading, 'A Message Of Love' has gone through many different incarnations and changes throughout the years until it finally settled upon what it is today. However, how and why did it all come about?

Ultimately the main reason why I set up the account and began 'posting' the messages of love online was because I needed them, they were for me first.

Yes I needed these messages too.

Some of you may be surprised to hear that, however only a few short years ago I was fighting a very secret battle and the messages contained within this book undoubtedly helped to save me and support me as I became the person that I am today.

To understand this fully there is something that you need to know. Something that I haven't publicly shared before, and that is that I have Obsessive Compulsive Disorder (OCD for short). My OCD which started from a very early age, reached its peak in my early 20's, which at the time, caused me to spiral down into a very unhappy and dark place. It was something that I struggled with and battled against for many years.

So lets start from the very beginning. My spiritual journey (and the journey of 'A Message Of Love') first began in my early twenties. In those moments of unhappiness, and if I'm being completely honest, despair, I searched for something that would be able to help me. Something that could help to ease the fear and the constant onslaught of the negative thoughts and feelings.

That is when I first heard about the teachings associated with the 'Law of Attraction'. However, sadly, instead of allowing the teachings associated with the 'Law of Attraction' to be able to help me, my OCD ended up distorting and 'hijacking' the core message.

I would think to myself constantly, "What if my OCD is creating horrible events in my life?" or "What if I just happen to think about something negative about myself or others for a few moments and then I create that?". Feelings of dread, shame, worry and guilt haunted me. Uncontrollably I began to obsess over that idea and perspective. My OCD ultimately made the 'Law of Attraction' teachings something to fear, rather than something to inspire and empower me. So I ended up walking away from the teachings all together.

It was also during this time that I found myself in long periods of unemployment with no real prospects. Fear and anxiety had become constant companions for me. However one day in the summer of 2013, something changed.

To be completely honest, I just had enough, something clicked within me. Instead of allowing OCD to define me and continuously defeat me, I decided that it was time to take back the wheel and time to steer my life in the direction that I preferred. I made a promise to myself that I would no longer allow OCD to continuously and consciously have full control over my life and my happiness any more.

I unknowingly began my 'spiritual journey' or 'spiritual awakening' as some people like to call it. I started to buy as many 'Law of Attraction' and Self Help books that I could afford. I watched numerous motivational seminars and read all of the spiritual magazines that I could find. From that point on, I started to focus my time and energy upon my dreams instead of my fears and anxieties. It was during this time that an idea popped into my head, that I should start an account on Twitter called, 'A Message Of Love', which I could use to help people who felt like me.

Armed with a purpose and the determination to help, I searched on Twitter for terms and sentences such as, 'I'm depressed' or 'Pray for me', and I would respond under each 'tweet' that I could find providing a simple message of love, something that I felt would be able to help them in their moment of need and let them know that they're not alone and that it does get better. I was unknowingly giving them the help that I needed but couldn't find. I loved the feeling of being able to help people and being able to see the very real difference that I was making in people's lives in real time. From that moment on I knew that I couldn't underestimate the power in helping someone and how the smallest of words can have a huge impact on someone else's life.

Pretty quickly the account took off. I would spend hours upon hours replying to people from all over the world, however since I was replying to so many comments in such a short period of time, Twitter automatically disabled my account on two separate occasions believing that I was a 'spam' account. I was devastated. My hard work and purpose was gone in a flash, so feeling sorry for myself, I gave up on 'A Message Of Love' and I continued on with my life.

I left the idea behind me (well I thought I did) however the experience had changed me considerably. I started to meditate daily and my OCD had begun to release its grip upon me. My life started to feel so much more brighter and more optimistic than ever before. I even had the courage to start my very own music publishing company, however after a few short months it all came tumbling down around me once more. The financial backing that I needed to continue my business pulled out and opportunities that I had lined up fell through, I had no other option but to close down my company and yet again start over.

I found myself at the end of December 2014 back in the same place that I was the year previously, feeling down and sorry for myself, but this time not defeated. It was during this time that yet again the same idea popped into my head. To start 'A Message Of Love'. So on a whim, I decided to start the account again, but this time on Instagram. I logged into an old Instagram account that I set up in 2013 but didn't use and changed the username handle to @aMessageOfLove. On December 28th 2014 I made my first ever post which read, 'To change your life, you have got to change your life'. It was an old quote that I had heard a few years previously that continued to resonate with me. I honestly believe that I posted that message to remind myself that in order for lasting changes to occur in my own life, things had to change and most important of all, I had to change.

A few months after I started the account, something incredible started to happen, I started to get insight without consciously trying. Without effort a sentence or an idea would pop into my head (which I now know to be a reflection and a manifestation of my increased frequency). The more that I helped people, the more insight that would continue to be revealed to me.

To make a very long story short, my 'A Message Of Love' Instagram account has gone from strength to strength and has over the years cultivated a small and ever expanding following from all over the world. I am forever thankful for each of my failures, setbacks and problems, because ultimately they were the making of me and not the breaking of me. Without those failures, you wouldn't be reading this book.

My OCD thankfully no longer has the same affect on my life that it once had, and I am now able to recognise it and step back from it whenever it happens to arise. I am able to reach out and accept help when I need it. Instead of my mind bringing me 'negative' thoughts and feelings, my higher self now brings me empowering and motivating messages of love for me and for all others.

I hope that my journey in creating 'A Message Of Love' can help to inspire you in some small way, maybe it can inspire you to keep going or maybe even encourage you to try again. Above all else, take my story as a reminder to not give up on yourself.

Always remember, that there is greatness in store for you.

A Reminder...

If you are going through a tough or a challenging time, please reach out and let your friends, family or a health care professional know how you are feeling and what you're going through, you're not alone. You're only ever the only one going through something until you speak up. There is no need to sort out or try and solve all of your problems on your own. It's impossible to see things clearly when you're feeling that way. Let others help you to see things clearly again. Things do and will get better, but they'll only get better once you open up and express how you're feeling.

Much Love,

Simon

Made in the USA
Middletown, DE
22 August 2020